FROM SOAPBO

D0488606

# From Soapbox to Soundbite

**Party Political Campaigning in Britain since 1945**

Martin Rosenbaum

First published in Great Britain 1997 by
**MACMILLAN PRESS LTD**
Houndmills, Basingstoke, Hampshire RG21 6XS and London
Companies and representatives throughout the world

A catalogue record for this book is available from the British Library.

ISBN 0–333–61944–7 hardcover
ISBN 0–333–61945–5 paperback

First published in the United States of America 1997 by
**ST. MARTIN'S PRESS, INC.,**
Scholarly and Reference Division,
175 Fifth Avenue, New York, N.Y. 10010

ISBN 0–312–16566–8

Library of Congress Cataloging-in-Publication Data
Rosenbaum, Martin.
From soapbox to soundbite : party political campaigning in Britain
since 1945 / Martin Rosenbaum.
p.   cm.
Includes bibliographical references and index.
ISBN 0–312–16566–8 (cloth)
1. Political parties—Great Britain.   2. Electioneering—Great
Britain.   3. Great Britain—Politics and government—1945–
I. Title.
JN1121.R69   1996
324.941—dc20                                           96–35408
                                                              CIP

© Martin Rosenbaum 1997

This book is printed on paper suitable for recycling and made from fully managed and sustained forest sources.

10   9   8   7   6   5   4   3
06   05   04   03   02   01   00   99   98

Printed and bound in Great Britain by
Antony Rowe Ltd, Chippenham, Wiltshire

To Jane

# Contents

# List of Tables

# Abbreviations

| | |
|---|---|
| ALC | Association of Liberal Councillors |
| BMP | Boase Massimi Pollitt (later called BMP DDB Needham) |
| BMRB | British Market Research Bureau |
| CCO | Conservative Central Office |
| CPA | Conservative Party Archive (located at the Bodleian Library, Oxford) |
| CPV | Colman, Prentis and Varley |
| CRD | Conservative Research Department |
| MORI | Market & Opinion Research International |
| NEC | [Labour's] National executive committee |
| NOP | National Opinion Polls |
| ORC | Opinion Research Centre |
| PEB | Party election broadcast |
| PPB | Party political broadcast |
| SCA | Shadow Communications Agency |
| Y&R | Young and Rubicam |

# Acknowledgements

This book is based partly on written sources – including internal party documents and archive material as well as published works – and partly on interviews (some attributable, some unattributable) with participants in the developments it describes. I am extremely grateful to all those who spared me their time to grant me an interview, including: Tom Arnold, Tim Bell, Keith Britto, Karen Buck, David Cowling, Barry Day, Barry Delaney, Michael Dobbs, Margaret Douglas, Julian Eccles, Bryan Gould, Joyce Gould, Philip Gould, Olly Grender, Robert Hill, Steve Hilton, Colin Hook, Gerald Kaufman, David Kingsley, John Lacy, Chris Lawson, Peter Mandelson, Deborah Mattinson, Alec McGivan, Tom McNally, Gerry McSharry, Henry Neuberger, Dick Newby, Jim Parish, Cecil Parkinson, Vicky Phillips, Chris Powell, Chris Rennard, Maurice Saatchi, Jeremy Sinclair, Norman Tebbit, Harvey Thomas, Geoffrey Tucker, John Underwood, Rob Waller, Robin Wight, Shaun Woodward, Bob Worcester and Johnny Wright.

I would like to thank others as well who spoke to me more briefly but nevertheless usefully: John Banks, Brendan Bruce, Andrew Lansley, Peter Luff, Adrian Slade, Mary Spillane and Mike Thomas. And I received helpful correspondence from Nigel Lawson and Ronald Millar.

I am also appreciative of the friendly cooperation of staff at the Advertising Association library, the Conservative Party Archive (Bodleian Library, Oxford), the Economic and Social Research Council Data Archive (University of Essex), the Labour Party library, and the National Museum of Labour History; and I am grateful to Alistair Cooke of Conservative Central Office for permission to quote from documents in the Conservative Party Archive. Additionally, I am obliged to David Deacon, Gordon Hands and Bob Whybrow for willingly supplying useful information in their possession.

Finally, many thanks to Ruth Willats who edited the text and to the following for their valuable and edifying ideas and/or comments on drafts: Bill Bush, Charles Grant, David Jordan, Andrew Marr, John Rentoul, Nick Robinson, James Stephenson, Henry Stewart and Damien Welfare; and assorted Rosenbaums – Danny, Laurie and Olga – and Ashleys – Jack, Jackie and Jane.

# 1 Introduction

*Winning elections is really a question of salesmanship, little different from marketing any branded article.*
Extract from electioneering manual, published in 1922[1]

*I regret very much myself the introduction of publicity experts – if that is the proper name for them – into the business of our general elections.*
Michael Foot, 1978[2]

In the nineteenth century aspiring MPs tried to win campaigns by hiring election agents to bribe voters. On polling day, candidates paid innkeepers to keep supporters happily refreshed. These options are no longer available to modern political parties.

Instead, today's politicians must rely on persuading the electorate. And to help with this task, they employ a huge array of people whose trade is not corruption but communication: advertising advisers, spin doctors, speechwriters, phrasemakers, opinion pollsters, logo designers, rally organisers, film directors, image consultants, and so on. The methods used by these contemporary electioneering professions are not quite as expensive as bribery and treating, but their effectiveness is harder to prove and their ethics is still a matter of debate.

Party political campaigning in Britain is now a much more elaborate and carefully orchestrated enterprise than it once was. This book examines how the techniques involved have developed. It is not about the political content of the messages which parties have put to the electorate; it is concerned with their increasingly sophisticated means of delivery.

The book covers the period since 1945, although I refer to earlier events when they illustrate the roots of post-war developments. However, it is important to note one overall point: in many ways electioneering before the second world war was more advanced than in the years immediately after it. The 1920s and 1930s saw major changes in political

1

campaigning, fostered by the growth in a mass electorate, technological progress, the use of propaganda in the first world war and the borrowing of commercial approaches. The extension of the franchise in 1918 and 1928 (to men who had not satisfied the previous property or residence qualifications and to women) virtually quadrupled the total eligible to vote to 29 million. To reach such a large number of electors parties conducted major national publicity campaigns, including supplying information and articles to the press, newspaper and poster advertising, mass distribution of literature, radio broadcasts, cinema newsreel appearances and even their own mobile film shows. This was expensive – the well-funded national Conservative campaigns in 1929 and 1935[3] cost, in real terms, a similar sum to that which the party headquarters spends today on a general election.

However, this kind of electioneering was interrupted by the wartime break in ordinary party competition. By 1945 there had not been a general election for ten years. Party organisations at national and local level had deteriorated, finances were in poor shape, equipment was lacking and expertise had been dissipated. Parties were almost starting from scratch, and even faced additional constraints remaining from the war, such as paper rationing. For these reasons the transformation in election campaigning between 1945 and the present day is particularly dramatic. Forty to fifty years ago politicians stood on soapboxes at street corners. Now they dispense soundbites to the media.

Today we are witnessing the beginnings of a communications revolution, in which computing, broadcasting and telephony will converge into powerful new media technologies. Like everyone else with a case to argue, political parties will be travelling down the information superhighway, and have in fact taken their first few tentative steps. This means that now is a convenient moment to look back at the communications era currently drawing to a close and explore how the parties have used the methods of this period in their striving for office.

The structure of this book is thematic. Chapters 2 to 10 are each concerned with a particular form of party political communication. I have tried to give a thorough, balanced and informed account, across the full range of electioneering techniques, of how each form of communication has evolved since 1945 into the shape it now takes. The book covers both direct channels of communication (such as advertising) and also indirect channels – the media; it describes how parties aim to impart impressions through the way they present themselves and their leaders; and it deals with both national and local campaigning.

Some notes on the text: (1) The chapters are slices through history, and the slices sometimes intersect. I have included some minor repetition from one chapter to another for the sake of making each chapter self-contained. (2) The word 'says' attached to a direct quote indicates that this is a remark which the individual quoted has said to me, usually in an interview for this book; 'said' indicates a quote taken from a published source. (3) The term 'third party' refers as appropriate to the Liberals, the SDP/Liberal Alliance and the Liberal Democrats. (4) 'Saatchis' is used sometimes as a shorthand form for the advertising agency, Saatchi and Saatchi. (5) I have generally referred to people who have acquired knighthoods or peerages according to their status at the time they are mentioned.

# 2 Advertising

*The Conservative Party placed itself in the hands of an advertising agency, which produced the so-called image of the Tory Party by advertising methods. I believe that in doing this it introduced something into our political life which is alien to our British democracy.*
Alice Bacon MP, chairman of the Labour Party publicity committee, 1960[1]

*Political advertising calls for blunter instruments. The bludgeon, not the rapier.*
Andrew Rutherford, creator of the Conservative 'Labour isn't working' poster, 1992[2]

*7.1 No advertisement should mislead by inaccuracy, ambiguity, exaggeration, omission or otherwise. . . . 12.1 Any advertisement whose principal function is to influence opinion in favour of or against any political party . . . is exempt from clauses . . . 7.1 . . .*
Extracts from British Codes of Advertising and Sales Promotion, 1995[3]

During the general election of 1812, the Conservative MP Sir Matthew Ridley spent 50 guineas on newspaper advertisements. He was then appalled to discover that the papers he had used charged for electoral ads at double their normal rates. The unfortunate Sir Matthew later told the House of Commons that this was a practice 'to be reprobated'.[4]

These days political advertising can still be a surprisingly expensive business. Indeed, if the relative importance of activities can be judged by the money spent on them, then advertising would seem to be by far the most important element in today's election campaigning. Its costs dwarf other aspects of electioneering.

The Conservatives spent £5.8 million on advertising in the run-up to and during the 1992 election, 52 per cent of their central election spending (and even this was less than the £6.4 million spent on advertising for the 1987 election, which constituted 70 per cent of the central total).[5] Labour spent £3.3 million on advertising for the 1992 election, 32 per cent of its central campaign expenditure.[6] The main political parties appear to be ardent believers in the power of advertising.

In fact, the purchase of advertising space can consume large sums more easily than other forms of electioneering. After all, news coverage can be obtained free of charge. So advertising does not play such a dominant role in winning votes as it does in campaign spending. Nevertheless, the millions of pounds devoted to it indicate the importance parties attach to advertising as a crucial means of direct, unmediated communication with the electorate. This chapter examines the development of electoral advertising. The first part covers strategy and creativity – the content of party ads and the use of professionals to create them. The second deals with media planning – the selection of which media to use for the advertisements.

## STRATEGY AND CREATIVITY

### The rise of political advertising

Advertising was established nationally as a significant political tool between the wars, as the parties slowly learnt to embrace the techniques of mass communications already deployed by business. All three main parties made some use of paid advertising during this period. The Liberals ran extensive newspaper and poster ads for the 1929 election, largely funded by the money their leader David Lloyd George had made as prime minister through selling honours. The Tories used commercial poster hoardings widely for the 1929, 1931 and 1935 campaigns, employing the agency S. H. Benson to design posters and obtain sites. Labour was more reluctant to adopt costly commercial methods, but, assisted by sympathisers from the ad industry, it advertised in the press for the 1937 London County Council elections.

After the war, substantial party advertising started again in the run-up to the 1950 election. Within ten years it had become a controversial centrepiece of electioneering. This was due to one company – Colman, Prentis and Varley (CPV) – which demonstrated powerfully the value of applying professional advertising discipline to the task of political persuasion.

CPV was appointed the Conservative ad agency in 1948. This decision was part of the thorough programme mounted by the Tories, under the reforming party chairman Lord Woolton, to rebuild their campaigning capability following the electoral disaster of 1945. In the first phase of its work for the party, the agency devised mainly poster, but also some press, ads for the periods approaching the elections of 1950, 1951 and 1955.

The posters went up on commercial billboards nationwide and were similar in format to most political posters of the time, including those produced by other parties. Mainly they featured plain designs with straightforward slogans and basic illustrations, such as photographs of party leaders. In 1950, for example, Tory posters ranged from 'Make Britain great again, vote Conservative' (this slogan above a stern-faced bulldog) to 'Socialism leads to Communism, vote Conservative'. Labour hit back with 'A million new homes – thanks to Labour' and 'The good neighbour votes Labour'.[7]

However, some CPV press advertising, which appeared largely in local newspapers, was more distinctive. It prefigured the style of the agency's most famous work, which it was to produce in the late 1950s. Although the ads were generally small and did not stand out, they were appealing and simple in their use of illustration and language. They combined pictures of ordinary people with a comparison of Tory and Labour policies on issues ranging from housing to nationalisation.[8] In 1950 CPV justified its approach to local Conservative associations as follows: 'These advertisements contain the faces of ordinary people and thus help the average reader to identify himself or herself with them. This campaign deals with the facts and figures of political propaganda but expresses them warmly and in terms of human feelings.'[9]

Modern political advertising really began on 30 June 1957, when several national newspapers carried an ad featuring a small girl looking through a five-bar gate. 'Will she be fenced in when she grows up?', the headline asked. The copy attacked regulation, praised the opportunity to enjoy one's earnings and concluded: 'For, despite all the Socialists say, we are human beings, not numbers in tables or figures on adding machines. The Conservatives believe in people.'[10]

This was the opening shot in a huge and unprecedented advertising campaign created by CPV. Launched at a time when the Tories were doing badly in the polls following economic problems, the Suez crisis and the resignation of Sir Anthony Eden as prime minister, it ran at tremendous cost for over two years until their victory at the 1959 election. The campaign was overseen by the party's deputy chairman Oliver Poole, a successful city businessman determined to modernise electioneering techniques. The ads inspired a flurry of indignant protests, of the sort still familiar today, that politicians were being sold to the electorate as if they were detergents, baked beans, cornflakes or some other archetypal fast-moving consumer good. The exercise was opposed by more traditional elements within the party, some of whom regarded commercial methods with as much distaste as did many Labour activists.

The length and extent of the campaign was revolutionary (see below under 'Media planning'). The content also represented a breakthrough in the accessible communication of political messages using contemporary marketing techniques.

First, it focused on long-term building of the party's image, rather than specific policies, tactical attacks on the opposition or imminent election winning. Second, it was driven by one clear strategy. This was to present the Conservative Party as champions of prosperity and opportunity for ordinary families, as opposed to defenders of a privileged minority. The exercise was particularly aimed at women and the better-off working class. It culminated with two posters that became classics: one featured an idealised happy family washing the car, the other the family eating dinner with a television in the background. Both were captioned with the famous slogan: 'Life's better with the Conservatives. Don't let Labour ruin it.'

Third, it advanced a general case through tangible and human examples. When the party told the agency that it wanted to promote the idea that Conservatives believed in opportunity, CPV converted this general proposition into a series of ads featuring photographs of young children and bold headlines asking whether they would be fenced in, make the most of their brains, or ever own a house of their own.[11] Fourth, the large size of the ads created a bolder impression than the small local ads used before.

- Two further aspects mirrored characteristics already seen in CPV's earlier press ads. The language was simple and avoided political jargon; and good use was made of photography, principally of ordinary people – for example, portraying representative occupational types as Tories (a cloth-capped lumber-yard hand in the *News of the World*, a young scientist in the *Observer*).

The contrast with Labour was stark. For the 1959 election Labour's most common poster was a drab picture of Hugh Gaitskell, captioned 'The Man with a Plan'.[12] Suspicious of commercial methods, Labour dismissed an offer of help from sympathetic advertising professionals – their proposal to spend £22 000 on press ads was rejected as wildly extravagant,[13] although it was minimal compared to Conservative expenditure. Labour politicians responded to the Tory campaign with a mixture of outrage and derision. However, their attacks succeeded in drawing further attention to the ads they objected to. The mere name 'Colman, Prentis and Varley' became a standing joke at Labour party conference, where advertising was denounced in motion after motion. It seemed less funny after the Conservatives were re-elected in October 1959 with a majority of 100.

This result and the CPV campaign (although the extent of their causal connection is another matter) convinced many that a few advertisements seen by millions were more effective than the traditional campaigning method of activists stuffing leaflets through letterboxes. Those persuaded included the Labour leader Hugh Gaitskell and several of his senior colleagues. Like its attitude to opinion polling, Labour's attitude to advertising was transformed between 1959 and 1962 or so. However, the party was still not ready to appoint an ad agency formally. In any case, it might well have been difficult to find one which was not put off by the possible reaction of its commercial clients to sharing an agency with Labour. Instead, the party found another (and cheaper) way to exploit professional expertise – the use of volunteers from the advertising industry.

The party's new director of publicity, John Harris, who was a Gaitskellite enthusiast for modern communications, set up a small voluntary group of publicity professionals in 1962. The most important advertising figure among them was David Kingsley, soon to set up Kingsley, Manton and Palmer, one of the most aggressive and fast-growing ad agencies of the 1960s. After Gaitskell's sudden death in January 1963, the publicity group found they had an even more enthusiastic backer in his successor as leader, Harold Wilson. Labour launched its first national press advertising campaign in May 1963, with an ad dominated by a large picture of Wilson. The party continued to run press and poster ads until the election was called in September 1964.

1964 was the first election which was a battle not only between politicians, but also between advertising professionals – at least in the case of the two main parties (Liberal resources were insufficient to allow advertising). This battle provided an interesting contrast in the styles of the advertisements, after some initial fluctuation on the Tory side.

The Conservative press ads in the first part of their 1963–4 pre-election ad campaign were old-fashioned – large blocks of text on specific policies, often without any illustration.[14] The livelier approach of CPV had never appealed to many senior figures in the party, and these forces had been strengthened by the appointment of a new, traditionally-minded chief publicity officer, George Hutchinson, in 1961. As the election approached, however, CPV acquired more freedom and its work then echoed 1957–9. Not only were the slogans (such as 'Conservatives give you a better standard of living – Keep it!') similar, but as before, the ads frequently used eye-catching photos of real people, along with a variety of typefaces and visual gimmicks.

In comparison, the Labour ads in 1963–4 tended to be simpler in design with one straightforward typeface, and were more often based on blocks of text and photos of the party leader.[15] Some more adventurous ads were rejected by Wilson. These included an appeal to women, which featured a photo of a mother bathing a baby – he dismissed it as 'beneath the dignity of the Labour Party'.[16] All this reflected a residual hostility among Labour politicians to the tricks of the advertising trade. But the style also suited a left-wing party seeking to communicate a reassuringly respectable image, while the Conservative designs fitted with a desire to convey an impression of modernity.

Although the formats of Tory and Labour ads were distinct, their political content was less so. Aimed at floating voters, this was often concerned with non-ideological themes like the need to modernise industry and improve schools. Within a week of the two parties launching their ad campaigns in May 1963, the *Sunday Times* was able to combine extracts from both parties' material to concoct an ad which could plausibly have been used by either.[17]

In the run-up to the 1964 election both sides also experimented with knocking copy. One Conservative ad featured an old-fashioned gramophone repeating Labour's pledge to nationalise the steel industry, while another ridiculed the Liberals by comparing them to toy soldiers. Labour ran ads headlined 'I've had enough of the Tories' and 'Don't Let Them Kid You!'[18] But in contrast to later elections, the overall impression of the advertising from both parties was a positive portrayal of themes, policies and leaders. A typical Labour ad was headlined 'What Labour will do about overcrowded schools', while Tory ads praised the government's record on road-building, health, housing, and so on. Both parties also placed more emphasis on policy compared to the image-building approach taken by the Conservatives in 1957–9.

The next important developments happened in the approach to the 1970 election. The content of party ads became more sophisticated and aggressive. On the Tory side, the long-standing link with Colman, Prentis and Varley ended in 1968. The relationship between agency and party had deteriorated since the glory days of the late 1950s. Following a change of management, the agency declared it was no longer interested in the account, although the party's new director of publicity, Geoffrey Tucker, was intending to terminate the contract in any case. In place of CPV he appointed Davidson Pearce Berry and Tuck, a comparatively new agency with a high creative reputation. He believed it would bring more passion to the cause. Labour's work was still done by its voluntary publicity group.

The Conservative strategy was to reinforce public dissatisfaction with the government, and attack Labour hard on taxation, inflation and the credibility of its promises. One pre-election poster showed a husband, wife and two children, captioned 'This family pays too much tax'. Another featured a man with a pound note being burned away in his hand.[19] The poster sites used by the Tories in the 1970 campaign were predominantly devoted to two negative ads. The most common was a picture of a wastepaper basket headlined 'Remember Labour's broken promises'; the other stated (at a time before decimalisation) 'The £ in your pocket is now worth . . . 15/7'. These appeared most often because they were the ones selected by local constituency agents from a choice offered by Conservative Central Office. They were more popular than the poster which featured Edward Heath.[20]

But it was Labour which devised the first really dramatic negative or 'attack' political advertisement. On 14 April 1970 a collection of Plasticine models of six Tory politicians (Heath, Maudling, Macleod, Douglas-Home, Hogg and Powell) was smuggled into Wilson's room in the House of Commons and 'unveiled before [Labour's] Campaign Committee with electrifying effect'.[21] Lurid in colour, unpleasant in expression, these were to star in the party's next ads under the dramatic headline 'Yesterday's Men (They failed before!)'. A photograph of the models was accompanied by short, unflattering biographies of each politician. When launched in May the ads caused outrage, not least within Labour's own ranks. Such pugnacious personal attacks were new to political advertising and prompted much criticism that the political process was being degraded. The angry reaction unnerved Labour leaders.

The ad was the result of a deliberate decision by Labour's professional publicity advisers to 'accentuate the negative'. Partly they wanted to combat recent Tory campaigning. This had been consistently more negative than Labour's ads over the past year or so, many of which had been aimed at rebuilding the enthusiasm of party supporters. 'The "Yesterday's Men" campaign was enormously controversial, but it was correct,' says David Kingsley.[22] 'It derived from research, and underlined what we knew people thought about the "funny old Tories".'

In fact, the campaign was the first half in a planned, two-stage strategy. The onslaught on Tory politicians was intended all along as a precursor to a positive presentation of Labour leaders and policies. However, the positive second stage failed to materialise. Wilson surprised his advertising team and disrupted their plans by calling the election in June 1970 rather than October. And 'Yesterday's Men' itself was then quickly overtaken by the campaign proper, to the relief of many Labour politicians.[23] For the campaign period the party had to fall back on three rapidly produced and unimaginative posters, all based on images of Wilson.[24]

The next few years proved a barren period for party advertising. The February 1974 election, prompted by Edward Heath's self-defeating determination to show striking miners who governed Britain, was called too quickly for specific ad strategies to be well developed. The content of the advertising in both 1974 elections was unremarkable. Labour attacked the Tories on issues like inflation and presented its own senior figures as a collective leadership team. Conservative ads fought back on inflation and proclaimed 'Vote for national unity'.

Both main parties also faced problems of continuity because of their failure to maintain consistent relationships with the people who planned and created their advertising. Following the 1970 election Wilson fell out with David Kingsley. In 1973, Labour brought in as its key adman in his place Chris Powell of Boase Massimi Pollitt (BMP), the agency which had done the TUC's advertising against the Industrial Relations Bill in 1971. Powell coordinated creative volunteers from a number of agencies, while BMP was officially used to buy the advertising space. However, Powell found some senior party staff difficult to work with and pulled out after February 1974. He and his agency were to play a much bigger role in Labour advertising from 1985 on. The Tories also chopped and changed in 1974. For February they used Roe Humphreys, and for October reverted to their 1970 agency, now called Davidson Pearce Berry and Spottiswoode.

## The Saatchi era

Party advertising was at a lull in 1974, but it took politics by storm at the next general election in 1979. This was thanks to the ad agency whose distinctive name was to become famous as a symbol of the professionalisation of political campaigning – Saatchi and Saatchi.

After 1974 the Conservatives dropped their agency, and in 1977 formed a committee of industry volunteers (coordinated by Robin Wight, creative director of Euro Advertising) to start planning advertising for the next election. Wight persuaded the party it needed a full-time agency again, and that as an important innovation the agency appointed should take charge of party political broadcasts as well as advertising to ensure the two modes of communication reinforced each other. Gordon Reece, the Tory director of publicity, selected Saatchis (its full title was then Saatchi and Saatchi Garland-Compton) in March 1978. Established in 1970 by brothers Charles and Maurice Saatchi, the agency had built a reputation for highly creative and aggressive advertising. Its growth had been rapid, and as it had become Britain's sixth largest agency it also had the resources to handle the large quantity of quickly turned-round work an election requires. It impressed Reece as a talented outfit which had achieved success, but was hungry for more.[25]

Saatchis brought strategic discipline as well as creative flair to its Conservative work. And the essence of the strategy was attack, attack, attack. After the successful 1979 campaign Tim Bell, who was the agency's chairman and ran the Tory account, commented:[26] 'Although it's an over-simplification to say that "governments lose elections, oppositions don't win them", it is true that an opposition must use communication techniques effectively to sharpen public dissatisfaction with the government rather than satisfaction with the opposition. Everything we did was directed towards increasing the salience of this dissatisfaction.' (In subsequent elections, however, Saatchis' equally belligerent work seemed to be based on the thesis that 'governments don't win elections, oppositions lose them', as it devoted itself not to sharpening public satisfaction with the Conservative government but dissatisfaction with the Labour opposition.)

The agency made its mark on the political world soon after starting work for the Tories. It assembled a motley group of individuals and photographed them in a straggling queue purporting to be unemployed. Headlined 'Labour isn't working', this picture was plastered on over 1000 sites across the country in August 1978. The ad was conceived by Andrew Rutherford, one of Saatchis' creative staff. The fake unemployed became the stars of what is still the most famous ad ever used to sell a British political party – in fact, one of the most well-remembered ads used to sell anything at all to the British public.

'Labour isn't working' was the most intrusive, dramatic and hard-hitting ad which had yet been created for a political cause. In its boldness, simplicity, accent on the negative and focus on a central issue – all reinforced by the heavy block capitals and strong visual – it established a style for much of what Saatchis has since done for the Conservative Party.

Ironically, Bell had 'the most awful battle getting the party's approval for the poster'.[27] Political objections were raised because the word 'Labour' was much larger than the slogan 'Britain's better off with the Conservatives', which was dimly discernible at the bottom. Jeremy Sinclair, Saatchis' creative director, says:[28] 'The politicians asked us: "Is it normal to have the name of our opponents in much bigger print than ourselves?"'

Its impact was bolstered by the vigorous and largely counterproductive attack launched on it immediately by Labour, led by James Callaghan, who said it was the first step in an unprecedented attempt to 'beguile the British public'. Labour made much of the allegation that the purported unemployed were Saatchi and Saatchi staff (in fact, they were Young Conservatives from the constituency of South Hendon).[29] Denis Healey, then chancellor of the exchequer, referred to 'the politics of rent-a-fake'. The usual analogies were drawn with the selling of soap powder. Within a week of the poster's first appearance it had become a major news story, hitting the front pages and television bulletins. Labour's response was a bonus.

The Conservatives launched their advertising blitz in the summer of 1978 partly because they anticipated an October

election. When that did not happen, they kept up the flow
of advertising in posters and print. To suit the medium, posters
were simple and bold. They included 'Educashun isn't
wurking' and 'Cheer up! Labour can't hang on for ever'.
The newspaper ads were less stark. Double-page spreads were
taken in the tabloids to explain 'Why every trade unionist
should consider voting Conservative'.

The 1978–9 Tory campaign was not necessarily a paragon
of advertising and persuasion. It contained its share of dull
and long-winded ads. But as a whole it was hard-hitting, well
targeted and highly visible. It was founded on a close and
productive relationship between Reece and Saatchis, while
politicians outside Margaret Thatcher's inner circle had less
influence on campaign themes than their counterparts had
previously. All in all, it showed what could be achieved when
a political party exploited the full resources of a top-class
ad agency, involved it at the core of campaign planning,
and gave it lots of scope and plenty of money over a period
of several months.

The agency's work did wonders for the profile of political advertising. By the next election in 1983 the advertising
battle was widely regarded, and reported, as central to the
electioneering war rather than a minor sideshow. Not only
was it more prominent, it had a more directly competitive,
confrontational tone. All three main parties made some use
of ad agencies, who were conscious that whether or not their
work boosted the electoral fortunes of their clients, its reception was important for their own reputation.

Saatchis unsurprisingly retained the Tory account for 1983,
which was again run by Tim Bell. But with its combative
style the agency found it more difficult to promote a government than an opposition. It solved the problem by behaving
as if its client was an opposition party, and concentrated on
attacking the other side. During the 1983 campaign the entire
national press advertising for the Conservative Party was solely
devoted to disparaging the Labour Party.[30] This was also true
of most of its poster activity.

Saatchis produced a number of highly memorable attacks
on Labour, which represented an easy target, thanks to its
unpopular radical manifesto and similarly unpopular leader,
Michael Foot. The most forceful identified 11 points in

common between the Labour and Communist manifestos
and headlined them '"Like your manifesto, Comrade"'.
Another listed 14 Labour policies, rewritten to make them
as unappealing as possible, and equated voting Labour with
support for these unattractive propositions, such as 'I do
not mind paying higher rates'.

In a rare move, one Saatchi poster directly assailed the
Alliance, which was moving up the polls and eventually came
close to beating Labour into second place. Seizing on the
close association (in popular satire, if not in reality) between
SDP membership and the drinking of claret, it asked, 'What
are the SDP's policies?'; and responded, 'Ten bottles of claret
can be won for the best guess'. Party chairman Cecil Parkinson
later described it as 'one of our less successful posters'.[31]
Soon after the ads went up, a group of Alliance activists
appeared outside Central Office clutching copies of their
manifesto, eagerly looking forward to claiming their claret.
But the poster was more notable for a different reason – as
a rare instance of a Tory ad devoted to knocking the third
party. Saatchis has generally prepared contingency material
to attack the centre party in case its bandwagon started to
roll during an election, but at other times it has not been
thought necessary to use it.[32]

The 1983 result meant that the Conservative Party and
Saatchi and Saatchi had enjoyed two electoral triumphs
together, but the harmonious relationship between party and
agency was soon to become more complicated. This stemmed
from a bitter internal conflict at the agency between Bell
and the Saatchi brothers, which resulted in Bell's departure
in 1984. Bell had established a unique rapport with Thatcher,
which the agency now lost. Saatchis continued to pay Bell a
retainer for him to be involved with the Tory account, but
when the time came in 1986 to start work on the next election, neither the agency nor party chairman Norman Tebbit
wanted Bell to take part, much to Thatcher's subsequent
annoyance. Bell later had strategy discussions with Thatcher,
which were kept secret from Tebbit and others.

The overall strategy adopted by the party and the agency
in 1986–7 was encapsulated in the slogan 'The Next Move
Forward'. This was intended to demonstrate that the government had not run out of steam. It required what for Saatchis

was a new approach to election advertising – most of it had to be positive. The plan was to have 'something like a 60:40 or 70:30 positive/negative ratio', according to Tebbit.[33] 'You can't measure it exactly', he says,[34] 'but this ratio was a way of saying, put more emphasis on the positive than the negative, but don't ignore the negative entirely. If we have been in government, then we should have a positive story to tell. It's not enough to rely on the other rascals being worse.' At a pre-election planning meeting in April 1987, Thatcher told Saatchis to come up with more positive work to bring the ratio into line. The agency was not convinced, but complied.[35]

The positive ads used in due course included a double-page listing of 23 government achievements, with the heading 'Don't undo eight years work in three seconds'. The negative work was more characteristic of Saatchis' style. The most emotive example showed books entitled 'Young, gay and proud' and 'The playbook for kids about sex', under the headline: 'Is this Labour's idea of a comprehensive education?'

However, the advertising was generally regarded inside and outside the party as uninspired and ineffective; the only well-remembered ad was a classic piece of negativity. This exploited Neil Kinnock's blunder in a television interview with David Frost, when he raised the possibility of a Soviet occupation of the UK. The Tories attacked Kinnock as willing to surrender, and the Saatchis ad showed a soldier with his arms up under the heading 'Labour's policy on arms'. Thatcher wrote later that it was 'the only good advertisement of our campaign'.[36]

Some well-publicised and dramatic accounts[37] of the 1987 Tory campaign have claimed that in the last week there was a comprehensive shift in advertising approach, which more or less saved the party from disaster. What is true is that on 'Wobbly Thursday' (a week before polling day), when some leading Tories were panicked by unfavourable polling information, a distinctly agitated Margaret Thatcher instructed that a last week advertising blitz should be based on ideas submitted by Tim Bell rather than proposals from Saatchis. The prime minister wanted advertising which was 'based heavily on our record of achievements', adding in a dig at Saatchis that this 'may have seemed dull to the creative and unpolitical minds of communications specialists'.[38]

Thatcher's decision did not please the agency, which was forced under protest to found its remaining work on Bell's suggestions. The resulting ads consisted of bold, simple statements in large type of Tory achievements, contrasted with assertions in smaller type of the dire consequences of Labour government. The Saatchi camp later argued that this was not very different from what it was planning anyway; while another ad agency which sought to claim credit after the election – Young and Rubicam – maintained that the new angle followed strategic advice which it had submitted to Downing Street.[39] The new ads improved Thatcher's morale at a difficult moment, but there is no evidence that they had much impact on the electorate. Before any of the ads appeared in newspapers, further polls showed that the figures which had led to the panic were blips to be ignored.

After the election, the three rival groups of advertising advisers fought over the plaudits for victory. The Saatchi brothers were deeply unhappy both about Bell's participation in the campaign and the reporting afterwards which denigrated their role. In October 1987 Maurice publicly resigned the Conservative Party account. The bitterness on both sides was such that all assumed it was a permanent end to the link between agency and party, a link which had symbolised the mass communication of Thatcherite doctrine.

The party did not attempt to replace Saatchis with another long-term agency appointment. For the 1989 European elections it tried out Allen, Brady and Marsh. This agency's ads reflected Thatcher's Eurosceptic sentiments, but were widely derided as obscure and alienating. One poster read: 'Stay at home on June 15th, and you'll live on a diet of Brussels.' Norman Tebbit, the former party chairman, called it the 'worst election advertising in living memory'.[40] Otherwise during the 1987–90 period the party depended for local election advertising (and also party political broadcasts) on a voluntary group of industry sympathisers, of which the leading figure was Tim Bell.

From 1989 the group was coordinated by the new Tory director of communications, Brendan Bruce, who regarded this arrangement as more flexible than employing a full-time agency. He sought to build up the voluntary team, so that when an election approached he would have the option of relying on it rather than an agency. This plan was disrupted by Thatcher's removal as prime minister, which brought a new team to Central Office. They wanted a different approach, including a formally appointed agency. And it was thanks to Saatchis' aggressive philosophy that it regained the account.

Early in 1991 Shaun Woodward, Bruce's successor, drew up a shortlist of agencies which did not include Saatchis. Even those leading Tories who were sympathetic to the agency had been antagonised by Maurice's public rejection of the account. But Woodward was persuaded by the agency chairman, Bill Muirhead, to let Saatchis pitch for the account on the understanding that Maurice would not be allowed near it. In fact, in the event he was closely involved.

Shaun Woodward says:[41] 'All the shortlisted agencies said what a nice bloke Major was and had ideas for a positive campaign. But when Saatchis gave their presentation, after the first half which was positive Jeremy Sinclair [creative director of Saatchis] said: "Now we need to tell you the other half. You need a hard-hitting, negative campaign as if you were the opposition party not the government." They felt we would have to run a campaign like that, even if we were not in a recession. My conclusion was that Saatchi and Saatchi should be our agency. While we could all convince ourselves that John Major's charm and niceness would win through, in reality that's not enough. It's not a campaign.'

In due course the positive half dwindled, and the bulk of Conservative advertising before and during the 1992 campaign was devoted to attacking Labour. It concentrated on two issues – trust and tax – which had been identified as Labour's key vulnerabilities. An imaginative range of sinister imagery was deployed to dramatise the Labour tax threat. The leading device was 'Labour's tax bombshell'. This became the primary visual symbol of the entire election, and its impact was crucial in keeping tax high up the media's campaign agenda. It was supplemented by a trio of leg irons ('taxes up, mortgages up, prices up'), a mosquito sucking blood ('Labour's tax on savings'), and 'Labour's double whammy' (two blows from a boxer, one representing higher taxes, the other higher prices).

There were some positive ads which represented interesting contrasts with the past. A poster of John Major apparently surrounded by smiling children (in fact, the pose was faked)[42] was used extensively in the last week of the campaign. Ads like this showing party leaders had gone out of fashion since the early 1970s, in line with the advertising dictum: 'only in the gravest cases, should you show the clients' faces'. But the Tories wanted to squeeze full value out of Major's popularity lead over Kinnock. Another ad listing government achievements also appeared in newspapers, but it only ran to ten, compared to the 23 achievements boasted of in its 1987 counterpart.

The Conservatives continued to use Saatchi and Saatchi after the successful 1992 campaign for local and European elections. But the company had been beset with financial problems and internal disputes, following over-ambitious expansion in the 1980s. Matters came to a head in December 1994, when Maurice was acrimoniously ousted as group chairman by other directors. Together with his brother, he set up a new agency, M & C Saatchi, and took with him many senior colleagues who had worked on the Tory account, including Jeremy Sinclair. Leading Conservatives attached great value to Maurice's strategic thinking and were determined not to lose access to it. In 1995 the party ended its contract with Saatchi and Saatchi, and in 1996 Tory advertising plans were in the hands of Maurice and Sir Tim Bell, who had patched up their earlier quarrel.

There are several clear characteristics applying to the bulk of Saatchis' work for the Conservatives since 1979. These are all visible in the most striking of the agency's ads in each campaign (1978–9: 'Labour isn't working'; 1983: 'Like your manifesto, comrade'; 1987: 'Labour's policy on arms'; 1992: 'Labour's tax bombshell'). These can be regarded as the archetypal Saatchi ads: they are all (a) simple, (b) negative, (c) hard-hitting and (d) about policy. The blunt tone is reflected in the heavy, solid, squashed Franklin Gothic typeface which Saatchis stuck to throughout its Conservative advertising.

'We just brought our aggressive advertising style to politics. One does advertising as hard as the client feels comfortable with. We did do some positive ads, but who remembers them now? It is not peace and tranquillity which attracts people's attention,' says Jeremy Sinclair,[43] who along with the two brothers was involved on the Tory account at all four elections. Or to use the term popularised into political discourse by the Conservative Party chairman, Chris Patten, their aim has been to do ads that 'gobsmack' the voters. The Tories' political opponents have never managed to produce ads which have rivalled the power or memorability of Saatchis' best work.

Whether the client was in government or in opposition, and despite disagreements with politicians who favoured positive ads extolling their achievements, the Saatchi philosophy has consistently been that great political advertising is negative advertising. According to the Saatchi view, the main benefit the agency brought to the Conservative Party was to teach it to campaign in government as if it were an opposition. The approach has been based on identifying the most potentially important political reasons people have for not voting Labour, and devising simple visual and verbal encapsulations which highlight those reasons and give them impact. In the words of Maurice Saatchi, 'Political campaigning is, above all, an adversarial activity. . . . A world of trial by combat, in which you would hit, and be hit.'[44]

**Saatchis' adversaries**

In the years since 1979, Labour's approach to advertising has changed enormously. In 1979 its advertising operation was about as dissimilar as possible to the way the Conservative Party and Saatchis worked effectively together. As before, Labour used a team of volunteers, although the individuals were different. James Callaghan's staff brought in new blood in place of the various advertising professionals who had helped Wilson. The key figures now were Edward Booth-Clibborn, head of the Designers and Art Directors Association, and Tim Delaney of the agency BBDO.

They faced the same major problems that had seriously hampered their predecessors – widespread distaste in the party for advertising in general, plus lack of coordination between the leader's office and party headquarters at Transport House. This led to too much infighting and not enough planning. In one especially unhappy episode, the party's campaign committee, angry at lack of consultation, ordered the withdrawal of a poster designed by the professional advisers, which had already gone up on some hoardings.[45] Many thought it was actually Labour's most striking ad. Referring back to the three-day week and power cuts under Heath, it featured a candle glowing in the dark and the headline 'Remember the last time the Tories said they had all the answers?'

And some Labour advertising was rather out of touch with the country's political situation. Posters with the slogan 'Keep Britain Labour and it will keep getting better' were devised for the expected October 1978 campaign. When Callaghan failed to call the election, they were then displayed on billboards during what turned out to be the strike-ridden 'winter of discontent'. By this time they probably seemed more like ads for the Conservatives. Party officials hunted down their own posters to have them removed from billboards.[46]

The impact of Saatchis' work in 1978–9 convinced both Labour publicity officials and the part-time advertising advisers that their party too should appoint a full-time ad agency. Labour had used agencies in the past to buy the media space, but creative work had always been in the hands of an ad hoc team of unpaid volunteers. However, everyone knew it would not be easy to find an agency which wanted the job enough to disregard any potential comeback from disapproving clients.

In 1981 the advertising trade magazine *Campaign* published a profile of Johnny Wright, managing director of the small agency Wright and Partners, which revealed he was a strong Labour supporter. He soon found himself approached by party officials. In due course Wright and Partners became Labour's first advertising agency, initially for the local elections of 1982. As this went well, the agency was later reappointed for the local and then general elections in the following year. Labour also maintained a small advisory committee of advertising sympathisers, who were consulted on Wright's plans (although several previous volunteers had defected to the newly-formed Social Democrats).

Wright's agency was responsible for producing party political broadcasts as well as creating the poster and print ads. The ads concentrated on Labour's usual themes of unemployment and public services, exhibiting a strong thematic unity in design and textual structure – some Tory-bashing followed by details of Labour policies. They had arresting visuals, such as a giant broom sweeping people down a drain, and two schoolchildren stranded at the bottom of a broken-runged ladder. But the headlines and copy were less forceful. The slogan – 'Think positive. Act Positive. Vote Labour' – was badly received and conflicted with the tone of the negative photomontages and headlines.

On the whole, Labour's experiment with an agency was not widely perceived as successful. Several leading politicians were unhappy with the work. With a staff of around 20 or so, Wright and Partners possessed a fraction of the creative talent available to Saatchis, which had 500 employees. But Labour also failed to take full advantage of the fact that an agency was willing to work for it. This was partly because many in the party regarded advertising as an evil necessity, and partly due to the chaotic nature of its 1983 campaign preparations.

Wright and Partners found Labour a difficult client thanks to the party's inefficient decision-making processes, which, under Michael Foot's weak leadership, at times came close to anarchy. 'When we first presented our creative work for the general election', says Wright,[47] 'there were 46 people in the shadow cabinet room. Being a good democrat, Michael Foot went round the room allowing everyone to express an opinion.' The party failed to involve the agency properly in strategic discussions. Wright and Partners was not even told that it would definitely handle the general election advertising until after Thatcher had announced polling day.[48]

After 1983, Labour reverted to the use of sympathetic volunteers rather than a full-time agency. This approach was formalised in early 1986 with the creation of the Shadow Communications Agency (SCA), often referred to as the Shadow Agency. It was set up by Peter Mandelson, Labour's new director of communications, and Philip Gould, an advertising industry executive who persuaded Mandelson that the party needed greater access to professional expertise. Over the next few years the SCA played a central role in devising and implementing Labour's communications strategy, and gave the party a new reputation for slick, well-organised publicity. Its members contributed not only to advertising but the full range of campaigning, including polling, party political broadcasts, press conferences and literature.

The Shadow Agency's advertising team was built around staff from Boase Massimi Pollitt, particularly those who had worked on BMP's 'Save the GLC' campaign for the Labour-led Greater London Council. Although ultimately unsuccessful, this well-planned and expensive campaign had shifted public opinion behind the GLC. Its impact did much to reduce left-wing hostility to political advertising. The SCA was chaired by BMP's chief executive Chris Powell, who had been Labour's key adman in February 1974 and had also advised the party on the work of Wright and Partners in 1983.

The advertising produced by the SCA for the 1987 election focused single-mindedly on the 'caring' issues – unemployment, the health service, schools – which were perceived to be Thatcher's main area of weakness. Sometimes they also attacked her personally. One ad was headlined: '800 000 people are waiting to go into hospital. They're being held up by the Prime Minister's heart problem.' The posters featured bleak depressing scenes, such as dole queues and dilapidated hospital wards. The press ads were clear and straightforward, generally relying for their impact on punchy copy rather than visuals. The slogan 'The country's crying out for change' became 'The country's crying out for Labour' in the last week. The advertising was well received in the party, the media and the ad industry, especially in contrast to the widespread criticism of Saatchis' work in 1987.

The SCA continued to produce the party's advertising from then up to the 1992 election. Its work retained several features which made it punchier than the ads Wright and Partners had done for Labour in 1983. Lengthy text was avoided; on the key issue of health the use of emotional individual cases was preferred over abstract argument; and there was no shirking from personal attacks on Tory leaders. In other respects there was a change in strategy and tone between 1987 and 1992. Strategically, there was more emphasis on the economy, particularly attempts to blame the recession on John Major. Within the caring issues, even more stress was placed on health, which was used to try to offset the tax issue. This was exemplified in a highly emotive ad about an 18-month-old girl with a heart condition, headlined 'Georgina Norris died because the NHS is short of money. Meanwhile, the Tories are cutting taxes to keep their election hopes alive.'

But on the whole the ads were not as hard-hitting as in 1987. Several employed cleverness at the expense of clarity, in line with the current advertising fashion for one-line witticisms or puns as headlines. One portrayed Chancellor Norman Lamont as 'Vatman', predicting increases in value added tax. Another pictured Major and Lamont under the headline 'Tory Defence Policy. "It's not our recession"'. The party later acknowledged some of its advertising messages had been 'too complicated and diffuse'.[49]

After the 1992 election, the Shadow Agency was disbanded. The new party leader, John Smith, a stolid, sober-minded character, had never warmed to its glossy presentational values. Many politicians resented the central strategic role played by Philip Gould, the Shadow Agency coordinator, and his colleagues. In 1993 Labour reverted to a full-time agency, contracting Butterfield Day Devito Hockney to produce ads and party political broadcasts. Following Smith's death and the accession of Tony Blair, a moderniser who had worked closely with Gould, Labour switched in 1995 to BMP, the much bigger ad agency which had initially provided the core of the SCA. Back in the mid-1980s, the possibility of BMP officially working for Labour had been vetoed by some of the agency's senior figures. This formal appointment illustrates Labour's new-found respectability in the eyes of business and the willingness of business to accommodate a party it expects to win.

As for the Alliance and the Liberal Democrats, the third parties have had particular problems finding professional adpeople who can successfully adapt to the demands of political advertising. The task of communicating their political message through what is now the largely negative instrument of advertising is harder because they have two enemies to attack. This makes it more difficult to devise a simple, powerful ad with one really sharp message that strikes home.

The creation of the Social Democrats in 1981 meant that the centre parties had some more money to devote to ads, but it made little difference to the overall nature of election advertising. In some ways this was surprising, since the SDP was the first British political party to be launched with an ad campaign aimed at recruiting members, and its publicity advisory committee included several leading figures from the industry. But together with its Alliance partners, the Liberals, it decided to devote most electioneering effort elsewhere. The Alliance ran no national press advertising during the 1983 campaign. The SDP did, however, employ an upcoming young agency, Gold Greenlees Trott, to produce five posters early in 1983. These included a picture of the 'Gang of Four' (the four party founders), smiling and distinguished-looking. The others were double-pronged attacks on the two main party leaders, Thatcher and Foot. The best presented them as characters from the *Wizard of Oz*, with Thatcher as the heartless tin-man and Foot as the brainless scarecrow.

For the following election the SDP wanted to appoint an agency again, but this was resisted by senior Liberals. With its emphasis on local community politics, the culture of the Liberal Party was distrustful of modern marketing and sceptical about the effectiveness of mass political advertising. They compromised by appointing as 'publicity consultant' David Abbott. He was creative director of Abbott Mead Vickers and the author of the initial 'Invitation to Join the SDP' ad, which broke the mould of political party recruitment by offering membership through credit card payment. Abbott was one of British advertising's most admired copywriters, but in the ads he created for the 1987 election campaign he found it difficult to apply his talents successfully to politics. One campaign organiser, Des Wilson, later wrote that Abbott 'never got within a hundred miles of what the Alliance is really all about'.[50]

For 1992 the Liberal Democrats employed an agency, TBWA Holmes Knight Ritchie. The main feature of their work was a badge-like symbol proclaiming 'My Vote', launched with much hype as a claimed breakthrough in political advertising. The point was to counteract the wasted vote argument which has bedevilled the centre party. It could also be incorporated into slogans or copy, for example, 'My vote will give my kids a future'. However, many Liberal Democrat strategists were dismayed that soon after the party had invested successfully in its new bird logo (see Chapter 8), another different visual device was being presented to the public. Moreover, it was generally regarded as obscure and confusing.


## MEDIA PLANNING

The effectiveness of advertisements depends not only on their content, but also on where they are placed. They need to be seen by the right people, at the right time, under the right circumstances and as often as possible. So the task of planning which media to use, and to what extent, is of crucial importance. In doing so, political advertisers face an important constraint. They have never been permitted to buy time on the most effective advertising medium of all – television. Nor have they been allowed to purchase radio time. This is despite the fact that commercial television started in 1955 and commercial radio in 1973. So the main options for party advertising have been posters and newspapers, and to a lesser degree magazines and cinema.

### Level and timing of expenditure

The story of the party political advertising industry since the war is one of growth, followed by recession, followed again by growth. The overall extent of national party advertising in different elections is shown in Table 2.1. (Many of these figures are estimates, which vary in source and accuracy; the table therefore provides a broad indication of trends rather than a basis for precise comparisons.) Spending on advertising peaked in 1963–4, and then fell back sharply. Since 1974 it has grown rapidly again. On the whole, the Conservatives and Labour have followed the same pattern of ups and downs, with Labour at a lower level. Third party spending was very limited until the creation of the SDP in 1981.

There have been two key dates since 1945 which have transformed the pattern of spending on political advertising. The first was 30 June 1957, when the Tories launched

*Table 2.1*   Advertising expenditure

| | Conservatives | | Labour | | Liberals/SDP/ Liberal Democrats | |
|---|---|---|---|---|---|---|
| | Current prices | 1992 prices | Current prices | 1992 prices | Current prices | 1992 prices |
| 1950 | 140[a] | 2300 | 0 | 0 | 0 | 0 |
| 1959 | 468[b] | 5200 | 23[l] | 260 | 0 | 0 |
| 1964 | 970[c] | 9700 | 267[m] | 2700 | 0 | 0 |
| 1966 | >30[d] | >270 | 0 | 0 | 0 | 0 |
| 1970 | 370[e] | 2900 | >192[n] | >1500 | >5[u] | >40 |
| 1974 (Feb.) | >297[f] | >1600 | 20[o] | 110 | 25[v] | 140 |
| 1974 (Oct.) | 400[g] | 1900 | 142[p] | 700 | 17[w] | 80 |
| 1979 | 1501[h] | 3800 | 617[q] | 1500 | 35[x] | 90 |
| 1983 | 2688[i] | 4400 | 878[r] | 1400 | 400[y] | 650 |
| 1987 | 6357[j] | 8500 | 2114[s] | 2800 | 410[z] | 550 |
| 1992 | 5800[k] | 5800 | 3338[t] | 3338 | 319[aa] | 319 |

*Note.* Estimates of sums spent on nationally organised advertising relating to the general elections in 1950 and from 1959 on, in thousands of pounds. (NB: The Conservatives also spent some money on national advertising for the 1951 and 1955 elections. It is not possible to give an estimate, but the sums involved were certainly much less than in 1949–50.)
*Sources:* See note 74.

their national newspaper campaign. Before this, party advertising mainly consisted of posters on hoardings. Roughly 90 per cent of the advertising money spent by the Conservatives in their biggest previous campaign of 1949–50 went on posters, when they occupied thousands of sites for nearly a year. The rest went on ads in regional and local papers and a few popular magazines.[51] The party continued with substantial, although briefer and smaller, poster campaigns in the approach to the 1951 and 1955 elections, but nationally organised press advertising was minimal.

The 1957–9 Conservative ad campaign was pathbreaking not only for its content, but also for its immense cost, unprecedented length and use of national newspapers as well as billboards. The ads ran on and off for over two years until the election was called in September 1959. For six weeks in the summer of 1959 the Conservative Party was the country's biggest press advertiser.[52]

The perceived success of this campaign established a pattern followed by the two main parties for the next election.

The Tories and Labour ran ad campaigns, using mainly national press but also posters, which both began in May 1963 and were more or less continuous until the election was called in September 1964. The 1963–4 Conservative ad campaign was briefer than its predecessor, since the vicissitudes of the Macmillan government and uncertainties about policy and leadership made long-term planning more difficult. But its greater intensity set a vast new record for spending.

By the mid-1960s, such a model for political advertising was well established. The received wisdom was that, just as for its commercial equivalent, effective political advertising required long-running campaigns in which a few credible messages were drummed home repeatedly. But this also caused a problem. Cost-effective work was therefore thought to need large sums over prolonged periods, stretching party finances to the limit. Disillusioned by their loss in 1964 despite the fortune spent on advertising, and handicapped by the substantial debts which resulted, the Tories did little paid advertising in the run-up to the 1966 election. Labour cut back similarly, its leadership demonstrating less interest in party campaigning once in government. The expected imminence of another election also precluded long-term advertising plans.

Towards the end of the decade both parties reverted to the established pattern, but in a more affordable way. Labour launched its 'Labour's got life and soul' press advertising campaign in summer 1969, followed by the 'Yesterday's men' ads in May 1970, which in turn would have been succeeded by a more positive campaign prior to the anticipated October election. The Conservatives initiated a press and poster campaign in September 1969, which ran until the election was called in May 1970.

The second key date was 15 February 1974. For once the Liberal Party was responsible. The party had modernised its approach to communications, and appointed Slade Monico Bluff as its ad agency (managing director Adrian Slade was a Liberal candidate). Eight days after Heath had called the election, the Liberals ran an ad in the *Daily Express*, later repeated in other papers. Featuring party leader Jeremy Thorpe gesticulating in front of shadowy portraits of Heath and Wilson, it was headlined 'You can change the face of Britain'. While the voters did not change the face of Britain in the way Thorpe desired, his ad succeeded in changing the face of British political advertising. For until then it had been assumed that it was effectively illegal for political parties to advertise in newspapers during the election campaign itself (that is, after the election had been announced).

In fact, the legal basis for the Liberal decision had been laid down over 20 years previously. In 1951 the Tronoh Mines company had placed an anti-Labour ad in several newspapers shortly before polling day. The company was prosecuted for incurring expenses in order to procure the election of non-Labour candidates, without these expenses being authorised by candidates' agents and counting towards candidates' tightly restricted constituency spending. But in 1952 the court held that the ad was not illegal, on the basis that it was general political propaganda not directed at assisting a particular candidate in a particular constituency.

This decision clearly also legitimised political parties in spending money during the campaign on national advertising not aimed at assisting particular candidates. Yet, until 1974, the judgment was ignored by the parties. They seemed to assume that the cost of any national press advertising would have to be allocated to individual candidates' expenses with the likely result that spending limits would be breached. So party press advertising campaigns ceased once an election was called. The costs of poster ads during the campaign were allocated to the candidates' expenses for the constituencies in which the hoardings were located. When local parties wanted to avoid the extra expenses, posters already displayed prior to the election announcement were blanked out.

The Liberals were not prosecuted in 1974. Thorpe presented their act as a triumph for free speech, which it may well have been – but not one to the long-term benefit of his party and its successors. The other two parties immediately took advantage of the Liberal trail-blazing. In September/October 1974 all three parties advertised nationally during the campaign period. The Labour and Conservative Parties considerably outspent the Liberals, who had to save their limited press advertising budget for the weekend before polling day. And today, the Liberal Democrats are hugely outspent by their better resourced opponents in the four weeks before voters make their final decision.

'We did not realise how pioneering we were being', says Adrian Slade.[53] 'We didn't think we were making history. We just took the view that it was acceptable to advertise in newspapers as we were not promoting individual candidates. We did not envisage that advertising spending in the campaign would grow in the way it has.'

The Liberal action led to a fundamental shift in the pattern of political advertising. The parties no longer devote their advertising budget to long-running print and poster ad campaigns in the months approaching polling day. Instead, they save much of it for sudden and intense activity once the election is called. Since 1974 advertising expenditure has generally been concentrated on the few weeks of the campaign proper.

This usually culminates in a final blitz in the last week or ten days. The most extreme instance of this was 1987, when following 'Wobbly Thursday' the Tory leadership panicked and bought huge quantities of newspaper space, almost regardless of cost. They spent an estimated £2.1 million on press ads in the last five days of the campaign,[54] taking three- or four-page ads daily in nearly every national newspaper. The philosophy of party treasurer Lord McAlpine was that it was better to be a poor party in government than a rich party in opposition.

The main exception was 1983, when Saatchis had written what they believed was the first three-page political ad and booked the space in papers for the last Sunday in the campaign. One page consisted of reasons for voting Conservative, the second of reasons for not voting Labour. The third, almost entirely blank, gave a single reason for not voting Alliance. The agency regarded the ad as its best work,[55] and was eagerly awaiting the stir the unprecedented three-pager would cause. It was bitterly disappointed when, at the last minute, the ad was pulled by Margaret Thatcher and party chairman Cecil Parkinson. They were confident of easy victory, keen to save money, and worried that buying so much blank space would be counter-productive. In Thatcher's words, 'Obvious extravagance is bad advertising.'[56]

The legal principles which affect general election advertising also apply to local government and European Parliament elections, so the parties are now able to run large national ad campaigns during these contests. The largest sum any party has devoted to national advertising for local elections was the £600 000[57] spent by the Conservatives in 1990. The Tories treated these elections as a vital contest because local government finance, in the form of the poll tax, was the top political issue of the time.

As for European elections (which started in 1979 when they were overshadowed by the general election), the Conservatives spent heavily in 1984 and 1989 – several hundred thousand pounds on each occasion. But, financially squeezed by some past items of extravagant expenditure, they could afford much less in 1994. Labour spent only £21 000[58] in 1984, but substantial six-figure sums in 1989 and 1994. In 1994 this led to the first national election campaign when Labour's central advertising budget has exceeded the Conservatives'. Labour spent an estimated £432 000 on advertising for the 1994 European and local elections combined, the Tories an estimated £211 000.[59] (For both parties the bulk of spending was related to the European elections.)

**Selection of media**

The press has usually been the main vehicle for party advertising since national papers were first used significantly in this way in 1957. This can be seen from Table 2.2, which shows estimated proportions of spending allocated by the Conservatives and Labour to different media. The table omits the 1966 to 1974 elections because of lack of specific data. Nevertheless, it is clear from the available information that in this period the majority of expenditure for both parties was also on press rather than posters. (The smaller Alliance adspend went almost entirely on posters in 1983 and almost entirely on press in 1987. In 1992 Liberal Democrat advertising was divided 69 per cent on press, 18 per cent on posters and 13 per cent on cinema.[60] As already noted, before these elections third party advertising was insignificant.)

Over the years both the Tories and Labour have assigned most of their spending on national press ads to mass circu-

Table 2.2    Press, posters, cinema

| | Conservatives | | | Labour | | |
| | Press | Posters | Cinema | Press | Posters | Cinema |
|---|---|---|---|---|---|---|
| 1959 | 70 | 30 | – | – | 100 | – |
| 1964 | 69 | 31 | – | 81 | 19 | – |
| 1979 | 51 | 39 | 10 | 42 | 58 | – |
| 1983 | 67 | 33 | – | 76 | 24 | – |
| 1987 | 71 | 29 | – | 81 | 15 | 4 |
| 1992 | 31 | 69 | – | 45 | 53 | 2 |

*Note:* Estimated percentages of spending by the Conservatives and Labour on press (national and regional newspapers and magazines), poster and cinema advertising, for selected elections.

*Sources:* As for Table 2.1, except the 1983 Labour breakdown also involves data from *MEAL Tri-media Digest 1983*, and the 1992 Labour breakdown is from Pinto-Duschinsky, M., 1992.

lation popular newspapers. They have also used provincial papers which serve large numbers of marginal constituencies. The Alliance and Liberal Democrats, constrained by tighter budgets, have focused on upmarket broadsheets with cheaper advertising rates to reach better educated voters and opinion-formers.

While 1978–9 was a partial exception to the dominance of press advertising, the only real exception was 1992. The Conservatives and Labour switched spending out of press and into posters, which suited the pithy, emphatic messages that both sides wanted to run. The change was most dramatic in the Tory case. It was a personal decision by the party chairman Chris Patten, who was not impressed by the effectiveness of large-scale newspaper advertising. The switch would have been even greater had it not been for pressure during the election from Saatchis, newspapers themselves and local constituencies who interpreted lack of newspaper advertising as lack of campaigning. Labour strategists wanted to ensure that they were not seen to be badly losing the battle of the streets, and also opted for a bigger outdoor presence.

The balance between the different media is not a simple matter of party preferences. It is often difficult to obtain decent poster sites at short notice. The Conservatives have traditionally benefited from long-term commercial advertisers passing sites on to them as an election approaches. This practice goes back at least to 1929.[61] In early post-war elections, sites were donated to the Tories by firms threatened with nationalisation by Labour, such as the sugar company Tate and Lyle.[62] In recent elections, the donors have usually been tobacco and brewing companies. In 1992, the Conservatives received a large number of hoardings from Imperial Tobacco. Saatchis also acquired many other sites for the campaign period by covertly pre-booking them in the name of other clients. Labour was only able to obtain most of the sites it used, and thus shift spending into posters, because the clothing company Benetton unexpectedly cancelled its deliberately shocking ad campaign after a flood of complaints.

While party advertising has predominantly been placed in national and provincial newspapers and on poster sites, a greater diversity of media has been employed in recent elections. This has been at the margins of campaigning, since floating voters are found in all demographic groups, and mass rather than niche media are needed to reach them. But the use of different media has provided parties with new opportunities to target particular categories of voters. One surprising obstacle to this trend has sometimes been certain media owners themselves, who have felt chary about carrying political publicity. Even now, political ads are not thought entirely respectable. They are still prohibited, for example, on the London Underground. Nevertheless, over the years they have gradually appeared in a wider variety of media.

Although the Tories used some popular journals such as *Picture Post* in 1949–50, from then until the 1970s party advertising in magazines was more or less limited to small-circulation weeklies read by the politically minded, such as the *Spectator* and the *New Statesman*. This was not due to party narrow-mindedness. Both the Conservatives and Labour tried to place ads in women's magazines in the 1960s, but were turned down by the publishers, who wanted to avoid controversial material.[63]

In the 1970s both main parties succeeded in running ads in mass-market magazines. Their biggest use was by the Tories in 1978–9. Gordon Reece and Saatchis believed that, thanks to the novelty of a woman leader, it made sense for them to target women. Their ads were rejected by one major publisher, IPC,[64] but the magazines they did use ranged from *Cosmopolitan* and *Family Circle* to *TV Times* and *Reader's Digest*. And the ads were designed to suit their environments. One aped the style of supermarket price-cutting ads, except that it showed how prices had risen under Labour. Another employed the quiz formula so beloved of such journals – 'Do this quiz to find out if you're Labour or Conservative'. Questions included: 'Which of these people is more likely to know what it's like to do the family shopping? a. James Callaghan; b. Your husband; c. Mrs Thatcher.'

This campaign represented the high point in the use of mass-circulation magazines. They have been employed by parties since, but in a more restricted way. Their longer lead-times makes them less convenient than newspapers, as it prevents responding to rapidly changing political circumstances. However, special interest titles have been used frequently since 1979 to target two more specific electoral groups. Labour in particular has tried to reach younger voters through the youth and music press. All parties have placed ads in ethnic minority publications, translated where necessary for non-English language journals. Labour did so as far back as 1979, if not earlier. 1983 was the first election when all three parties used the ethnic press – in fact, this was the only print ad run by the Alliance in that campaign.[65]

The first cinema commercial for a political party was produced by Saatchis for the Tories in 1978. Cinema audiences are generally young, and the commercial formed part of the strategy of appealing to first-time voters. The 60-second ad, shown at over 1000 venues, adopted a lighthearted tone to suit the target audience and the nature of cinema as an entertainment medium. It featured a cinema-going young couple in search of the queue for the stalls. Instead they come across queues for the unemployed, urgent operations, buying your council house ('It's hardly moved in the last four years') and leaving the country. He says he doesn't want to see Labour in power again. She says, 'Is that the Marx brothers?' He says, 'No, another bunch of comedians.' The endline was: 'Coming shortly, the Conservatives – a great programme for all the family.'

Its impact was boosted by its innovatory nature. It took audiences by surprise at first viewing, and generated much additional publicity. Launched in September 1978, the commercial ran until the election eight months later at a cost of £144 000, nearly 10 per cent of the party's adspend[66] – a significant proportion. This is despite the fact that it was banned by some large cinema chains who objected to political advertising.[67]

Cinema can only be peripheral in electioneering, since its reach is mainly restricted to young voters. Even among these, an ad has to run for months rather than weeks to build large-scale coverage. Such ads cannot react to political developments. Cinema commercials also involve higher production costs than press and poster ads. The Tories have not used the medium since 1979, although it has been considered and in 1992 Saatchis drafted some possible scripts. However, both other parties have taken it up in a limited way. Labour spent £86 000 on a cinema campaign in 1987 (4 per cent of total adspend)[68] and £70 000 in 1992 (2 per cent).[69] Both were original films – the 1992 one featured the comedian Stephen Fry as a buffoonish Tory candidate. The Liberal Democrats also ran a cinema commercial in 1992 (cost £40 000, 13 per cent of adspend).[70] They saved money by using a cutdown version of one of their party political broadcasts. In it a train hurtles through a dark tunnel. Text appears on the screen: 'Imagine Britain governed not by the Tories, not by Labour . . . but by common sense.' When in due course the train reaches the light at the end, up come the words 'Liberal Democrats'.

A different new medium of political communication was born in 1983 – the moving poster. This was thanks to the Liberal/SDP Alliance. Unable to book poster sites in central London for the May local elections, it hired an 'advan' – a lorry to drive around with the 48-sheet (10ft × 20ft) posters fixed to its sides. This worked well, and for the general election a month later the Alliance employed 20 mobile poster lorries to tour the country, displaying pictures of Roy Jenkins and David Steel looking amicable together. The idea has since been adopted by the other parties, who have employed small fleets of lorries for particular campaigns. Advans are convenient for photo opportunities of poster unveilings, since they are usually available at short notice and provide freedom of choice for location. They have also been used for acts of publicity-seeking impertinence, such as visits to other parties' annual conferences.

The poster which moves from place to place has been followed by another new technique in electioneering – the poster which hardly appears anywhere. In the run-up to the 1992 election, the parties realised they could often receive national news coverage with the claim they were launching a new poster campaign on a new theme. These 'campaigns' consisted of one central London site or advan (booked some-times for only a couple of hours) where the poster would be unveiled to the TV cameras and photographers, plus perhaps a few other disparate billboards. Labour usually purchased ten sites in major cities.[71] However, after several well-reported launches of this kind, the broadcasters got wiser and were no longer so easily manoeuvred into providing audiences of millions for the smallest of ad campaigns. Since the 1992 election, such unveilings have generally been pre-sented to the media as what they are – photo opportunities.

Poster unveilings represent a recent instance of what in the United States is sometimes called a 'newsad' – the con-version of an advertisement into a news event. This is a tac-tic used by political parties from time to time, most effectively by the Tories in 1978–9. They arranged a number of well-publicised 'previews' of Saatchi ads, based on the novelty of their approach. In this way, parties can get maximum pub-licity for minimum spend.


CONCLUSION

In summary, national party advertising up to the 1955 elec-tion consisted largely of poster campaigns on commercial hoardings. These posters generally conveyed simple messages (both positive and negative) with straightforward slogans. In the next phase, both main parties – first the Tories in 1957, next Labour in 1963 – became committed to a new model of party advertising. This involved a long-running, expensive campaign over at least several months, which was created by advertising professionals, made use of the most important available media (newspapers primarily, but also posters), followed a well-defined strategy and was predominantly positive in tone. To commercial advertisers, this model would represent a classic exercise in brand-building.

The late 1960s and 1970s were a period of transition between the two times of plenty in party advertising. Political advertising moved away from classic marketing principles, and adopted rules of its own. Its content became more negative, and lengthy campaigns were cut back in favour of a sudden election-time blitz. These aspects of party ads conflict with everything professional advertisers have been taught about how to build brands and sell products. But there are good reasons why winning votes is different.

First, parties are in the news all the time, while the key 'buying' opportunity only occurs every four years or so. What parties say about themselves through their advertising takes a very small 'share of voice' in the continuous cacophony of political messages communicated to the public. To maximise impact, it makes sense to concentrate activity in the period immediately prior to the public's decision-taking.

Second, the nature of the political 'marketplace' is such that negative political advertising can fulfil a number of useful functions which do not generally apply to most commercial advertising. It can help set the agenda, so that as much as possible of the political cacophony is at least concerned with your preferred issues. It can motivate your own activists and supporters. It can convert opponents into abstainers, which (in the two-party battle) is as useful as persuading abstainers to vote for you. And it can win votes on the basis that someone has to run the country, and you are the least of two or more evils.

There are four other factors which have encouraged negative political advertising. First, party political advertising has always been excluded from the provisions of the British Code of Advertising Practice which prohibit unfair denigration of competitors. Second, like all forms of communication, advertising is most effective when it builds on beliefs people already hold, and most beliefs already held by voters about politicians are negative rather than positive. In other words, negative political advertising is more credible. Third, British political parties are increasingly accepting the common wisdom of US politics, that negative messages are more powerful than positive messages. And fourth (except in the case of the two big parties attacking a smaller one), it does not run the risk of merely raising your competitor's profile, since the two main parties already have such a high profile that their opponents' advertising makes no difference.

Throughout their work for the Conservatives, Saatchi and Saatchi always understood the need to approach political and commercial advertising differently. Jeremy Sinclair says[72] about the 1992 election: 'After we presented our ads to John Major, he said: "Are all the ads you do knocking ads?". We said that if we were selling baked beans, then they wouldn't be.'

There has been one interesting recent exception to the trend towards negative advertising – Labour in 1983. This illustrates the danger of believing that voters are honest, whether to themselves or to pollsters, about what influences them. Wright and Partners, the party's agency, took seriously the private polling which appeared to show that 'slanging' was unpopular with the electorate. Voters claimed they preferred to know about Labour's plans for the future rather than the alleged iniquities of Tory government. While Labour ads (and broadcasts – also produced by the agency) did attack the Conservatives, they accordingly gave more space and time to Labour's proposals. The agency even came up with the slogan 'Think positive. Vote Labour', which was pointlessly amended by the politicians to 'Think positive. Act positive. Vote Labour'. The experience of the election changed Johnny Wright's mind. He says:[73] 'I now think hard-hitting knocking copy is legitimate, which I didn't think then. I was naive enough to believe people when they said they didn't like knocking copy.'

Although in these ways party advertising has diverged from commercial advertising, there is another general advertising trend which it has followed. This is a shift towards the visual rather than the verbal, accompanied by a move to shorter, sharper content. The text used in newspaper ads has become briefer. Indeed, these are now often not much more than a visual image plus headline, a kind of poster in print. Greater use has been made of visual symbolism to dramatise the message and give it immediate impact.

Since the 1980s, the new model for party advertising has had the following general characteristics:

1. It is predominantly negative and confrontational, focused on highlighting the weaknesses of the other side. An ad with 'Labour' in big letters is probably a Conservative one; an ad with 'Tory' in big letters will be Labour; and the exception is, of course, an ad with both parties' names in big letters, which must stem from the Liberal Democrats.
2. Millions of pounds are spent in an instant burst over a few weeks when polling day is announced, so much of the parties' advertising money goes on what could be called a 'single whammy'.
3. As well as pursuing long-term strategic themes, advertising has become part of the tactical cut and thrust of electioneering. This ranges from trying to set the short-term agenda to responding to the other side's gaffes.

# 3 Party Political Broadcasts

*I was the Peter Mandelson–Bryan Gould of the 1959 election. I fought a brilliant campaign and lost.*
> Tony Benn, who devised Labour's innovative 1959 election broadcasts, 1992[1]

*I'll give you five seconds to switch over. For anyone left, here's some Alliance propaganda.*
> John Cleese, opening a party political broadcast, 1987

*How can you operate at an emotional level for ten minutes? You might go for the height of emotion for thirty seconds or a minute – maybe two minutes if you've actually got something really good like a murder taking place on screen.*
> Sir Tim Bell, 1992[2]

Political parties benefit from a unique privilege denied to anyone else trying to influence the public. Although unable to pay for advertising on television or radio, they get regular quantities of airtime under their own editorial control for free.

Party broadcasts are often derided as the most boring and unwelcome of programmes. Nevertheless, they give parties the chance to convey their message to viewers and listeners in the way they want and without the mediation of reporters, presenters or interviewers. And since TV broadcasts are shown in peak time on the two main channels, they reach large audiences. During the 1992 election, the average party television broadcast on ITV was seen by 7.7 million people and on BBC1 by 4.7 million.[3] At one stage party broadcasts were the only form of political programme during elections. Now they are a drop in the ocean of political broadcasting, but one which, if well-aimed (such as Labour's film biography of Neil Kinnock in 1987), can still make large ripples. This chapter examines how parties have used an increasing variety of techniques to try to boost the impact of their broadcasts.

In formal terms there are two categories of party broadcast. Parties are allocated a certain number of 'party political broadcasts' (PPBs) each year, whether or not elections
occur. This is sometimes called the 'annual series'. Parties
are also given 'party election broadcasts' (PEBs) during campaigns for general, local and European elections. However,
the term 'party political broadcast' is often used to cover
PEBs too, and I have used it in this way in this chapter and
throughout the book.

## ALLOCATION OF BROADCASTS

Theoretically, the allocation of broadcasts is decided by the
Committee on Party Political Broadcasting, composed of
representatives from broadcasting organisations and political parties. However, the Committee has not actually met
since 1983, when the quota for the newly forged Alliance
was the subject of a fierce dispute between the Alliance and
the two main parties. After this bruising affair, the broadcasters resolved that controversial decisions were better dealt
with behind the scenes than through face-to-face conflict.
The arrangements are now sorted out via informal negotiation between broadcasters and parties, conducted through
the office of the government chief whip (the confluence of
the 'usual channels' of inter-party communication). When
agreement has not been reached, the broadcasters have
imposed a solution.

Excluding general election broadcasts, the Conservatives
and Labour have generally each had between five and seven
television PPBs annually and a similar or slightly greater
number of radio PPBs. The third party has usually received
a lesser but fluctuating allocation. The Scottish and Welsh
Nationalists get a smaller number of broadcasts.

At general elections, since 1964 it has been standard for
the Tories and Labour each to have five TV and seven radio
broadcasts. The third party quota has ranged from three
TV and five radio up to parity with the two larger parties.
The Nationalists and other small parties putting up more
than a specified number of candidates have also been given
election broadcasts. The election allocations are important

not only for PPBs themselves. Broadcasters have traditionally used the ratio between the party quotas as a guideline
for the party balance of their own election coverage. This is
largely why over the years the third party has fought hard
over its ration.

Television broadcasts are currently transmitted by BBC1,
BBC2, ITV, Channel 4 and Sky News, although Channel 4
does not screen the annual series. Radio broadcasts are carried on Radio 2 and Radio 4.


RADIO DAYS

Party political broadcasting began on radio in the 1920s as
the BBC was becoming established. During the 1924 election campaign, the BBC was allowed to broadcast appeals
from the three party leaders for the first time. MacDonald
and Asquith opted for speeches they were giving at public
meetings to be transmitted. John Reith, head of the BBC,
advised MacDonald that 'it was a mistake to append an invisible audience of millions to a visible audience of two or
three thousand',[4] but to no avail. Baldwin, however, had
the sense to come to a BBC studio to deliver a special talk.
The first official party broadcasts took place during the 1929
campaign. The practice was repeated at the 1931 and 1935
elections, when the broadcasts attracted large audiences and
were regarded as increasingly influential. Press comment
talked of elections as won or lost 'at the fireside'. The high-
est praise went to Stanley Baldwin, the first politician to
demonstrate that radio required a conversational style distinct from that suited to platform oratory.

After the war, party political broadcasting on radio was
the main method used by parties to communicate directly
with the mass of the electorate from 1945 to 1955 or so.

1945 was certainly a radio election. This followed the central
role radio had played in the war as the means by which the
nation was addressed (the incipient television service was
off air from 1939 to 1946). The nightly party broadcasts were
regarded as the major events of the campaign – particularly
Churchill's notorious opening broadcast in which he said
the establishment of socialism would require a Gestapo, and

Attlee's effective rejoinder, skilfully done as more in sorrow than in anger. The average audience was estimated at 45 per cent of the adult population. This figure was normally only reached by the most popular entertainment programmes, and greatly exceeded the numbers who attended election public meetings. The effect of the broadcasts led the authors of the first Nuffield general election study to write:[5] 'It may well be that this method of radio campaigning has revolutionised the nature of British elections.'

It was a revolution that lasted for about ten years. At the next two general elections in 1950 and 1951, senior party figures often considered radio broadcasts as their key contribution to the campaign. They took great care over their texts, and sometimes went through lengthy rehearsals prior to the live broadcast to improve their delivery. Conservative Central Office decided that politicians giving broadcasts should be relieved of other election commitments for four days beforehand.[6] Not only did the programmes reach large audiences, they were also reported prominently in the press. But in the 1955 election television broadcasts, which had started in 1951, achieved around the same significance.

During the 1945–55 period there was little originality of radio presentation. The parties stuck to the simplest of formats: one individual delivering a talk. This was despite their length – Conservative and Labour broadcasts were 20 or 30 minutes long, and Liberal broadcasts 10 or 20 minutes (minor parties got 10 minutes). Occasional attempts to include brief recorded material were sternly ruled out by the BBC, which provided the broadcasting facilities, as 'a breach with custom'.[7] The only party which managed to experiment with more than one speaker in a radio broadcast was the Liberal Party, which did so in 1954 and 1955 when they transmitted the same programme on radio and television. Their 1955 campaign broadcast featured three Liberal candidates being interviewed.[8]

As befitted their importance, most broadcasts were delivered by leading politicians, a few of whom knew of techniques appropriate to the intimate nature of radio. In 1945, foreign secretary Anthony Eden delivered his broadcast in the light of advice he had once received to imagine one individual as his listener and talk as if addressing that person directly.[9] Occasionally, the parties also used radio personalities with experience and understanding of the medium. In 1950, one Labour broadcast was delivered by the playwright J. B. Priestley, while a Tory broadcast was given by the 'radio doctor', Charles Hill. His well-received talk was notable for its lighter, folksy tone, becoming famous for his dismissal of his fellow celebrity's arguments with the vernacular line, 'Chuck it, Priestley.'

After 1955, the restriction to a single speaker was abandoned. Labour produced an adroitly imaginative broadcast prior to the 1956 local elections, which included a humorous sketch about canvassing, a satirical song and a series of short interviews with councillors.[10] It was devised by Anthony Wedgwood Benn (as he then called himself), who became the driving force in modernising the party's approach to both radio and television broadcasting (see below). By the 1959 general election, both main parties were using signature tunes and usually several politicians in a broadcast. Labour, which was more adventurous, also experimented with anonymous vox pops in which ordinary people briefly stated opinions.[11]

From then on, radio PPBs were eclipsed by their television counterparts in audience ratings and political importance. The parties became reluctant to devote much effort to their preparation, and agreed with the BBC to make them shorter. The 1964 election broadcasts were simpler than their predecessors, and the broadcasts during the 1966 campaign even more so: they contained no music, no slogans and at most two speakers reading a script.[12] During the 1970 and 1974 elections the broadcasts became somewhat less sedate and more varied as the parties made more use of vox pops, interviews and celebrity endorsements. But they still remained conventional and unadventurous, especially in comparison to the changes taking place in television PPBs. And the politicians used were generally obscure compared to the leading party figures employed in the 1940s and 1950s.

When Saatchi and Saatchi took charge of Conservative advertising and PPBs in 1978, it introduced a more creative and accessible approach. One early Saatchi radio broadcast featured a mock argument in the pub, during which a Conservative trade unionist, Bill, persuades his Labour-supporting mate, Ted, that life under the Tories would mean higher growth and lower unemployment. But there was no long-lasting attempt to devote time and money to the production of high-quality radio broadcasts.

Since the early 1980s, most radio PPBs have simply been the soundtracks of television broadcasts transmitted on the same day, with the minimum of changes required due to the absence of pictures. This has the advantage of reinforcing the same message, as well as saving on money and effort, but it means that the radio versions are often badly suited to a purely auditory medium. Today, audiences and direct response levels for radio PPBs are a small fraction of the TV equivalents. The parties treat radio as so insignificant that by early 1996 none had yet taken up their legal right to have PPBs transmitted on the national commercial radio stations, which have been established since 1992.

## TELEVISION

### Phase one: 1951–68

Initially, politicians treated the emergent medium of television with great wariness. Many found the thought of appearing on it rather frightening, and there was little grasp of how important it would quickly become. They were unenthusiastic about the prospect of televised party broadcasts. In 1949 the parties unanimously rejected the idea when it was proposed by the BBC for the forthcoming election, which took place in 1950.[13] They relented, however, in time for the following election in 1951, when the three main parties were each given one 15-minute slot.

The first televised party political broadcast was transmitted live at 8 pm on 15 October 1951. It was not an auspicious beginning. The broadcast was delivered for the Liberals by one of their elder statesmen, the former home secretary Lord Samuel. He spoke to the camera from prepared notes, having informed the programme's BBC producer that he would indicate the end by putting down his notes. Unfortunately, when already overrunning on his 15-minute allocation, he paused and shuffled his notes. This was misinterpreted as the closing signal, and thereupon he was faded out without having reached his conclusion.[14]

Samuel had approached the exercise exactly as if it were a radio broadcast. The other parties, however, immediately appreciated the difficulties in inexperienced television performers successfully delivering monologues to camera (this was before the autocue was in use), and devised different tactics. For the Conservatives, deputy leader Anthony Eden was interviewed by the experienced television presenter, Leslie Mitchell. The entire broadcast was planned and rehearsed word for word, down to Mitchell saying (of the charge that the Tories were warmongerers) 'I wonder, sir, whether I may introduce a question which I'm sure will infuriate you', and Eden responding 'I do resent that question'. The act was carried off sufficiently well that newspaper reports praised Eden for his spontaneity and sincerity.[15] Labour's first broadcast relied on a pair of presenters, cabinet minister Sir Hartley Shawcross and backbencher Christopher Mayhew.

Both parties also employed visual aids in a controversy which was dubbed 'the battle of the graphs', an early attempt to exploit the visual potential of TV propaganda. Eden showed viewers a graph of prices rising steeply under Labour. The following night, Mayhew countered with his own set of graphs. These demonstrated that the impression given by Eden's chart depended on how the horizontal and vertical axes were calibrated.

After the campaign, the parties and the BBC agreed that, as with radio, televised PPBs should also take place regularly outside election time. The first of these was given on 1 May 1953 by the Conservatives, who developed ambitious plans for this novel event. Churchill wanted 'to try out the technical tricks of television'.[16] Whereas the 1951 election broadcasts had been entirely studio-based, this 20-minute PPB contained 5 minutes of film,[17] including some rather stilted interviews with ordinary families grateful to have benefited from the government's large housebuilding programme. Along with studio discussion by housing minister Harold Macmillan and backbencher William Deedes, the broadcast also featured stills, music and title sequences. It was a fairly elaborate piece of television for its time.

After this, in the run-up to and during the 1955 campaign, the parties started to explore ways in which television could strengthen the presentation of their case. While the bulk of their output consisted of talking heads, and they stuck to using senior politicians rather than established TV personalities, the variety of television formats tried out was sufficient to contrast sharply with the monotonous form of radio broadcasts.

Both Labour and the Conservatives introduced basic studio props to provide visual elucidation of economic arguments. In its first non-election broadcast in October 1953, which attacked the Tories over their management of the balance of payments, Labour used a wall to represent imports, a ladder placed against it to represent exports, and a soapbox under the ladder to represent the surplus on invisibles.[18] Sometimes problems were difficult to rectify since broadcasts were transmitted live. In the 1955 campaign, Labour displayed shopping baskets of standard goods to illustrate a broadcast on inflation. The butter and cheese melted under the studio lights.[19] One Tory broadcast in 1955 employed small and large money boxes to dramatise the difference in personal savings under Labour and Conservative governments. Trick camerawork was needed when it turned out the larger box had been constructed not, as ordered, 30 times as big as the smaller one, but 30 times as long in each dimension – that is, 27 000 times as big.[20]

Both parties also used short film sequences introduced by politicians in the studio, while for some entirely studio-based broadcasts, they both tried another technique – mimicking the style of BBC current affairs programmes. In the 1955 campaign, the Conservatives ran a half-hour broadcast involving Eden, now prime minister, and four senior colleagues, being quizzed by ten newspaper editors. This was similar in style to a BBC programme called *Press Conference*. Labour imitated another show, *In the News*, with a broadcast consisting of a panel discussion among four politicians.

For the final Tory broadcast of the 1955 campaign, Eden took the brave decision to speak direct to camera for 15 minutes of live television. He had no script and held no notes, but relied on large cue cards placed out of the sight of viewers.[21] Generally well received as conveying calmness and competence, this inspired emulation from other politicians and paved the way for the straight talk to camera format, which in due course became characteristic of televised party political broadcasting. It also helped establish the tradition, largely although not universally followed ever since, that each party's final television PPB contains a direct personal appeal from leader to voters.

After the 1955 election Labour's broadcasting adviser, William Pickles, concluded that the best formats for television PPBs were in order: 1) 'straight talk'; 2) 'straight interview'; 3) 'straight talk with simple visuals'; 4) 'press conference, especially with apparently hostile questions'.[22]

1955 had been widely hailed in advance as the first television election. This was based entirely on party broadcasts, since at that time other television and radio programmes still avoided covering any matter of the remotest political controversy during election campaigns (see Chapter 4). Over a third of the public now had sets, and for those who didn't the parties organised 'At home' sessions so that they could watch the broadcasts at the houses of those who did.[23] The Tories also showed some broadcasts at public meetings.[24] But the average audience for the TV broadcasts was still slightly less than for radio, and the impact of television was not as great as anticipated. It was not so much the first television election as, in the words of a *Times* editorial,[25] 'the transitional election'. In the following election in 1959, which was also the first reported on TV and radio news and discussed in current affairs programmes, the party television broadcasts attracted six times the audience of their radio counterparts.[26]

Labour's 1959 broadcasts achieved a higher level of professionalism and inventiveness in the production of PPBs than anything done before. They adopted a flexible, fast-moving magazine format similar to the BBC's successful *Tonight* programme, which since its creation in 1957 had pioneered such a style of popular current affairs programming.

The key figure behind the Labour broadcasts was Anthony Wedgwood Benn, who had been a BBC radio producer before becoming an MP and was an enthusiast for new methods of political communication. A close student of early political broadcasting, Benn was determined to educate his party in the ways of the television era. Entitled – in line with the party manifesto – 'Britain Belongs to You', the broadcasts (mainly 20 minutes long) were presented by Benn and two other young Labour politicians with experience of current affairs television, Christopher Mayhew and Woodrow Wyatt.

The trio were located in a businesslike mock office which was described as 'Labour's radio and television operations room', but was in fact a BBC studio. They introduced film reports, animated cartoons, interviews, short talks to camera by party leaders and testimonials from non-political celebrities. The opening music was a phrase from Holst's *Jupiter*, chosen by Benn because it was 'strong and powerful'.[27] (In 1987 Saatchi and Saatchi also found *Jupiter* a good source of strong and powerful music for PPBs on the merits of Thatcherism.) These thoroughly planned, tightly paced and easy to watch broadcasts caused an enormous stir. During the campaign the Tories were forced to change their less professional approach and make more use of television expertise.

In fact, this series was the highpoint of party political broadcasting for years to come. Labour broadcasts at the following elections in the 1960s suffered from lack of advance planning and confusion over who was in charge. Leading politicians favoured giving maximum time to talking heads, especially if it was their own head which was doing the talking. While Harold Wilson fostered a modern approach to advertising and polling after becoming leader in 1963, his attitude to party broadcasts was distinctly conservative. Ironically, it was precisely because the politicians regarded broadcasting as more important than advertising that they refused to leave it to those with professional skills.

Although it was mainly Labour which advanced the techniques of party broadcasting in 1959, there were two linked innovations for which the Conservatives were responsible. Their final broadcast was a straight to camera talk by Harold Macmillan, with a number of props, notably a globe which he twirled with the authoritative air of a man seasoned in foreign affairs. It was recorded in advance at the studios of Associated Television (ATV), one of the recently established commercial television companies. Macmillan was coached by Norman Collins, a former controller of BBC television and now ATV deputy chairman, who to help him relax allowed Macmillan to do the recording under the impression it was a rehearsal. This made it the first studio-based PPB to avoid the risks of live transmission by being pre-recorded, and also the first to be produced using independent facilities rather than those of the BBC. By the next election in 1964, party political broadcasting was almost entirely pre-recorded.[28]

The broadcast was widely lauded, and so was Collins. In 1964 he was given the equivalent if trickier task of trying to coax an effective performance for the final broadcast out of Macmillan's successor, Sir Alec Douglas-Home. He failed. Douglas-Home, largely protected from the party battle as a peer before he became prime minister, had never read an autocue, although its use was by now common. Collins decided it was too late to teach him. Nor could he be expected to memorise his entire 15-minute talk. Instead, he learnt it in 2-minute sections. In the film these were linked by shots of him looking at notes he was not actually using. The effect emphasised the contrast between the elderly, amateurish aristocrat and his opponent – the modern, competent Wilson. In the 1966 election the new leader, Edward Heath, abandoned the use of Collins and the ATV studios, reverting to the BBC's production facilities.

Generally, until the late 1970s the dominant mode of party political broadcasting was the talking head. Broadly, this could take two forms: the politician being interviewed (either rehearsed with a stooge interviewer, or genuinely unrehearsed with a reputable interviewer like Robin Day) or the politician talking straight to camera.

The interview did have some advantages: as a conversation rather than a monologue it was a more natural form of discourse for a medium watched in people's living rooms; and for the politicians it was easier, especially once they were accustomed to ordinary television interviews. The most extreme example of this was Douglas-Home, who later acknowledged his failure to master the set-piece talk to camera: 'On question and answer I was adequate because that is a reproduction of a natural occasion, but on the set-piece unhappiness and distaste was written all over my face . . . "Imagine that you are speaking to two other people in a room," the producer would say. In vain I would retort that I usually let them get a word in.'[29]

But the use of interviews in PPBs had one overwhelming defect: by inviting comparison with the impartial and increasingly probing interviews of ordinary television, they seemed false and lacked credibility. This was confirmed by Conservative private opinion research in the early 1960s, which concluded: 'First, that any questioner is suspect in a party political broadcast: the impression is that the whole thing is rehearsed – a put-up job. Second, speaking direct to the viewer is much more successful – though some of the effect is lost if the script is read from notes.'[30]

And talking straight to camera without the embarrassment of notes had become easier and less of a feat of memory or fluency due to technological progress – the import to Britain from America of the autocue or teleprompter.[31] This used a system of mirrors to pass a written script over the lens of the camera so that it could be read by the person broadcasting but was invisible to the viewer. Done well, it gave the impression that the speaker was not reading but was talking informally to those watching. However, it was not easy to do well.

Conservative officials decided that Eden should not use the device for his 1955 straight to camera election broadcast because they thought at that time 'anyone who read the teleprompter gave the appearance of having extraordinary rolling eyes that looked as if they were seasick'.[32] When Eden tried out the system a few months later he encountered another problem: he was too shortsighted to read it.[33] It turned out that this was not uncommon for middle-aged politicians with imperfect eyesight who did not want to be seen wearing glasses on television. Eden's successor Harold Macmillan also found it difficult, complaining that he had to screw up his eyes so much that he 'presented the appearance of a corpse looking out of a window'.[34]

The first major politician to become an accomplished user of the autocue was Harold Wilson, who was determined with characteristic thoroughness to seize the opportunities offered by television and to exploit every means for improving his performance. In the first talk he gave to camera in a PPB, in February 1963 soon after his election as Labour leader, he insisted on using the autocue.[35] Wilson had eyesight problems too (on occasion he needed the camera to be brought nearer),[36] but he did not let this prevent him from mastering the technique and learning how to read his script while hardly moving his eyeballs.

The autocue did involve one small disadvantage – it made late changes to text more inconvenient. But this was easily outweighed by its benefits. As the machinery became more sophisticated and easier to use and politicians became more practised, in the 1960s the autocue-assisted talk to camera almost entirely displaced the interview in PPBs. This became the stereotypical form of party political broadcasting, especially in its most conventional setting – beginning with a shot of the politician at an imposing desk in an authoritative office and then closing in to head and shoulders.

Although the talking head was dominant, in the late 1950s and 1960s the parties did incorporate into their broadcasts numerous elements of ordinary television, linked by studio presenters. After their initial experimental approaches, they became accustomed to producing what were in effect television programmes of between 10 and 25 minutes, with most effort going into the election broadcasts transmitted during campaigns.

As well as the simplest visual elements – captions, stills, diagrams and cartoons – broadcasts often had brief film sequences, with a soundtrack or backing music or a studio voiceover. When these were not filmed interviews or discussions, these were usually fairly general shots – such as schoolchildren to illustrate education and cars to illustrate transport, and scenes of prosperity or poverty, construction or dereliction, according to political need. However, editing film was then a time-consuming and cumbersome process. It made sense to shoot the film well in advance, but this also involved the risk that changing political circumstances would render it irrelevant. So the preponderance of talking heads over film was due not only to the vanity of politicians, but also to the practicalities of film-making at the time.

Apart from politicians, broadcasts made use of two other categories of people – the ordinary and the famous. Initially, ordinary people (whether passers-by in the street or an invited audience) were generally used to ask questions, in an attempt to show that politicians were willing and able to respond to the real concerns of real voters. However, the 1960s saw more use of vox pops, which were also becoming increasingly common in television news and commercials. This gave a feeling of authenticity and immediacy, and fostered the impression that the party was supported by a wide cross-section of the population. They could be exploited as well to voice sentiments which politicians themselves could not be seen to express directly. For these reasons – and their cheapness to film – vox pops have remained a mainstay of party political broadcasting ever since.

The most systematic use of celebrity endorsements was by Labour in 1959, when those given cameo roles in the party's election broadcasts included the jazz musician Humphrey Lyttelton, the philosopher A. J. Ayer, the scientist Ritchie Calder, the actress Jill Balcon and the writers Compton Mackenzie, Wolf Mankowitz and John Osborne. After that, celebrities continued to appear occasionally, at least in the case of Labour and the Liberals. Show business stars used in PPBs in the 1960s included the actor Harry H. Corbett for Labour and the actress Honor Blackman for the Liberals.

In imitation of ordinary programmes, the party broadcasts also sometimes had opening and closing titles and theme music. Labour's 1964 election broadcasts, for example, featured a signature tune specially composed by the jazz musician Johnny Dankworth.

The main problem the parties faced was the tendency of viewers to switch off when a PPB came on. There was no point then in switching over. From 1956, the year after it started, ITV showed PPBs at the same time as BBC1. BBC2 joined in simultaneous transmission when it began in 1964. From time to time, special efforts were made to seize the attention of viewers right at the beginning. One of the more imaginative gimmicks opened a Conservative PPB featuring Macmillan in 1962. His press secretary, Harold Evans, wanted an initial shot which would hold the immediate attention of viewers through its novelty. His idea was to show the apparatus of television production, normally kept out of the camera's view at all costs: camera, microphone, lights, cables, technicians, down to the floor manager giving Macmillan his cue.[37] Another effective example was a Liberal broadcast in 1966 presented by Ludovic Kennedy – it opened melodramatically with mysterious silhouettes of Kennedy himself and Harold Wilson in a manner reminiscent of a popular television crime series.[38] On the whole, however, these attention-grabbing devices were noted for their rarity.

The 1960s also saw the first notable use of fiction in party political broadcasting. This came from the Tories who ran what became known as their 'soap opera' in August 1964, when the start of the election campaign proper was imminent. The bulk of the broadcast was given over to a touching miniature drama, featuring a warm-hearted if quarrelsome married couple. The film begins with the husband saying goodbye to his wife as he leaves for work. She leans on the vacuum cleaner and sulks because he has clearly forgotten their wedding anniversary, then she muses on how things have improved in the 13 years since then (and, coincidentally, since the last Labour government). He phones. Not only has he remembered the anniversary, the present he has bought is her dream come true, their first car – affordable thanks to the rise in personal allowances in last year's budget. But he still supports Labour and when she queries that, he says: 'Don't you talk about things you can't understand, my girl.' She says: 'I know I don't know much about politics and that sort of thing, but I do know we've done all right these last few years.'[39]

This early use of fiction to make a political case about increasing prosperity provoked an outburst of indignation from press and politicians. It was strenuously defended by the Conservative Party vice-chairman Lord Poole, who had commissioned the broadcast from a company which specialised in producing television commercials, TV Advertising Ltd.[40] But it was regarded with distaste by many senior Tories and there was no attempt to continue with this approach. However, by the late 1980s such techniques became acceptable.

**Phase two: 1968–78**

The next major improvements in party political broadcasts on television came at the end of the 1960s. This followed the appointment in 1968 of Geoffrey Tucker as the Conservative director of publicity. Tucker regarded TV PPBs as central to his strategy, particularly in terms of presenting Edward Heath. He was determined to improve their impact and technical quality.

To do this, Tucker assembled a talented team of television and advertising specialists. It included James Garrett (a leading producer of TV commercials), Barry Day (creative director of ad agency McCann-Erickson) as scriptwriter, and the television/film directors Bryan Forbes, Terence Donovan and Dick Clement. This was the first time outsiders rather than politicians had so much influence over PPBs, right down to Day providing scripts for the politicians' talks to camera. To maximise his control over production, Tucker also abandoned the use of BBC studio facilities.

The group produced original and striking work in their initial, pre-election PPBs. This was facilitated by technological developments in filming which were neatly suited to overcoming the party's main presentational problem – Heath's stuffy and remote image. It was now possible to use smaller hand-held cameras that could work in natural light, instead of bulky cameras which were fixed to a tripod and required powerful lights. This meant that a camera crew could easily follow a politician and record vision and sound of unscripted encounters.

The Tories used footage obtained in this way (variously described at the time as newsreel, reportage or cinéma vérité) in two PPBs, one set in Heath's Bexley constituency and the other on a trip to Newcastle. They filmed Heath enjoying himself and seeming relaxed in ordinary settings – in shops, constituents' homes, pubs and at a football match. The party's research confirmed that the public preferred this kind of material to the straight to camera format of conventional PPBs. This filming technique was also used extensively in the final Tory broadcast of the 1970 campaign, described below under 'Bio-pics'. And it was copied at the time of the election by Labour, who transmitted film clips of Harold Wilson's walkabouts.

'The old guard didn't like it,' says Geoffrey Tucker.[41] 'They thought the leader of the Conservative Party should never be seen in a pub talking to ordinary people. But he enjoyed it and came alive. Much to our surprise he was very good at it. It was important that he should be seen talking to people and drinking with people.'

For the 1970 campaign itself Tucker and his team modelled the studio setting for their broadcasts on the recently established *News at Ten*. The aim was to fit into the television environment and borrow the authority of the programme. It was reinforced by using Geoffrey Johnson Smith and Christopher Chataway, MPs who were both well-known former television reporters, as the two anchormen. This was planned in advance, and it was an unexpected bonus when the broadcasters and parties decided the party election broadcasts would be transmitted at 10 pm. The presenting duo read pieces of party propaganda as if they were news items, and briskly introduced film sequences, vox pops and talks straight to camera from senior party figures.

Most of the broadcasts had a 'commercial break' in the middle with two or three mock commercials, after which the presenters said 'Welcome back'. The self-contained 'commercials', lasting up to 30 seconds, were used to make simple, stark, anti-Labour points. A particularly memorable one featured a pound note being trimmed by a pair of scissors. This illustrated how inflation continuing at the current rate would reduce its purchasing power, ending with a menacing prediction of the 'ten-bob pound'.

'Having created the "editorial" context of the programme format, we still felt the need for the capsulisation the TV commercial can uniquely provide,' said Barry Day,[42] who wanted to emulate the single-minded simplicity of TV commercials and exploit public familiarity with them as a means of communication. 'We couldn't buy commercials, but there was nothing which said we couldn't put them into our own programmes.'

The most inventive broadcast of the series was largely devoted to a film of the household chores and daily activities of Sylvia, a young, working-class housewife from south London. It was accompanied by her straightforward but engrossing musings on life, its hardships and the cost of washing powder. No PPB had ever starred an ordinary person in this way before. The political point was to detach working-class women worried about rising prices from their unionised and Labour-supporting husbands, who were pleased with their rising wages. Sylvia concluded: 'I think my husband will vote Labour 'cos he's always voted Labour and generations before him have . . . but I certainly won't. I shall vote Conservative.'

After the 1970 election, Tucker's team was disbanded. Heath, who had never showed much voluntary interest in mastering presentation skills, was even less willing once installed in Downing Street. Members were quickly summoned back for the February 1974 election but the essential planning and preparation, such as the extensive pre-shot footage, which went into the 1970 broadcasts was absent. There was no attempt to repeat anything like the imitation of *News at Ten*; instead the broadcasts mainly followed the simple formula of a straight to camera talk, topped and tailed by brief film sequences.

The 1970 Conservative broadcasts were pathbreaking in the emphasis placed on carefully shot and edited film. But, widely regarded as a central feature of the campaign, they were also important in augmenting several trends which affected not just PPBs but electoral campaigning generally. They encouraged the attempt to persuade through image and connotation rather than fact and argument; interest in personality rather than policy; the use of dramatic visual symbolism (such as the vanishing ten-bob pound and, in another broadcast, the 'frozen wage packet' retrieved from a freezer); and, often linked to such symbolism, harder hitting negativity. 'We were in the forefront of negative advertising,' claims Barry Day.[43]

The 1974 broadcasts took this negativity further. One Conservative broadcast in the February campaign featured a puppet of Harold Wilson spewing forth pound notes for the miners and nationalisation, while the voiceover asked: 'Where does Harold Wilson get his money? From you.'[44] Another was by far the most controversial PPB of either 1974 election. To the sound of eerie music, it showed photographs of Labour's pragmatic leaders Wilson and James Callaghan fading into the left-wing bogey figures of their shadow cabinet colleagues Tony Benn and Michael Foot. This was followed by symbols of bank accounts, mortgages and even wage packets being stamped 'state-owned'; quotes from Communists about their purported influence on Labour policy; and then chancellor of the exchequer Tony Barber warning that if Labour won, democracy itself would be in peril. Labour was so outraged that it replayed the broadcast to journalists at its regular press conference the following morning. The broadcast was badly received in the press. And at a time when both main parties believed too much mud-slinging drove voters into the fast-growing Liberal camp, it caused consternation within Conservative circles as well.

The growing importance of film in broadcasts continued. It was less apparent in February 1974, when all parties were inadequately prepared for the snap election. But it was clear in October 1974, when there was greater use (particularly by Labour) both of film specially shot on location and stock library film. The camerawork was also becoming more imaginative. In the October campaign only one television election broadcast consisted entirely of a solo straight to camera talk – the Liberal Scottish 'opt-out' (a specific broadcast for Scottish viewers different to the one seen elsewhere).[45]

## Phase three: Since 1978

So by the mid-1970s the proportion of PPB time allocated to talking heads was decreasing, while the use of film, music and visual devices to emphasise the party message was becoming more creative. These trends were rapidly accelerated when Saatchi and Saatchi was appointed as the Conservative advertising agency in March 1978. For the first time, the party gave control over advertising and PPBs to the same group of people. This meant not only that the content and style of the two forms of communication were more closely integrated, but also that broadcasts were now entirely in the hands of an advertising agency.

Naturally the Saatchi approach to the broadcasts reflected the styles and techniques of TV commercials. In the words of the agency's then chairman Tim Bell, 'Basically we made long commercials rather than short films.'[46] This meant faster cutting, the use of professional actors, more special effects, more imaginative visual and dramatic devices, and the reduction of talking politicians to a bare minimum. From the start the Saatchi broadcasts set new standards of slickness and professionalism in the production of PPBs.

Saatchis' first party political broadcast was transmitted in May 1978, two months after the agency gained the Conservative account. It was the agency's first public piece of work of any kind for the party, and it succeeded in getting noticed. The broadcast was heralded by novel teaser ads in the press that morning, stating that if you did not watch television at 9 pm that night you might regret it for the rest of your life. Scripted by creative director Jeremy Sinclair, it claimed Britain was going backwards – and showed film of people walking backwards over Waterloo Bridge, the hands on Big Ben going round the wrong way, and so on. The appearance of politicians was limited to brief takes in which they delivered only a couple of sentences.

This and the other early Saatchi broadcasts attracted much media attention, in which the agency was presented as having invigorated television's most lifeless output. ('Why the nation has stopped switching off party political broadcasts,' said the *Daily Mail*).[47] Labour's advertising advisers recognised the challenge. One of them, Tim Delaney, stated after the 1979 election: 'We had said to the party: look, the name of the game has changed. You can no longer cut to a picture of a man at a lathe every time you talk about industrial relations or to an old-age pensioner every time you talk about a caring, sharing society. . . . You must borrow some of [the Tories'] techniques. At the very least, you must acknowledge that the Conservative broadcasts are going to condition people to expect different things from party political broadcasts.'[48]

The Saatchi style was expensive. The broadcasts produced by the agency in the year from its appointment up to and including the 1979 election cost £425 000.[49] Saatchis carried on working on Tory PPBs for some time after the election, but then Conservative Central Office decided to produce PPBs in-house to save money. This was reversed by Cecil Parkinson after he became party chairman in 1981. In his view the in-house productions resembled 'very amateurish home movies',[50] and he determined to find the money to pay Saatchis to do the job properly again.

Saatchis' use of professional actors and actresses speaking scripts and purporting to be ordinary housewives, shopkeepers or trade unionists was vehemently attacked by Labour (although in the late 1980s Labour broadcasts were to use actors extensively and successfully). Central Office appeared defensive in response, and by the time of the 1983 election Saatchis used only actors to present the broadcasts or do voiceovers. The use of actors as presenters, sometimes in the manner of television reporters, has since become a standard PPB technique for other parties too.

Other aspects of the early Saatchi approach proved durable. These included not only the reduction in talking heads, but also the basis of selection of those heads which were occasionally still required to talk. The control given to the agency – and the concomitant reduction in influence of politicians – meant that politicians could be casted for the PPBs on the basis of communications logic rather than status or Buggin's turn which had so often been the criteria in the past. It also meant Saatchis could largely script what they said. Early Saatchi broadcasts on 'caring' issues used the gentle-toned deputy leader William Whitelaw, 'since he was a good person to speak on care and compassion'.[51] Party chairman Lord Thorneycroft was used in 1978/9 because, as a former chancellor of the exchequer, he was regarded as a voice of authority and experience. On the other hand, in the first 40 minutes of Saatchi political broadcasting the then unpopular party leader Margaret Thatcher appeared for only one minute.

And there was another factor at work, then and later. 'We quite unashamedly chose people we thought looked good, such as Michael Heseltine and Humphrey Atkins,' says Bell.[52] 'Cecil Parkinson was the prime choice as he was so handsome. Geoffrey Howe was not good in visual terms – he looked too scruffy.'

Saatchis also frequently exhibited a fondness for a tongue-in-cheek, less serious, even sometimes satirical tone to some PPBs. While this often appeared to go down well in 'electoral peacetime', it was widely regarded as too flippant during actual election campaigns. The agency's first election broadcasts in 1979 included a mock athletics race (the 'international prosperity race') in which the British runners were weighed down by government-imposed burdens of tax and inflation, and a Scottish broadcast written in the doggerel style of William McGonagall. These were not well received. Nor was a later 1987 election broadcast in which Labour was presented as an unsuccessful magician whose tricks aimed at tackling the nation's problems never worked.

But there was one special difficulty which the agency faced from the start. Used to producing commercials which rarely exceeded one minute, Saatchis found the process of creating ten minutes of television somewhat testing. Tim Bell says:[53] 'Filling up ten minutes of television is a nightmare. You end up trying to think of things to put in it, which is crazy. Ten minutes on any subject is bound to be unbelievably tedious. Advertising people believe the shorter and pithier the message, the better.'

Before the 1979 election, Saatchis and the Conservatives sought to replace the allocated ten-minute PPB slots with five of two minutes. This was rejected by the broadcasters who thought such short PPBs would be too similar to ordinary commercials. After the election the party voluntarily started to cut its annual PPBs from ten minutes to five, a length which the broadcasters found acceptable. This policy was also adopted for the 1983 election, when four of the five Tory broadcasts were five minutes long, while Labour and the Alliance ran all theirs at the full allocation of ten minutes.[54] 'It was regarded by many people as madness to give up free airtime,' says Bell,[55] 'but five minutes is ample to convey a message.'

This view was shared in retrospect by his adversary, Johnny Wright of Wright and Partners, the ad agency which did Labour's 1983 broadcasts. Wright says:[56] 'The Tory decision to have five minutes was right. Theirs were seen as short and snappy, ours were seen as long and boring.'

The Conservatives initiated another change in party political broadcasting around this time. Until the late 1970s PPBs had been transmitted simultaneously on all channels, so that viewers had to watch them or nothing. After Margaret Thatcher became leader, the Tories unilaterally abandoned this for broadcasts outside election periods, allowing the different channels (BBC1, BBC2 and ITV) to schedule their broadcasts at different times. This was in keeping with Thatcherite notions of freedom of choice for viewers, but it also meant the broadcasts were less resented. Their audiences, if smaller, were more willing. In 1980 all parties agreed on non-simultaneous transmission for most broadcasts. In due course simultaneous transmission was abandoned entirely.

While Saatchis was transforming the presentation of Conservative PPBs, Labour was also modernising its broadcasts, if at a slower pace. As with the Tories, 1979 was the first election when responsibility for most Labour election broadcasts was taken away from politicians and party officials and given to advertising advisers. However the decision, taken at the insistence of James Callaghan, only occurred at the last minute after the election was announced. This rendered effective planning impossible.

During the 1979 campaign, Labour was briefly accused of one rather sinister innovation – the use of subliminal techniques. In one broadcast a voting-type cross flashed momentarily on the screen while Denis Healey was speaking. This led to the claim in a *Daily Express* lead story[57] that 'when confronted with a ballot paper in a polling booth a person's subconscious may be triggered by the vision of a cross over the face of Denis Healey and be compelled to vote Labour'. The cross turned out to be an editing mark which should have been removed, but had not been owing to the haste with which the broadcast had been prepared.

In the 1983 campaign the Labour PPBs were produced by the party's ad agency, Wright and Partners, also appointed at the last minute. Their broadcasts lacked the flair of those produced by Saatchis for the Conservatives, but with rapid cutting, graphics and location shots they did take Labour further down the road to professionalism.

As with other aspects of campaigning, Labour PPBs became more rigorously directed to winning votes once Neil Kinnock became party leader in October 1983. He removed their supervision from the national executive committee, the arena for much party infighting, and passed it to a newly-formed campaign strategy committee, which was more directly under his control. And for the first time the party gave the job of producing its non-election broadcasts to outsiders – John Gau Productions, an independent television production company (managing director John Gau was an experienced producer and formerly head of BBC TV current affairs). This approach increased costs, especially because Gau avoided the free studio facilities offered by the BBC and produced complete films ready for transmission,[58] but it resulted in broadcasts of a higher technical quality.

Gau's first PPB focused on the new party leader, with shots of him speaking triumphantly at conference, talking concernedly to nurses, hugging Glenys and coaching his son's

rugby team. Gau then continued to produce Labour broadcasts until after the 1987 election. During this period the
PPBs became more closely integrated with the party's other
campaigning, as Labour's increasingly glossy and well-organised mid-term campaigns were launched with slickly professional broadcasts. And more care was taken to feature those
politicians deemed telegenic, although this caused resent-
ment among some senior figures who felt they had been
unfairly snubbed on political or personal grounds. The decisions were partly based on private polling data. According
to this, the frontbencher consistently thought most likely to
make people vote Labour was Denis Healey, while the frontbencher thought most likely to deter Labour votes was Gerald
Kaufman.[59]

The most prominent PPB of the 1987 campaign itself was
Hugh Hudson's panegyric to Neil Kinnock, described below under 'Bio-pics'. But Labour's most controversial broadcast
involved a direct personal attack on Thatcher, uniquely ferocious in the history of party political broadcasting. Trad-
ing on the prime minister's occasional use of the royal 'we'
and other apparently quasi-regal behaviour, it was captioned
'Thatcher's Glorious Reign 1979–87' and featured a succession of caricatures and unflattering stills of Thatcher, inter-
spersed with scenes of deprivation, violent policing and other
alleged aspects of Thatcherism. It was all skilfully cut to the
sound of 'A regular royal Queen' from *The Gondoliers*. In
retrospect, however, it was widely considered excessive and
counter-productive, including by senior Labour figures.

This broadcast certainly constituted a stark contrast to
Saatchis' adulatory portrayal of the prime minister. One Tory
broadcast in the 1987 campaign featured 29 clips of Thatcher
as world leader, running for nearly $2\frac{1}{2}$ minutes and accompanied by a triumphalist theme specially composed by Andrew
Lloyd Webber – at that time it was 'the longest non-verbal
sequence in the history of party broadcasting'.[60]

After 1987 John Gau Productions ceased to work for Labour. From 1988 to 1990 party broadcasts were written by
adman Barry Delaney, creative director of the agency Delaney
Fletcher Delaney (and brother of Tim who had worked for
Labour in the past). Delaney introduced a novel and imaginative approach. Many of his PPBs were fictional narratives.

Some were highly stylised – in one, a trendy middle-class couple with baby are harangued by a disembodied Thatcher-like voice coming from above, sloganising about market forces and moaning minnies. Others were quite naturalistic. One featured a young northerner who had sought work in London, musing on how the poll tax, social security changes and NHS waiting lists had affected his family; another starred a prosperous businessman influenced by scenes of deprivation he witnesses while driving home.

The broadcasts were driven by clear, simple creative ideas and were well executed, being filmed by directors of TV commercials. The use of professional actors did sometimes bring problems – the 'young northerner' promptly told the press that in real life he had no intention of voting Labour. The party's private polling also showed that people said the use of actors in PPBs was inappropriate. But this was dismissed by Delaney as irrelevant to how viewers actually responded to the broadcasts. Overall, these PPBs represented a more accessible, less hectoring way in which to make political points. The technique also suited Labour particularly well at the time of its wide-ranging policy review in 1987–90 when it had little positive to say.

Delaney ceased to write Labour PPBs after John Underwood succeeded Peter Mandelson as the party's director of communications in 1990. Underwood wanted broadcasts to have greater policy content and to present a wider range of Labour politicians to the public.

Conservative broadcasts in the 1987–90 period were generally less well received. This was acknowledged by the party's director of communications, Brendan Bruce, who said:[61] 'Labour have got ahead of us in this field, and I do think we could do our party politicals a lot better.' Over this period the Tories involved several different advertising agencies and production companies in work on PPBs. This was partly because they were testing out possible arrangements to succeed Saatchi and Saatchi, which had resigned the party account after the 1987 election. When Saatchis was reappointed in 1991, the new director of communications, Shaun Woodward, told the agency to devote more money and effort to improving the executional values of PPBs. As a former television producer, Woodward considered this important. Fourteen broadcasts produced in the 12 months up to and including the 1992 election cost the party £2 250 000,[62] much more than it had ever spent before on this side of campaigning.

These Saatchi broadcasts were notable for their close integration with other party campaigning, not only in their themes but also in their visual symbolism (such as the 'tax bombshell' and 'double whammy'). There was also a greater use of repetition, with broadcasts structured so that certain filmic elements or modules could be repeated in different PPBs. The broadcasts focused on attacking Labour, the overall tone was stark and doom-laden, and as usual for Saatchis they featured short dramatic scenarios.

Talking heads still figured in broadcasts in the late 1980s and early 1990s, if to a lesser extent than before. In some ways, however, their manner of presentation changed. Due to advances in make-up, lighting and filming techniques, such as the use of colour filters, the broadcast producers could exercise more control over how the politicians actually looked on screen. 'With a combination of make-up, lighting and lenses you can make anybody look like anything you want,' according to Brendan Bruce. In 1989, when worried that the public might start to think that Thatcher was too old, he arranged for her to be filmed for one PPB in such a way that it had 'taken about ten years off her age'.[63] Unfortunately for Bruce, his research showed that viewers found the result unrealistic. Similar techniques have been used, for example, by Hugh Hudson in Labour broadcasts.

The party broadcast battle of the 1992 election was dominated by one particular Labour film, whose repercussions far eclipsed those of any other PPB in that campaign. Screened on 24 March and later nicknamed 'Jennifer's Ear' (although officially entitled 'Mandy'), it was the most emotive party political broadcast there has ever been.

The broadcast intercuts the tales of two young girls painfully afflicted by glue ear. There is no speaking or commentary, but throughout a soulful soundtrack of the B. B. King song, 'Someone Really Loves You'. The opening caption announces: 'The story of two girls with the same problem. One can afford private treatment. The other can't.' Initially both girls sit suffering in hospital, accompanied by their

anxious mothers. Rich girl is told she can have the operation now. Poor girl must wait. Rich girl recovers in hospital,
surrounded by flowers and a happy family. Poor girl sits
stoically through school lessons in agony, then cries by herself in the toilet. And all because, the ending reveals, rich
girl's mother can write a cheque to pay for private treatment. The four-minute drama is followed by Neil Kinnock
talking calmly to camera about Labour's intention to enhance the National Health Service for all.

Using child actresses, directed by Mike Newell (who later
directed *Four Weddings and a Funeral*), and written by John
Webster (of the ad agency BMP DDB Needham), the broadcast was moving, hard-hitting and made to top creative standards. No previous PPB had used 'faction' or 'docudrama'
in this way to squeeze the maximum emotional impact out
of real-life case histories. No previous PPB had appealed so
emphatically to the heart rather than the head, to emotion
rather than argument. Members of research groups with whom
it had been pre-tested were moved to tears. No one knows
how many English and Welsh viewers of the real thing responded in the same way (it was not shown in Scotland,
which instead had to make do with an opt-out broadcast
about devolution). It represented a powerful blow on Labour's best vote-winning issue of health. The broadcast was
denounced virulently by senior Tories ('wicked', 'despica-
ble', 'shameless', 'ruthless'), but for some Labour strategists
it constituted a major step forward in party political
campaigning.

However, the direct influence of the broadcast was swept
aside by the extraordinary row which gradually unfolded
around it. It emerged it was based partly on the case of a
young girl called Jennifer Bennett. An increasingly bizarre
dispute then dominated the media for three days, accounting for about half the election news on BBC1 and ITV.[64]
The principal parts were taken by Jennifer's father who had
informed Labour of her plight and backed the broadcast,
her Tory mother who was deeply angered by it, her grand-
father – a former Conservative mayor – who had warned
Central Office about the broadcast in advance, her medical
consultant who claimed it was inaccurate, health secretary
William Waldegrave who advised the consultant to speak to

the *Daily Express*, and Kinnock's press officer Julie Hall, who
suddenly took over her boss's press conference and denied
emotionally that she had inadvertently disclosed Jennifer's name.

The affair led to many similar cases being highlighted in
the regional media, but the overall impression it created
was of a confused slanging match between the two main
parties in which the real issues were submerged. The result
was to boost the opinion poll rating of the Liberal Democrats.[65] An effective piece of party propaganda was undermined, and the power of health as a Labour issue was seriously
weakened. Labour's internal report[66] on the election concluded: 'The problem on this PEB was ... that it was wrongly
briefed on and badly researched. The indication that it was
based on one single case (which it never was) was mistaken,
and that case proved highly vulnerable. There was a serious
crisis in the campaign at this point ... [The row over the
broadcast] meant that we had not managed to gain the high
moral ground in this campaign and looked not a little grubby.'

While the PPBs of the two main parties became much
slicker from the late 1970s to the early 1990s, this trend
had less effect on the centre party in its various incarna-
tions during this period. Due to lack of resources, it remained more dependent on talks to camera and vox pops
than the other parties, even though the Alliance did spend
more heavily on broadcasts than the minute sums the Liberals had previously paid.

The 1979 Liberal and 1983 Alliance election broadcasts
were mostly produced by Justin Cartwright, a television director highly regarded by the Liberal leader, David Steel.
After this more use was made of advertising expertise. The
adman David Abbott wrote some Alliance broadcasts in 1987
in collaboration with Cartwright, although to poor reviews.
The broadcasts 'looked appalling', according to chief campaign organiser John Pardoe,[67] who added: 'Unfortunately
we had just enough money to give some creative people
the idea they could create something. They did; they created an absolute mess.' The most derided broadcast was
devoted to the new SDP MP Rosie Barnes talking politics
while cuddling a pet rabbit. In 1992, the Liberal Democrat
broadcasts were scripted by another advertising creative director, Jeremy Bullmore.

Because of their political marginality and financially constrained production, third party broadcasts have rarely had
much impact. There is, however, an interesting exception
to this. In 1986 and 1987 the comedian John Cleese wrote
and presented two SDP broadcasts, which deftly mounted
satirical attacks on the unproportional electoral system and
extremism in local government, while gently mocking the
notion of PPBs themselves. Cleese skilfully deployed not only
his own comic talent, but also the understanding he had
gained from his work for his flourishing training video company of how to use humour to make serious points.

The first of the two broadcasts was particularly successful.
Since it had been well trailed in advance in the press, people
switched on to watch – a rare phenomenon for PPBs. The
broadcast attracted 7500 responses from the public,[68] whereas
a standard response rate is about 1000. And the SDP claimed
that, according to its private polling, support for proportional representation jumped in the week spanning the broadcast from 39 to 64 per cent of voters.[69] It was all an excellent
achievement for a PPB which began with its presenter yawning
on the self-confessed grounds that party political broadcasts
are so boring, adding that 'this one, I am afraid, promises
to be outstandingly tedious'.

### Bio-pics

There is one genre of party political broadcasting which it
is worth discussing separately – the biographical documentary or 'bio-pic'. Numerous British PPBs have contained some
biographical or personal material on party leaders and senior figures, but in contrast to US political advertising the
full-blown bio-pic has been a rarity. Nevertheless, the few
instances that have been produced are all among the most
well-known and important of party political broadcasts.

The first was the final Conservative broadcast of the 1970
campaign. Entitled 'A man to trust', it strove to suggest that
the public perception of the image was a poor reflection of
the private reality of Edward Heath. It began: 'Cold, aloof,
distant. These were the kind of words the press were always
ready to trot out about Ted Heath. But as the election battle got into its stride they began to use them less.' In a

quick-cut montage of images, it showed him happily electioneering, moving amiably through crowds, chatting in a
pub, signing autographs, being enthusiastically received at
public meetings. The scenes were carefully selected from
huge quantities of film which had been taken. It ran through
his achievements: scholarship boy at Oxford, self-made man
with no inherited money, cabinet minister, negotiator of the
UK's bid to enter the Common Market, the first elected
leader of the Conservative Party – and, not least, winner of
the classic Sydney to Hobart race in his yacht, *Morning Cloud*.
It portrayed him as likeable, determined and dutiful, if neither
light-hearted nor passionate. The film concluded: 'Perhaps
he's not an easy man to know. But when they know him,
people feel he's a man worth knowing. A man to trust.'

The broadcast ended with an apparently heartfelt talk to
camera from Heath delivered from an imposing desk in a
studio replica of his flat. It avoided policy detail in favour
of a grander philosophical approach about his personal
determination to give Britain 'a better tomorrow'. The broadcast was very well received by politicians, the media and,
according to Tory private polling, the voters.

'Every US politician has a biographical documentary, showing the private man. That's where we took it from,' says the
scriptwriter Barry Day.[70] 'It wasn't an original idea but it
was innovative in Britain. We set out what people thought
about Ted – cold, aloof and distant – and we showed it
wasn't true.'

Despite its perceived success the Heath broadcast did not
establish a pattern for party leaders. Such an approach did
not fit with Labour's traditional campaigning style in the
1970s and early 1980s, and Heath's successor as Conservative leader was similarly unkeen. Although some Tory PPBs
featuring Margaret Thatcher contained biographical elements
(in her very first PPB as leader she talked about her up-
bringing in Grantham),[71] a full Thatcher bio-pic was never
transmitted.

This is despite the fact that one was made. Nicknamed
the 'Grantham tape'[72] and inspired by a commercial for US
president Gerald Ford, it was produced for the 1983 election by Saatchis. Opening with a shot of her father's corner
shop in Grantham, it covered Thatcher's early years, the

birth of her children and her entry to the Commons, as well as her career as party leader and prime minister.[73]

'It was to show the "grocer's daughter" on her way through to the top,' says Tim Bell.[74] 'It aimed to appeal to the C1/C2s, saying to them "you can aspire". It wouldn't have had the glossy techniques of the Kinnock broadcast in 1987, but if it had happened the Kinnock one wouldn't have looked so original. But Margaret Thatcher rejected it for reasons of personal embarrassment.'

In fact, Thatcher was never keen on seeing early film of herself in party broadcasts. During the 1987 campaign Saatchis produced a PPB illustrating her career as prime minister. A film clip from 1979 was removed because, according to party deputy chairman Lord Young, Thatcher was 'very conscious how her appearance had improved over the years'.[75]

As it was, the Kinnock bio-pic screened during the 1987 campaign appeared not merely original but astonishing, in both the skill of its production and its daring, single-minded concentration on Kinnock's personal character. It was the first party broadcast for many years to become a major campaign event, and the first PPB ever to be repeated. The broadcast acquired a variety of nicknames of which the most common was probably 'Kinnock – The Movie'.

The opening shots marked out its differences from any previous PPB: a warplane zooms across the sky, a seagull soars in the air, then Neil and Glenys Kinnock appear walking romantically hand in hand along windswept cliffs. Through the voices of the subject himself and others, the broadcast covered his school-days, parents, early career and marriage, as well as his underlying philosophy and patriotism. Kinnock was interviewed dressed casually in a pullover in his own home, and shown with his family at the breakfast table. Testimony to his character was provided not only by Labour elders such as James Callaghan and Barbara Castle, but also by his Aunt Sadie and Uncle Bill. To a throbbing, menacing soundtrack he was shown denouncing the far left Militant grouping in his speech at the 1985 party conference. The broadcast closed with a single word superimposed on a shot of Westminster – 'Kinnock'. (For many viewers and commentators this endframe symbolised the broadcast's brazenness, but in fact it was a last-minute suggestion accepted because those involved were too tired to think of anything else.)[76]

Strongly influenced by American bio-pics, the broadcast depended on an array of film-making talent. It was directed by Hugh Hudson, most famous for his Oscar-winning direction of *Chariots of Fire*, but also an experienced maker of distinctive and successful television commercials. The script was by Colin Welland, who also won an Oscar for his work on the same film, and the score by Michael Kamen.

The decision to run a broadcast about the 'real Neil' had been taken several months before the election. Labour strategists wanted it to counter the unflattering image of Kinnock portrayed in the media, especially the right-wing tabloids, and to offset the 'negatives' attached to him in the public mind (inexperience, weakness, and so on). It fitted with their overall plan of fighting a presidential-style campaign based around the party leader, and with the need to combat the inevitable personal attacks on Kinnock from the other side. Reminding voters of his attack on Militant was an important part of this, since it had raised his poll ratings at the time and was regarded by his advisers as one of his biggest public relations successes.

According to Labour's private polling, the broadcast produced a dramatic and literally overnight shift in public attitudes to Kinnock. It clearly even swept along some who had not seen it themselves, but had just heard or read about it. The proportion of interviewees who thought he would make an effective prime minister jumped from 45 per cent immediately before the broadcast to 55 per cent the day after; while those who thought he would be ineffective dropped from 47 per cent to 41 per cent.[77] This represented an overall switch from a net score of −2 to +14. However, although Kinnock's ratings improved following the broadcast and generally over the campaign, they started from such a low base that he still trailed Thatcher.

Labour's polls also revealed that just one in four voters had actually seen the broadcast, its first of the campaign, when transmitted on 21 May. The party decided to abandon the prepared film for one of its later PPB slots and repeat the Kinnock show, due, it claimed, to 'popular demand'. On second screening the endline 'Kinnock' was changed to 'Labour'.

Hudson went on to direct a number of other Labour PPBs. These included a kind of compilation bio-pic in April 1991, a broadcast which briefly portrayed the family backgrounds and roots of Labour's frontbench economic team – John Smith, Gordon Brown, Tony Blair and Margaret Beckett. The party was trying hard to promote this foursome at the time. Later that year, Hudson made a PPB which became nicknamed 'Kinnock – The Movie II'. With the help of romantic footage from the Welsh valleys, much choral music and enthusiastic endorsements from constituents, it updated the earlier film, but was somewhat less presidential in style.

In response, the Conservatives found their own celebrity film maker, John Schlesinger, the Oscar-winning director of *Midnight Cowboy*. Schlesinger's first contribution to a Tory PPB was in 1991, when he directed some shots for a glossy 'day in the life' account of a happy, prosperous, sunlit Britain – a country which appeared to be, in John Major's oft-quoted words, 'at ease with itself'. His main task, however, was the Major bio-pic which constituted the opening Tory broadcast of the 1992 campaign, costing around £250 000 to make.[78]

Entitled 'The Journey', it was the story of a boy made good and his passage from humble childhood in Brixton to premiership in Downing Street. It thus demonstrated Major's achievements and ordinary roots at the same time as identifying the Conservative Party as the party of opportunity. The broadcast shows Major driving through Brixton in the back of his prime ministerial limousine, reminiscing about his childhood, tracking down the dilapidated houses in which he once lived, appearing surprised that one former abode is still standing, identifying the spots where he played cricket or declaimed politics from soapboxes, meeting the current locals, and buying tomatoes and kippers in Brixton market. He talks about being unemployed as a young man, getting married, his time as a Lambeth councillor, his parents' dependence on the NHS in their last years, and his election to the Commons.

In some respects the broadcast was derivative of its Kinnock predecessor. Major was interviewed in an informal setting wearing a casual pullover, just as the Labour leader had been five years previously. But in other ways it was a much simpler, less glorifying, less dramatic film. No family, no

testimonials, no seagulls or airplanes or clifftops – it concentrated on footage of the prime minister, whether being
interviewed, meeting world leaders, or tripping down memory
lane in south London. This reflected Major's personal feelings about the broadcast. A reserved man who feels uncomfortable with personality politics, he was reluctant to do it
in the first place, insisted that references to his wife and
children be deleted, and could never bring himself to watch
the final version.[79] Its understated, whimsical tone fitted Major's
character, but was a striking contrast to the hard-edged aggression of the Saatchi-produced Tory broadcasts in the 1992
election.


CONCLUSION

Party political broadcasts have declined dramatically in importance since the second world war. This is due not so much to
their own content as to a major change in the broadcasting
environment – the fact that other political broadcasting has
greatly increased.

The 1945 radio broadcasts were the landmarks of that
campaign, the only political programmes on the most important medium. As television eclipsed radio in the 1950s,
it was the televised party broadcasts which became the fore-
most election events. This was true, for example, of Eden's
and Macmillan's closing broadcasts in the 1955 and 1959
campaigns respectively.

But from 1959, television and radio started to cover general election campaigns, and in the 1960s and 1970s party
broadcasts became less and less prominent. This change has
been gradual. In 1970 the Conservative broadcasts were still
central to the image of Edward Heath, because party leaders had much less television exposure then than now through
extended interviews, parliamentary reporting, and so on. But
as time has passed, other political coverage has expanded
enormously, so that party broadcasts have been virtually
crowded out. Today a party political broadcast has to be as
stunningly innovative as 'Kinnock – the Movie' or 'Jennifer's
Ear' to have similar significance to its predecessors of 40
years ago. The Conservatives became sufficiently disenchanted

with the impact of their PPBs that in 1995, burdened by financial difficulties and deep unpopularity in government, they voluntarily abandoned almost their entire allocation.

Party broadcasts have declined not only in importance but also in length, generally as a matter of agreement between the parties and broadcasters. Radio broadcasts contracted rapidly in the 1950s. In the 1951 election the Conservatives and Labour each had two 30-minute and three 20-minute broadcasts; in 1959 this had come down to four 15-minute and four 5-minute broadcasts. Since then the maximum length has been 10 minutes. And since 1966, 10-minute broadcasts have only occurred at general election times – otherwise they have been just 5 minutes long.[80]

Television broadcasts, to which the parties attached more importance, shrank slightly more gradually. In the 1950s some ran to 30 minutes, and in the early 1960s the longest took 25 minutes. The last 20-minute broadcast occurred in 1964, the last 15-minute one in 1974.[81] The maximum duration since then has been 10 minutes, although in the 1980s following the lead set by the Tories the parties often ran 5-minute broadcasts in place of 10-minute allocations. At the last general and European elections 10-minute broadcasts were allowed, but otherwise they are now restricted to 5 minutes.

In the past 15 years, the parties and their ad agencies have occasionally pressed for them to be shorter still, believing they could make punchier broadcasts which would hold the audience until the end. This was last raised in 1995 by Labour. But the broadcasters, especially the BBC, have remained resistant to transmitting anything that would seem like political advertising.

As for the actual format of broadcasts, the main change has been the decline of the studio-based talking head. At its most extreme in the 1950s and 1960s, this phenomenon involved 15- or 20-minute television broadcasts entirely devoted to one politician talking straight to camera, or 30 minutes of straight talk in the case of radio. This form of communication is now foreign to our modern television culture in which viewers are used to the rapid conveying of visual information. Party political broadcasting has moved with the times, if somewhat more slowly than other forms of television.

Virtually from the start, parties introduced other elements into some of their television broadcasts – simple film sequences, music, stills, props, captions and graphs – and later vox pops. Over the 1960s, 1970s and 1980s the use of film became much more extensive, and in some cases elaborate with more sophisticated camerawork and tighter editing. Music became increasingly prominent as well, sometimes specially composed. And PPBs today rely on a range of modern televisual devices such as highly stylised sets, animated graphics (often particularly effective for making statistical points), and various special effects. The best party broadcasts now constitute high quality productions.

Talking heads are nevertheless still a staple constituent of party political broadcasting, for reasons of cheapness, ease of production, tradition and the self-importance of politicians. But today the politician's contribution to a party broadcast is more likely to be a 30-second clip following a 4-minute film. This is a common feature of PPBs, although Labour's 'people-metering' (see Chapter 6) of party broadcasts since the early 1990s has found a sharp increase in negative reaction when the politician appeared. There has often been tension between politicians and those making broadcasts over the politicians' role. 'The politicians always wanted to appear as party spokesmen. Our task was to make it palatable,' says Barry Day.[82]

In terms of television genres, party political broadcasts were once largely imitative of news/current affairs programming, with their talks to camera, interviews and short film reports. Indeed, the two most significant and acclaimed early series of broadcasts were those which took furthest the idea of replicating the style and production values of ordinary news/current affairs programmes – Labour in 1959 and the Conservatives in 1970.

Today, PPBs with their shorter duration, tightly edited film and evocative use of music are more often compared to commercials. This is only partly true. The expense, time and degree of care-per-second-of-output involved in the production of ads on television greatly exceeds that of party broadcasts. And while PPBs have been getting shorter, so have commercials: in the 1960s and 1970s, 60-second ads were common and 10-second ads a rarity, while now it is the other way around. Advertising professionals have found making 5 or 10 minutes of television an unfamiliar task.

In fact, PPBs have become more varied in genre. While some still come closest to current affairs, and others do seem like long commercials, we have also had the party political broadcast as fiction, as faction or docudrama, and as situation comedy – while the most insipid resemble corporate videos.

The development of PPBs has been linked to change in the sort of people responsible for them. Once they were under the direct control of politicians and party officials. Now they tend to be made by advertising professionals, television production companies or even celebrity film directors. And since the production of party broadcasts has been professionalised, it has also become more costly.

Thus over the years televised party political broadcasts have become shorter and slicker, more elaborate, more entertaining and more expensive. They count for less politically, but on the other hand they are better television.

# 4 Using the Media

*Television is the greatest, best and most important thing that has happened to British politics.*

Tony Benn, 1950[1]

*We're not having a party political broadcast. We're having an interview, which must depend on me asking some questions occasionally.*

Sir Robin Day, trying to interview Margaret Thatcher, 1987[2]

*I've never understood why the photo opportunity should be criticised even standing on its own, because supposing for example that you have a picture, as the cliché goes, which speaks more than a thousand words, why waste everyone's time, if they are getting the message very definitely through the picture ... and of course you're much more a hostage to fortune of something going wrong if any politician of any party opens his or her mouth.*

Harvey Thomas, former Conservative director of communications, 1992[3]

*Happily, it is still a convention that you should say something when you appear on television. But that convention will wither away. One can imagine a time when politicians will simply appear with a suitable expression and a carefully chosen tie and the image will speak for itself.*

Douglas Hurd, 1994[4]

*Our news today is instant, hostile to subtlety or qualification. If you can't sum it up in a sentence or even a phrase, forget it. Combine two ideas or sentiments together and mass communication will not repeat them, it will choose between them .... The truth becomes almost impossible to communicate because total frankness, relayed in the shorthand of the mass media, becomes simply a weapon in the hands of opponents.*

Tony Blair, 1987[5]

The average British voter is not an enthusiastic consumer of party political propaganda. Few people set their video so as not to miss a party political broadcast, scour the streets for party billboards, or rush to their letterbox when they hear it open and shut in the hope of finding the latest circular from a local candidate. And the rare individual who is an avid peruser of a party's publicity material is probably a committed supporter and almost certainly not an all-important floating voter.

So the electoral battle must also be fought through the media which millions of people do happily consume on a daily basis – television and radio programmes and articles in the press. This sometimes has the advantage that a party message may gain credibility when it is carried by a neutral source. But the media has one big disadvantage for parties compared to their own propaganda – they cannot directly control what is said. Instead, their task is to seek to influence it.

## THE CHANGING MEDIA CONTEXT AND ITS CONSEQUENCES

The evolution of party media strategies has naturally depended on the development of the opportunities presented by the media for reaching the electorate. By far the most important change has been the growth of television, which has ruled political communication since the end of the 1950s. While newspapers are not as crucial as they were before the domination of TV, they are still important channels of political information. Other media, however, have been eclipsed by television. Cinema newsreels reached large numbers in the years following the second world war, but have since disappeared entirely. Radio was vital for the official party broadcasts from 1945 to 1955, but by the time broadcasting was allowed to cover electoral politics in other ways in the late 1950s, its audiences were exceeded by those of television.

Cinema newsreels provided an early indication of the impact moving pictures could have on politics. Indeed, some claims often made for television in fact apply to newsreels. In the 1930s they became the first medium to show the electorate what its leaders both looked and sounded like, as well as the first to allow politicians to appear before more voters and address them directly than they would reach in a lifetime of public meetings. In this way they contributed to the personalisation of politics, as television was also to do.

The most effective political newsreel performer was Baldwin, in the age of mass cinema before the second world war. He mastered the art of conveying calmness and dependability. After the war, cinemas still attracted weekly audiences of 20 million, and newsreels mattered to politicians for the way they covered their actions and speeches. The three party leaders – Attlee, Churchill and, for the Liberals, Clement Davies – made filmed appeals at election time. The newsreels also carried reports of campaign events and round-ups of constituency electioneering. But there was no debate or discussion. By the mid-1950s newsreels were rapidly declining owing to the rise of more up-to-date television news. They soon became less newsy ciné-magazines and then, in the 1970s, finally ceased altogether.

The BBC had started a regular public television service in 1936, but it went off the air during the war. Transmission began again in 1946, and TV ownership grew rapidly during the 1950s to take in most of the population. Initially, television had little impact on political communication, because of the reluctance of both the party leaderships and the BBC.

Although there were MPs and party officials who soon realised the potential importance of television, Attlee and Churchill were elderly men loath to adapt to newfangled technology. Some more junior politicians took to appearing on the small screen with enthusiasm when they got the chance, but there were few current affairs programmes and those that did exist were handicapped by the '14-day rule' – they could not discuss any matter which was likely to be debated in Parliament within the next fortnight. This rule, which also applied to radio, had first been proposed by the BBC during the war and was then insisted on by the politicians until 1956.

Election coverage was even more constrained – it was non-existent. Keen to avoid any unnecessary political controversy, the BBC hierarchy interpreted electoral law restrictively as forbidding campaign reporting in case it illegally promoted the election of particular candidates. Although the corporation transmitted the parties' own election broadcasts between 1945 and 1955, its news bulletins on both TV and radio contained no mention of the campaign. Other programmes which might have had any bearing on the contest were cancelled.

This self-censorship was eventually swept aside by the more robust approach adopted by ITV, which began transmitting as the country's second television channel in 1955. Less cautious and establishment-minded than the BBC, it broke the taboo by covering a by-election at Rochdale in 1958 without legal or other repercussions. BBC television and radio then joined Independent Television News in reporting the 1959 general election, which was thus the first to be covered on the electronic media beyond the standard party election broadcasts. It featured in news bulletins (which collectively had larger audiences than the party broadcasts),[6] and some candidates took part in televised debates. Parties took their first small steps towards adapting their electioneering to these new circumstances. Leading politicians found they sometimes had to deliver their speeches earlier than usual so that film could be developed in time for the evening news. And the broadcast coverage speeded up the exchange of argument between the parties, as the combatants found they could convey to the voters their response to the other side's claims on the same day.[7]

By the following election, in 1964, it was clear that television was the central feature of the campaign. Coverage was much expanded, now including more analysis and interviews with party leaders. Around 90 per cent of the population had sets, and television was the source of political information on which voters said they relied most.[8] With Harold Wilson as leader, Labour regarded the medium as its main lever in achieving power. Other politicians, such as Harold Macmillan, had already succeeded in using TV appearances and staged news events (in Macmillan's case, notably visits from US presidents) from time to time to bolster a personal image and get a message across to the public. But Wilson was the first party leader really to feel at ease with television and to put it at the heart of his communications strategy. He saw television as an essential opportunity to counter the predominantly Conservative press. Not only did he use the medium consistently to project himself and his desired image to the electorate, he also took care to maximise beneficial TV coverage of rallies and other aspects of the party's electioneering.

Ever since then, television has been the most important battleground of party political campaigning. TV ownership is nearly universal. News bulletins with a fair amount of political content are watched each day by millions of people whose views span the political spectrum, including floating voters whose political loyalty is wavering or undecided. Television has become the main means through which most of the electorate acquires political information, hears political argument and forms an impression of political personalities and events.

Furthermore, the requirement for broadcasters to be impartial means that all main parties are effectively guaranteed substantial TV reporting of their activities and statements. The broadcasters have traditionally tried to satisfy the principle of impartiality by ensuring among other measures that the parties get coverage during the campaign roughly in proportion to their allocation of party election broadcasts.

On top of this, the messages conveyed by television, whether implicit or explicit, hit home particularly hard for two reasons. First, the visual nature of TV gives it much more impact. To the human brain, pictures are usually more compelling and memorable than words, and moving pictures are even more striking and influential. A picture is worth a thousand words, but a moving picture is worth ten thousand. Second, the polling evidence[9] consistently shows that the public generally regard both the BBC and ITN as impartial, honest and trustworthy purveyors of political news – and to a much greater extent than they think this of newspapers or political parties themselves. This gives television more authority and credibility than the press, particularly the partisan tabloids, which account for the vast majority of newspaper circulation.

Politicians and parties also gradually realised that the visual nature of the newly dominant medium encouraged a different approach to persuading voters. Instead of the emotional rousing of large crowds at public meetings or the rational argument facilitated by the written word, the visual spectacles of television can be used as powerful creators of associations in the minds of viewers. Visual appearances build impressions and foster connotations between an individual or a party and certain characteristics or qualities. In other words, TV is effective at nurturing an image.

In the words of Sir Tim Bell, one of Margaret Thatcher's closest advisers:[10] 'TV is the most critical input into voters' choice. And TV is about imagery – the way it works is by giving impressions. It's hard to get people to listen to the words, it's the image that counts. So we put effort into thinking about how everything would look – politicians, Margaret's entourage, the stage-sets, the 'battlebus', everything. It was all very important in order to create the right impressions.'

Over the past 30 years the supremacy of television has strengthened, to the extent now that for many voters the TV campaign more or less is the election campaign. The parties have focused their efforts more and more on television electioneering, subjugating other campaigning activities – leaders' tours, rallies, press conferences, and so on – to the visual and logistical needs of TV.

The main agents of these developments were three officials who were at one time in charge of their party's campaigning. Geoffrey Tucker, the Conservative director of publicity from 1968 to 1970, 'dinned into all of us his conviction that the [1970] election would be won or lost on television,' according to Edward Heath's private secretary, Douglas Hurd.[11] One of Tucker's successors, Gordon Reece, who had the same job from 1978 to 1980 after advising Margaret Thatcher from the mid-1970s, made her picture poses a centrepiece of Tory campaigning.

Peter Mandelson, Labour's director of communications from 1985 to 1990, made his party even more meticulously attentive to the demands of television than his Conservative opponents had become. Mandelson's determination to think visually was often attributed to his brief career as a TV producer. In fact, most of his work had been on the highly cerebral *Weekend World*, a current affairs programme so scornful of picture-led journalism that in the TV industry it was nicknamed 'television for the blind'. His understanding of mass communication via television developed while he worked for Labour. In terms of TV coverage, his key goals were (in order of priority) to lead the news, to produce a charge against the Conservatives which stuck and to provide crisp pictures of attractive people.[12]

The growing emphasis on TV electioneering went together with a tremendous expansion in television coverage of politics. While this also applied between elections, it was especially dramatic during the campaign period, involving extensions in news coverage, an increasing number and variety of interview or discussion shows, and greater analysis in current affairs and specialist programmes. The factors behind this included the creation of new channels (BBC2 in 1964, Channel 4 in 1982) and the expansion of TV news into more hours of the day (lunchtime news programmes, the arrival of breakfast TV in 1983, increasingly frequent short bulletins during the day). These trends combined in the establishment in 1989 of the 24-hour satellite news service, Sky News, watched by few ordinary viewers, but carefully monitored by party staff and journalists.

The proliferation of TV news and current affairs has had three important consequences. First, it means that television has taken a gradually greater share of voice in the cacophony of politics. Second, parties have to put more time and energy into trying to influence all this output. Third, together with the development since the late 1970s of faster and more flexible ENG (electronic newsgathering) cameras and equipment in place of film, it has accelerated the pace of campaigning. The TV bulletins structure the campaign day, each one providing an opportunity (or sometimes the necessity) to launch a new initiative, refresh a running news story with a new development, or combat the other side's latest move. 'We had to be ready to move our story on, to provide new pictures for new bulletins; we had to be absolutely up to date with what the other parties were saying, we had to be ready to react, to try and blow out the story that they were trying to run,' explained Patricia Hewitt,[13] Neil Kinnock's press secretary in 1987 and a key Labour strategist, 'so that the whole communications and campaign day was structured around the demands, outlets and deadlines of television.'

The importance of TV to politics was further boosted by the televising of the House of Commons which began in 1989. This gave MPs new opportunities to exploit the medium, and naturally affected the way they treated the Commons chamber. Extracts from Commons proceedings soon became a standard feature of national and regional TV news. Politicians now often use their appearances in the Commons to speak to the nation, or at least to be seen by their constituents, rather than to address their colleagues in the House.

After television, newspapers (especially the popular press with readerships of millions) are by far the most important direct source of political information for voters. In fact, TV and newspapers constitute more or less a political information duopoly – radio and the other media are insignificant in comparison.[14]

The key difference between newspapers and television is that the free press is under no obligation to be fair. For political parties, the impartiality demanded of broadcasters is sometimes an obstacle to the coverage they would most like, and sometimes a lever to be used through pressure or complaints to get a better showing. Newspapers offer different problems and opportunities. Bringing pressure to bear on them can sometimes bring results, but it may also be simply brushed aside. It is difficult for parties to prevent hostile assaults in unsympathetic papers. But instead they can collaborate with the ones that back them to generate the newspaper content most favourable to their cause.

Close cooperation with supportive newspapers has been a traditional feature of British party politics. Parties keep friendly papers in touch with their strategy and themes, and steer them on what is important and what is not. Liaison involves planting stories in newspapers, feeding them information and propaganda points, using them to try to set the agenda for other papers and media, and encouraging them to launch virulent personal attacks on opposing politicians of the sort which would rebound if made by the party itself. It also involves pampering editors and proprietors, and making them feel appreciated.

This was widespread before the war, and it continued afterwards. In his report on the 1945 election,[15] Labour's press and publicity secretary, William Henderson, stressed the value of off-the-record talks with 'a small group of friendly newspapermen . . . who can be trusted to make no improper use of the news and views imparted to them'. On the Tory side in the early post-war period it was the *Daily Telegraph* which was most nearly recognisable as a 'press mouthpiece for the Conservative Central Office'.[16]

The intensity of national press partisanship has fluctuated considerably since.[17] Early elections after the war (1945–51) were marked by aggressive campaigning by both pro-Labour and pro-Tory papers. The period from the mid-1950s until 1970 was a calmer time of consensus politics, in which newspapers were more willing to give space and consideration to opposing political views and criticise their own traditional party. The February 1974 election, fought in the tense atmosphere of the miners' strike, witnessed a return to partisan belligerence, which has continued since.

The most important change between the two periods of fervent press partisanship was in the balance of political forces among the popular press. In the period after the war Labour was supported strongly not only by the *Daily Mirror* but also by the *Daily Herald*, which was controlled by the TUC and constitutionally committed to the Labour cause, and additionally *Reynolds' News*, a smaller Sunday paper linked to the Cooperative Movement. By the mid-1970s *Reynolds' News* had folded, and more importantly the *Daily Herald* had been relaunched as the *Sun* and bought by Rupert Murdoch.

In the late 1970s Gordon Reece went to great lengths to cultivate the editors and proprietors of the pro-Tory tabloids, breaking new ground for his party in focusing on the downmarket but mass-circulation *Sun* and *News of the World* (also owned by Murdoch), as well as the mid-market papers, in his attempt to reach skilled working-class voters. Back in the 1960s, Harold Macmillan had formed the view that he got a bad press 'because I do not cultivate sufficiently their rather unpleasant proprietors'.[18] Margaret Thatcher never made the error of failing to pay enough heed to newspaper hierarchies. She recalled of her time as leader of the opposition:[19] 'Whatever the other demands on my diary, when Gordon [Reece] said that we must have lunch with such-and-such an editor, that was the priority.'

She later courted them as assiduously in government as she had in opposition.

It was during the late 1970s that the *Sun* became both Britain's biggest selling daily and an ardent champion of Thatcherism. Combined with the *Daily Mail* and the *Daily Express*, traditional Tory cheerleaders, this meant that the Conservatives had the preponderance of the popular national daily press on their side. The Tories thus had more scope for mobilising supportive papers than Labour, which was now restricted to the *Daily Mirror*.

Although some partisan content of the tabloids is directly inspired by the Conservative and Labour parties, much of the time this is unnecessary. The papers are generally only too willing to oblige with their own helpful lines of attack. Parties often do not have to ask their favourite tabloid journalists for particular kinds of propaganda, because (to adapt Humbert Wolfe's famous ditty)[20] seeing what the hacks will do, unasked, there's no occasion to. However, the papers may not always produce what the parties want most.

The personal relationships carefully nurtured between Thatcher and her key advisers on the one hand, and newspaper proprietors and editors on the other, helped ensure that for the 15 years she led the Conservative party the collaboration between the two was remarkably close and productive. In contrast, while the *Mirror* produced some powerful pro-Labour propaganda, it did not follow party strategy as closely as the Conservative papers stuck to their side's. In 1987, for example, the *Mirror* concentrated on attacking the alleged depredations of Tory Britain, whereas Labour strategists would have liked more emphasis on what the party would do in government. The discrepancy occurred partly because of poor personal relations between leading party managers and key figures on the *Mirror*.[21]

For political parties, the primary function of a particular medium is usually the communication of political messages to the voters who consume that medium. But parties are also aware that some media have a secondary function. They can be used indirectly to shape the approach of more influential media. This gives additional importance to the press – television often takes its cue from newspapers, which raise topics that TV then covers. And although radio has small audiences, some programmes are vital for their ability to set the agenda of both television and the press. This is especially true of the *Today* programme, which over the past 30 years has been transformed from a light programme with soft features into the favourite media outlet of cabinet ministers. Its former presenter Brian Redhead described politicians appearing on *Today* as 'whispering in the nation's ear'. In fact, most of the nation isn't listening, but those politicians certainly are shouting in the ear of the rest of the media.

## FROM PRESS OFFICER TO SPIN DOCTOR

Political parties' attempts to influence the press have generally been conducted at two levels: the behind-the-scenes cultivation and lobbying of proprietors and editors, undertaken most effectively by leading politicians and senior party managers; and the direct transmission of information and argument to writing journalists, often the job of party staff. This work at the base has increased dramatically in importance in recent years. (Since this book is about party campaigning, this chapter does not examine the development of government press machinery or themes such as how the government handles the lobby. This has in any case been covered extensively in other books.)[22]

The press offices run by the parties in the decade after the war were not the driving forces of electioneering which they are today, but small, routine and low-key operations, largely reactive to events and subsidiary to other facets of party campaigning. Their main tasks were notifying the press of meetings, distributing texts of speeches and party broadcasts, arranging logistical facilities, promoting new party publications, supplying background information and responding as necessary to queries from journalists. Even these tasks were sometimes undertaken in a rather amateurish manner, which indicated their low priority. When Toby O'Brien, a professional PR man, took charge of Conservative publicity in 1946, he found that Central Office's idea of issuing a press release was simply to post it to *The Times*, the *Daily Telegraph*, the *Financial Times* and the Press Association.[23]

At election time the major self-initiated enterprise of party press officers consisted of 'article factories' – writing and trying to place feature articles composed in the names of senior politicians. They rarely sought to devise news events simply for the sake of good publicity. In trying to reach voters the party publicity departments generally devoted more effort to producing literature than seeking to influence the press.

All this changed in the 1960s and 1970s. The parties adopted a more systematic approach to the media, and employed press officers who had more status and resources within the party and adopted a more energetic approach to creating and managing news. Some of this was done through the use of devices like press conferences and photo opportunities – (see below). However, this activity was still on a much smaller scale than it is today.

The current structure of relationships between party press officers and journalists owes much to Peter Mandelson. He intensified a trend already started on behalf of the government by the equally energetic and aggressive approach of Bernard Ingham, Margaret Thatcher's chief press secretary, who directed most of his notable vehemence at journalists rather than editors. After Mandelson became Labour's director of communications in 1985, he made himself the main point of contact between party and media. He adopted a more proactive and assertive role than his predecessors, cultivating or berating individual journalists. His strategy was to influence the broadsheets in particular, which may sell comparatively few copies, but, he argued, set the agenda for television. The classic description of his technique appeared in a newspaper profile:[24] 'He wheedles journalists, cajoles them, takes them into his confidence, spurns them, adapts his tone to theirs . . . Then if they fail to present the party his way, he bullies, pesters and harries them.'

Although Mandelson instituted many changes in Labour's campaigning approach, most of his time was spent on dealings with the media. At points his personalised approach alienated some journalists, but overall he was undoubtedly highly effective in improving the presentation of the Labour leadership's case, whether against its opponents in the Tory Party or sometimes those in the Labour Party itself. This was based on a shrewd grasp of how news stories developed, an effective combination of charm and ruthlessness, and the level of authority granted him by Neil Kinnock.

Mandelson's accomplishments helped establish a new pattern of relations between party officials and journalists, in which the latter were subject to more extensive and intensive attempts at persuasion. A similar style was also adopted by Conservative Central Office, although to a lesser extent. Over the past ten years it has tended to be less proactive and robust in its contact with individual journalists than Labour. But while the Tories are in power, the CCO press office inevitably plays second fiddle outside election time to the government press machine, which is much better resourced and closer to the real action.

The main strategic difference between Labour's approach to the press now and ten years ago is that it pays more attention today to the high circulation tabloids, which most actual and potential Labour voters read. This is primarily due to Alastair Campbell, Tony Blair's press secretary and a man at ease with tabloid values thanks to his time as the *Daily Mirror*'s political editor. In the 1980s the Tory tabloids evinced such adulation for Thatcher and hostility to Kinnock that Labour could do little about it. But now that some proprietors and editors seem to find Major less praiseworthy and Blair less threatening, Campbell has successfully followed the twin tracks of seeking to place frequent articles in Blair's name and to ameliorate news coverage, most notably in the *Sun* and the *News of the World*. Labour strategists take seriously the research by Martin Linton,[25] published in 1995, which suggests that in 1992 readers of the Conservative tabloids swung dramatically to the Tories as the election approached.

It has today become commonplace to refer to party media work as 'spin doctoring'. Imported from the US, this term originally referred to the efforts by party officials to impose a favourable interpretation or 'spin' on the bare facts of what politicians had done or said. Now it is often used more loosely to cover all contact between party officials and journalists in an attempt to influence the media. Nevertheless, the narrower meaning does illustrate a significant change. Twenty or 30 years ago, most political reporting was news. Now, especially in the broadsheets, there is much more analysis and commentary. In part this is due to the need for broadsheets to find a different role, given the news supremacy of TV. But latterly broadcasting too, notably on the BBC, has provided more analysis. The growth of interpretative coverage of politics has meant that parties do have to attach more importance to pushing interpretation rather than just facts.

As the role of spinning (in the narrower sense) has become institutionalised, one result is that politicians' statements frequently come as a package with the spin attached. Politicians have often had to talk in code, so they can make their points deniably or tentatively. Now speeches may be planned in conjunction with the spin to be put on coded remarks. The most striking instance was Tony Blair's speech to the 1994 Labour party conference, in which he blandly said that Labour required a 'modern constitution'. This was accompanied by background briefing to the media indicating that what this really meant was an intention to revise Clause 4 of the party constitution, which pledged Labour to 'common ownership'. Thus he conveyed his message to the public without threatening the warmth of his standing ovation from the party faithful, who had little idea of the significance of the words they heard.

SOUNDBITES

Parties have to provide the media with words and pictures. The challenge they face is to ensure it is their chosen words and pictures that get reported and remembered.

In terms of words, their main weapon is the soundbite – a brief, self-contained, vivid phrase or sentence, which summarises or encapsulates a key point. This is how to communicate quickly and effectively to most people, who take only a superficial interest in politics.

Its potential impact is well illustrated by what may be the most famous soundbite in recent political history. This was spoken by an embattled Margaret Thatcher when addressing the 1980 Conservative party conference. The economy was in deep recession, her government was highly unpopular and she was facing tremendous pressure to change policy. She said: 'To those waiting with bated breath for that favourite media catchphrase, the U-turn, I have only one thing to say. You turn if you want to. The lady's not for turning.' This twist of the title of Christopher Fry's play, *The Lady's not for Burning*, was featured countless times on TV and radio that day and constituted the main headline in five national papers the following day.

The line was supplied to the prime minister by one of her most talented speechwriters, the playwright Ronnie Millar, who wrote material for both Edward Heath and Margaret Thatcher for many years. In Thatcher's time, one of his main functions was to spice up texts with witticisms and verbal finesse, a process known to her entourage as 'Ronniefication'. The soundbite more than succeeded in his aim when composing it – to find 'something that might fit a headline space. Not too short, not too long, crisp and easily remembered for maybe an hour or so or even, hopefully, a day or two.'[26] It hit home not only because of its wit, but also because it went to the heart of current political debate. And to many people it represented a crucial facet of Thatcher's personality – that which was regarded by her admirers as determination in the face of adversity and by her critics as stubbornness in the face of the facts.

The key verbal skill for politicians today, or those who write their words for them, is not (as it once was) grand and persuasive oratory, but colourful and memorable encapsulation. Or – to encapsulate the point – the ability to talk in headlines. Publicity-hungry politicians think consciously in terms of soundbites. They never give a major speech, interview or statement on the doorstep without planning the morsel of their text which they want to be gobbled up and regurgitated by the media.

Some politicians, of course, are much better than others at squeezing their views into 15–20 seconds or so. The best are highly practised at expressing their message in exactly the number of seconds that reporters need for their pieces. And when being interviewed for a brief recorded clip to go into a broadcast news report, the most determined (such as Labour's shadow chancellor Gordon Brown) will merely repeat their intended soundbite whatever question they are asked, so that broadcasters have no option but to use the exact point the politician wants. The disadvantage, however, with these learnt soundbites is that they are more difficult to deliver with natural inflections, and they often sound forced.

The basic idea of the soundbite is not new. Even in the 1930s, Baldwin's staff prepared deliberately brief speeches to get round cinema newsreel editors who had reduced earlier speeches to short extracts of their own choosing.[27] And media-conscious campaigners have always been aware of the advantages of delivering a highly quotable sentence. But it was in the 1960s that politicians and their advisers first made it a priority to provide the media with brief, compelling phrases or sentences. This was linked to the new factor of political coverage on TV. Television news is much more selective than newspapers in its direct quotes from politicians, so those hoping to be reported had to become more succinct.

The parties had yet to master the art of 'concocting quotable sayings' in the 1959 election, the first reported on TV, according to David Butler and Richard Rose. They noted:[28] 'The bulletins . . . were well supplied with brief taunts and slogans, but these appeared to have been collected through the assiduity of reporters more often than with the planned assistance of the parties.' The first politician who systematically sought to create soundbites for television was Harold Wilson, after he became the Labour leader in 1963. Wilson liked to associate himself with the modern, youthful image presented across the Atlantic by John F. Kennedy, and sought to emulate Kennedy's victorious campaign for the US presidency in 1960. Having discovered that Kennedy had included certain passages in his speeches purely for them to be reported in the television news, Wilson put this same idea into practice in the 1964 general election.

While Wilson was eagerly learning the technique of the soundbite, the Conservatives were slower to pick up on it. In 1963 Harold Macmillan's press secretary had difficulty trying to persuade him always to have a quotable sentence ready for Prime Minister's Question Time.[29] By 1970, however, the Tories had caught up. Edward Heath's publicity advisers realised the need to 'sum up what we thought the election was about in a simple phrase that could be used in speeches, quoted by the media and generally stick in the public mind'.[30] Their key issue was inflation, and they came up with 'The shopping basket election'.

Since then the soundbite has become an increasingly important feature of political communication. Parties and the media concentrate more and more attention on the brief statements intended for wide consumption, and less and less on the rest of the verbal output from politicians. This is just as true in Parliament, particularly since the Commons has been televised, where the ability to make a powerful, full-length speech is today less important than the nimble intervention, the quick-witted response or the well-aimed jibe at Question Time.

The evidence suggests that the length of televised soundbites has been diminishing. In the 1964 election most excerpts from speeches shown on the TV news were 'under ninety seconds',[31] which is a pretty substantial mouthful by today's standards. In 1979 the median length of speech extracts was 45 seconds on the BBC's *Nine O'Clock News* and 25 seconds on ITN's *News at Ten*.[32] Similarly, Harold Macmillan complained that when he gave prime ministerial TV interviews at airports, 'in the editing your carefully chosen phrases are all boiled down to 50 seconds'.[33] Today, politicians' answers are distilled much further. During the 1992 election, party leaders could expect TV soundbites of around 22 seconds on the *Nine O'Clock News* and 16 seconds on *News at Ten*.[34] (Paddy Ashdown usually got longer soundbites than the two main party leaders, as the broadcasters padded out reports on the Liberal Democrats to ensure they received their quota of election coverage.)[35]

This change partly stems from technical factors. Since it is easier and quicker to edit videotape than the old technology of film, TV news reports are edited to a greater extent and contain more elements of shorter duration than they used to. But it also reflects more fundamental facts about our modern televisual culture. TV is generally much faster moving than it was. Audiences have shorter attention spans, assimilate information more quickly and are increasingly accustomed to briefer messages.


## PHOTO OPPORTUNITIES

Politicians today who want to seem caring visit hospitals and talk to nurses. If they want to seem up-to-date, they tour high-tech factories and stare in awe at complex equipment. If they want to seem popular, they get themselves surrounded by cheering crowds. And if they wish to appear capable of normal human pleasures, they might walk a dog along a beach. But there has to be one extra ingredient: they must be photographed or televised at the same time.

Photo opportunities are the means by which political parties supply the media with the pictures they require. And these pictures are important in forming the public image of politicians and parties.

The photo opportunity has a long history in electioneering which well pre-dates the use of the term. Politicians have always been keen to pose for pictures they think likely to be flattering. During the 1945 election, the photographs of Winston Churchill in the press included scenes of him resting at the roadside during his speaking tour by car, being presented with a box of cigars, shaking hands with a soldier and meeting a mother and her triplets.[36] Conservative-supporting papers were eager to publish these pictures of Churchill in appealing settings.

Some more flamboyant politicians conceived more elaborate visual stunts for the sake of the cameras. During the 1950 campaign, for example, the senior Tory frontbencher, Sir David Maxwell Fyfe (former Attorney General, later to be Home Secretary), was pictured marching through his Liverpool constituency surrounded by supporters sweeping the street with brooms and others holding posters declaring 'The Tories will clean up the mess'. This was before television reported elections but when cinema newsreels were still important. Maxwell Fyfe's style of electioneering was seen in cinemas across the country.[37]

The early precursors of the modern photo opportunity were generally much less sophisticated than the contemporary version. For many years most pictures or filming of politicians involved activities they would have been doing anyway – pressing the flesh, participating in meetings or ceremonies, arriving or departing from somewhere. Nevertheless, imagination and skill was involved in setting up the right kind of photogenic occasion. By the late 1950s Labour 'had begun to cultivate the (for us) neglected art of the photo-call,' according to Barbara Castle, party chairman in 1958/9. She was particularly proud of a widely used and well-posed picture of her sandwiched between Hugh Gaitskell and Aneurin Bevan, their arms aloft, on their return from a trip to Moscow during the 1959 election.[38] The photo implied a spirit of party unity, in contrast to the bitter internal battles which had actually been waged between Gaitskell and Bevan.

As television grew in political significance in the 1960s, parties became increasingly conscious of the role of visual imagery in communicating impressions. They were willing to go to greater lengths to create the right visuals. In 1966 the Conservatives wanted to emphasise the difference between their young, dynamic-seeming new leader, Edward Heath, and his elderly, aristocratic predecessor, Sir Alec Douglas-Home. They organised a photo opportunity of Heath in a helicopter to back up their slogan, 'Edward Heath – Man of Action'. In later years Tory publicity advisers had to devise ideas to counter negative perceptions of their leader. In 1970 Heath interrupted his election tour to eat egg and chips at motorway services, but his image as aloof and remote was too deeply rooted to be undermined by such tactics. Heath's adversary Harold Wilson was more suited to this kind of presentation. When he wanted to be portrayed in the media as a normal human being, he liked to be pictured kicking a ball for the family dog.

It was during the 1979 campaign that the photo opportunity suddenly became one of the few most important devices in the electioneering tool-kit. The person responsible was the Conservative director of publicity, Gordon Reece. A former TV producer, Reece appreciated the value to television of striking and unusual pictures. As an adviser to Margaret Thatcher in the Tory leadership contest of 1975, he had already encouraged her to pose for publicity-grabbing pictures, such as while doing the washing-up. He had also closely studied techniques of television campaigning in recent American elections. Reece thought he could boost Thatcher's appeal to women, skilled workers and the young, by softening her image and showing her relating well to ordinary people. His plan was to use interesting visual content to get appropriate scenes of her onto both national and regional TV news, especially in the early evening, when his target voters were watching. He said privately that he wanted his leader 'to be seen but never heard'.[39]

The most celebrated instance of Reece's new approach to electioneering was Thatcher's close encounter with a calf. During her election tour she visited a farm in East Anglia to court the agricultural vote. While there, she picked up and cradled a newborn calf, holding the uncomfortable animal for nearly 15 minutes until all the cameramen and photographers were satisfied they had got everything possible out of this peculiar scene. Although her tour had been planned in meticulous detail, this had not extended to teaching the party leader how to hold a calf. Her technique led her husband Denis, in attendance as always, to mutter, 'If we're not careful, we'll have a dead calf on our hands.' But the animal survived the ordeal, and enjoyed a starring role on television that night and newspaper front pages the following morning.

This was only one of the numerous acts Thatcher performed for the benefit of the cameras – and, of course, the voting public – in various factories, shops and other locations during the campaign. She also tasted tea, sorted chocolates, stitched overalls, sampled butter, tested a heart monitoring machine, carried her shopping basket, bought the Sunday joint, chatted about the price of bread, and brandished a broom in a brush factory while pledging to 'sweep away the cobwebs'.

These stunts did indeed provide the TV news bulletins with excellent pictures, which they proceeded to relay to the viewers at home. Thatcher was successfully presented, in partial counterbalance to her image otherwise as strident and distant, as an ordinary housewife-turned-party leader who could relate naturally and sympathetically to people at large. Much of the credit was due to Thatcher's own professionalism. She proved good at unselfconscious small talk and at portraying curiosity in the mundane details of the work and lives of others. She also complied readily with the requirements of cameramen and photographers, for example, by happily repeating poses and actions. On one such occasion she justified this on the basis that they were 'the most important people on this campaign'.

In contrast, the Labour leader James Callaghan fought a

staid campaign in which he rejected entreaties from the media to provide equally engaging pictures. His photo opportunities were of a more traditional kind, such as attending Easter church services with his grandchildren. At the following election in 1983, Callaghan's successor, Michael Foot, was even less willing to perform for the cameras, and Labour's publicity staff made even less effort to organise photogenic events for their leaders. Instead, the pictures of Foot which were used on television and in the press often tended to emphasize his age and dishevelment.

The Conservatives in 1983 organised another round of well-planned photocalls for Thatcher in factories, farms and shops. Compared to 1979 these lacked novelty value and had less impact, but one was a triumph of the art of the photo opportunity. On the day before polling, Thatcher posed in front of the largest Union Jack in the world on the hangar doors of the British Hovercraft Corporation on the Isle of Wight. This image associated her with patriotism and revived memories of her role in the Falklands conflict the previous year. It was impossible for her opponents to attack without strengthening these connotations. If she had explicitly and verbally brought the Falklands War into the election campaign, she would have been vulnerable to the charge of exploiting soldiers' deaths for party politics. But the visual image, whose meaning was only implicit, sidestepped this problem and (along with various other campaign devices) helped ensure that the Conservatives got the party political benefits of military victory.

However, at the next election it was Labour that won the battle of the photocalls. The photo opportunity was one of the greatest fields of advance in the transformation of Labour's campaigning capability between 1983 and 1987. By the 1987 election, Labour had learnt the skill of setting up attractive visuals in photogenic locations. Party managers tried as much as possible to show Neil Kinnock warmly meeting people or in front of welcoming crowds, whereas Thatcher's pictures, in which she was often the only figure, sometimes created an impression of isolation. And Labour scored heavily over the Tories through better campaign coordination – it carefully tied photo opportunities to its political theme of the day. This meant they fitted naturally into television reports of that day's campaign issues, reinforcing the party's daily messages.

The effectiveness of this deeply impressed Shaun Woodward, then a BBC news producer before he became the Conservative director of communications. He said:[40] 'If the theme of the day was health, you would find great footage of Neil Kinnock, who had visited a hospital that day, but nothing usable of Margaret Thatcher, who had been sent to a JCB factory in the Midlands. And you just had to go with what you'd got.'

The photo opportunity is now a key form of political communication, used by politicians to convey a message, modify their image, or just to get on television and in the papers. We have become accustomed to seeing our politicians wear unusual headgear to tour factories, brandish cricket bats, peer through binoculars, drive dumper trucks, lay bricks, conduct bands, sit in airplane cockpits, mess about in boats, vault fences, meet guide dogs, feed their children hamburgers and all the other activities that the imaginations of their image-makers have been able to come up with. Some politicians are keen on any kind of publicity-generating gimmick. Others see photo opportunities as a necessary evil and may draw the line at the most absurd. There are only a very few politicians, such as Douglas Hurd, who have remained altogether aloof.

Political parties must exploit to the full the potential of television, the dominant medium of the age. That means they have to supply the pictures which television craves. As Peter Mandelson, who transformed Labour into a much more televisual campaigning force, explained:[41] 'Television is putting tremendous pressure on us . . . to turn out strong visuals so that they have interesting pictures for their news bulletins. I have to provide those. If my opponents have got more interesting, more exciting, colourful, glitzy, jazzy pictures than me, then I may be losing out. I can resist up to a point, but if I want my people and my message on the news bulletins, then I have to supply the pictures.'

Often the best way for parties to fulfil this need is to arrange for eye-catching footage of the party leader, which they hope will boost the leader's image and reinforce the party's message. The result now is that the leaders' election tours are largely structured around photo opportunities. Great care is taken to find suitable settings months in advance of the campaign. The resulting pictures often take up a significant proportion of campaign coverage on television news. This has helped to increase further the dominance of the party leaders in election reporting and thus the 'presidential' aspect of the campaign.

The parties know that some TV coverage will contain disdaining commentary from the reporter highlighting the stage-managed nature of the event. This has been the case ever since photo opportunities rose to prominence in 1979. But while it is a good thing for journalists to remind the public about the crafted artificiality of these proceedings, it does little to undermine their purpose. Pictures have more impact and are more memorable than words. Whatever the words say, the visual image still makes the point. And sometimes commentary which points out the motives of the stage-managers strengthens rather than weakens the event's purpose, by making it clear to those viewers it might have escaped (for example, when reporters pointed out that Neil Kinnock wanted to be filmed travelling by train to associate himself with public transport).[42] In any case, many contextualising remarks by reporters are positive ones which reinforce the visual message – the grammar of television dictates that the commentary cannot deviate too far from the nature of the pictures.

The occasion is only subverted by the reporting at the rare times when the pictures of the artificiality become more compelling than those of the publicity stunt itself, such as when the surrounding media cause chaos and damage in a supermarket. Photo opportunities can fail for this reason. They can also backfire if the central activity goes wrong, such as the famous incident when, on the morning of his election as party leader in 1983, Neil Kinnock slipped while walking along the beach at Brighton and was caught by an incoming wave. And sometimes due to poor planning the activity may go well, but the pictures convey unintended messages, such as Thatcher's appearance as isolated during the 1987 campaign.

Photo opportunities work by fostering impressions. They do not assert clear propositions which can be the focus of argument, they establish connotations and communicate subliminally. This is well illustrated by the instructions Labour gave in the run-up to the 1987 election to researchers seeking suitable locations. They had to find venues which would associate the party with progress, youth, enterprise and dynamism. Labour's campaign planners were determined to feature Neil Kinnock in positive settings – not alongside closed factories or run-down hospitals – and with 'bright, attractive people ... not people who present an image of old-fashioned Labour diehards.'[43]

The basic desire of politicians to be pictured in ways which encourage the right impressions and make the right associations has not altered since 1945. What has changed, primarily due to television, is the prominence of visual imagery. And this has led to dramatic shifts in the level of care, ingenuity, artificiality and planning which goes into creating the right kind of photo opportunity.

The extensive coverage of photo opportunities is often condemned as crass, which indeed it is. But it happens for reasons. The logic of party competition dictates that parties must arrange the pictures, and the logic of broadcasting competition (even the BBC is far from immune from questions of ratings) that television must show them. If ordinary viewers wanted their main news bulletins to abandon nice pictures of party leaders in favour of worthy argument about detailed policies, then that is what would happen. But they don't, so it doesn't.

## INTERVIEWS

The interview is a crucial form in which politicians appear on television and radio. It can vary from the briefest of exchanges during a news programme, to a detailed, probing and lengthy interrogation on a flagship current affairs show. But whatever shape they take, interviews are one of the main chances most politicians get to project their message and their personality to the electorate. For them to do this to best effect depends both on their performance skills during the interview itself, and also on arrangements made prior to their appearance, such as the 'rules of engagement', casting and choice of programme.

The history of the political interview can be broadly divided into four phases. While these categories disguise much variation according to different politicians, interviewers, programmes and aspects of the relationship between parties and broadcasters, they nevertheless summarise what happened as first broadcasters and then politicians adopted a more assertive and less cautious approach. They are: 'the age of deference', lasting until the late 1950s; 'the age of ordeal by television', from then until the mid- to late 1960s; 'the age of gladiatorial combat', thence until around 1980; and, since then, 'the age of politician ascendancy'.

During the 1950s many politicians had to get used to the fact that they were sometimes going to appear on television. Although constrained by the '14-day rule', the BBC gradually and warily expanded its coverage of current affairs. Early questioning of politicians ranged from the polite to the obsequious. After 1955 Independent Television News provided another source of political television. ITN adopted a more forthright attitude, employing less deferential interviewers such as Robin Day.

Although a few MPs took to the new medium extremely well – ironically, in view of his later experience in the 1983 election, early TV stars included the young Michael Foot – for most it caused something between unease and torment. Harold Macmillan, although often a purposeful and effective TV performer, described television as a 'twentieth-century torture chamber'.[44] Many politicians found it uncomfortable to see themselves on screen and worried about the public impact of their physical appearance. Old dogs brought up on public meetings and parliamentary debate found it difficult to learn new communication tricks. Many did indeed fear 'ordeal by television'.

But some politicians and party managers quickly realised how important it was to master the skills of broadcasting. For many years parties had tutored their representatives in the art of public speaking, so it is not surprising that they moved into 'media training' once it appeared that broadcasting would displace the public meeting. The way was led by the Conservatives, who were better resourced, more open to new techniques and determined, in the words of party chairman Lord Woolton, to use 'to the full the latest devices of science – the radio and television'.[45] In the late 1940s the Tories sent MPs on radio training courses.[46] In 1951 the party established its own television and radio training studio at Central Office.[47]

The initial equipment was hardly sophisticated. At first Central Office did not possess a TV camera, so it constructed a mock one consisting of a wooden box on a tripod with a lens-like piece of glass facing the speaker. But this clumsy pretence did not obstruct the key message the trainers tried to convey to politicians – that on television they must talk in a conversational, not a rhetorical, style. The trainees were told to imagine that they were talking to someone who had just invited them into their living room for tea.[48] Those who grasped the lesson included Harold Macmillan, who noted:[49] 'Almost everything that one has learnt for public speaking has to be forgotten for a television performance. One has to remind oneself all the time that it is not a speech but a conversation; and that the audience, however large in the aggregate, in fact consists of two or three persons sitting quietly in a room, not subject to any of the emotions which can be stirred in a great public gathering.'

The Conservative broadcasting specialists also realised from early on that television was a medium of fleeting impressions rather than complex argument. In 1956 the party's first television officer, Winifred Crum-Ewing, reported:[50] 'American research places the four winning qualities in this order:– friendliness, conviction, sincerity and intelligence. Nothing in our experience contradicts this finding.'

Labour also entered the media training business. It set up its own closed-circuit TV and radio studio at party headquarters in 1958.[51] In the run-up to the 1964 election at least 250 Labour candidates were coached in television techniques.[52] Thus through the 1950s and 1960s politicians slowly discovered how to cope with the television interview. The more receptive politicians from both parties mastered the elementary points: how to avoid visual gaffes – what not to wear, how not to sit, where not to look; and the need to talk simply and directly without hectoring.

The first senior politician who fully understood that television appearances were not a problem to be managed but an opportunity to be exploited was Harold Wilson. He participated in interviews for his own purposes, not those of the broadcasters. 'He didn't go to the TV studio to answer the questions,' according to his former press officer Gerald Kaufman.[53] 'The questions were an irrelevance which had to be listened to. . . . He decided what he wanted to say – the message he wanted to communicate to the people who were watching and then, regardless of the questions that were put to him, he said what he meant to say.'

Wilson was thus the leading early exponent of an approach to interviewing which has become standard for politicians (and indeed other people with points to get across to the public). It can be partly counter-productive, creating an impression of evasiveness which is bad for the individual politicians involved and for politicians as a class. But, as well as ensuring that interviewees get home their key points, it has the important advantage that they appear fluent and confident rather than defensive. The most effective exponents are those who can successfully disguise evasion by 'bridging' from the questions to their prepared responses.

This approach is reflected not only in the behaviour of politicians, but also in the media training advice which they receive. Early television coaching had focused on making politicians familiar with TV studios, boosting their confidence, encouraging a conversational manner and avoiding various visual disasters. Modern media training is more concerned with teaching politicians how to be proactive – to seek to control an interview and use it for their own objectives (even by the mid-1960s Labour MPs were being taught to say what they wanted to say regardless of the questions).[54] Media training today also stresses the importance of appearance and body language; the use of this to construct a desirable image is covered in Chapter 7.

Edward Heath was never as comfortable as Wilson in front of the cameras, and was coached intensively by his publicity advisers prior to important interviews. While he found it difficult not to seem stiff and remote, he did try to keep the interview on his terrain. 'We trained him to take over the programme, dictate terms to the interviewer and score points to the audience,' says Geoffrey Tucker.[55] 'Each one was a gladiatorial contest, and we determined to win each one.' Or as Heath himself put it:[56] 'The thing to do before a big programme is to be clear in your mind about what you want to say, because the interviewer will always try to deal with something else.' But Heath was not quite as ruthless as Wilson. An analysis[57] of several interviews with each of them found that Wilson consistently evaded more questions than Heath did.

The growing assertiveness of politicians resulted in increasingly combative interviews in which the two participants struggled for ascendancy. As the doyen of interviewers, Robin Day, saw it from his perspective in 1972, 'the problem is not whether [politicians] will be able to state their case but whether I'll be able to get a word in edgeways on behalf of the viewer.'[58] Politicians could employ a variety of tactics. Heath's advisers, for example, aimed for psychological advantage by deliberately trying to lure the interviewer into interrupting, so that it would appear rude and could be brushed aside. They also encouraged Heath to raise topics early which they thought the interviewer intended to come to later, in order to disrupt the interviewer's plan of battle.[59] James Callaghan's preferred strategy was to pretend to be angered by questions on particularly sensitive subjects.[60]

In the 1970s, politicians also had to start becoming accustomed to a different type of interview – one where they were questioned by members of the public. Radio phone-in programmes became popular, partly due to the growth of local radio. Television became keener on shows where politicians were quizzed by studio audiences or viewers from locations outside the main studio. It is generally easier for politicians to deal with ordinary people, who usually ask less penetrating questions and have less opportunity to follow up or less proficiency at doing so. Politicians also benefit from being seen to be in dialogue with real voters. But such programmes are sometimes dangerous – ordinary people can be more unpredictable and aggressive than professional interviewers, and base their questions on personal circumstances or specialist knowledge, which it may be difficult to refute.

During the 1980s politicians became even more adept at using interviews as platforms for their own purposes. The younger generation of MPs brought up on television approached the medium with greater confidence; they found it a more familiar, less intimidating experience than their predecessors had. Media training became a booming industry (and not only for politicians). The parties extended training programmes for their senior figures, MPs and candidates. Some politicians were happy to proclaim the benefits they derived from television coaching. Lord Young, a Conservative cabinet minister in the 1980s, reckoned it was 'by far the most valuable single day's education of my life'.[61]

Party leaders continued to run most interviews in the way they wanted. Research[62] into the interviewing styles of Margaret Thatcher, John Major and Neil Kinnock found that all three evaded just over half the questions they were asked (between 50 and 60 per cent); and that by far the most common feature of their non-answers was the making of their own political points. This applied to two-thirds of Major's and Kinnock's non-answers, and three-quarters of Thatcher's.

While the equivocating behaviour of these party leaders was in some respects remarkably similar, there were also interesting contrasts in their other preferred methods for evading unwelcome questions. A technique favoured by Thatcher, but not at all by Kinnock, was to criticise the interviewer. This may well have fostered her reputation for intolerance of dissent. On the other hand, a technique used by Kinnock, but not by Thatcher, was to claim he had already answered the question, when in fact all he had previously done was avoid it. Then sometimes he would even repeat his non-answer. This is the sort of conduct which would give one a reputation for vacuous waffle.

It is now so routine for politicians to give predetermined answers that some of them are not embarrassed to state this openly. 'I always make a habit of writing down three or four points I want to make,' said the former Liberal leader Sir David Steel, 'and proceed to make them regardless of the questions the erudite interrogators or their even more erudite researchers have dreamed up.'[63] For some frustrated interviewers it means that politicians have won the battle of the interview. In the opinion of Sir Robin Day,[64] 'This technique has gradually brought about the decline of the major television interview. It is now rarely a dialogue which could be helpful to the viewer.' But for Kaufman, Wilson's press officer who later became Labour's shadow foreign secretary, it is merely a legitimate and effective strategy. He says:[65] 'Interviewers can't combat it except by being rude and objectionable. And in any case you owe them nothing – they're just paid employees who represent no one.'

Politicians seek to get the most out of being on television and radio not only through how they handle the interview itself, but also through the conditions they may negotiate in advance for their appearance – 'the rules of engagement'. This can cover the topics of an interview, its timing, the physical set-up of the studio, who else appears on the programme, who is recorded and who is live, who gets the last word and even who the interviewer is.

Such negotiations have gone on ever since political interviews have been broadcast. During the 1950s politicians being interviewed on television often expected to be told in advance the exact questions they would be asked, a condition which today would be most unlikely. The parties were also sometimes wary about subliminal impressions that interviewing situations could create. In 1964, for example, Harold Wilson refused to be interviewed in front of a desk behind which the BBC interviewer sat, on the grounds that it made him seem like a schoolboy being interrogated by his headteacher.[66]

However, in the past many constraints on broadcast interviews were ones imposed by the political parties collectively, rather than by individual politicians or parties seeking a competitive advantage over their rivals. The parties generally sought to avoid placing their spokespeople in circumstances which could be difficult or unpredictable. Thus during the 1964, 1966 and 1970 elections, the parties combined in refusing to participate in programmes in which politicians would be questioned by studio audiences. They also usually prevented discussions in which frontbenchers of different parties confronted each other directly.

In the 1970s the broadcasters broke free of such constraints, and these programme formats are now commonplace. In due course many politicians became more assertive in agreeing the rules of engagement under which they would appear on individual programmes. This applies especially to members of the government, who tend to be more concerned about notions of status and have greater negotiating clout. In the late 1970s some Labour ministers were reluctant to appear in discussions with their Conservative shadows. This aggressive approach went further in the 1980s. Conservative ministers regularly insisted, for example, on appearing live and after a filmed package in which the opposition featured, or on having the last word in a studio discussion.

Whereas the early restrictions politicians sought to impose on interviews stemmed from fear of television, now they act from knowledge of television. As parties acquired familiarity with the medium, helped by employing former TV producers in their press offices, they gained greater understanding of what concessions they could realistically obtain from broadcasters. 'Over the years I've been doing political interviewing the negotiation over the rules of engagement has got tougher,' says the experienced interviewer Jonathan Dimbleby.[67] 'It's territory where both sides have got rights. The politicians are now more aware of their rights. The sophistication of party officials is also much greater. They know what they think is to their advantage.'

Politicians have another weapon – the choice of which programmes to appear on. There have always been some politicians with dislikes for particular interviewers and programmes, which they are determined to shun. But the first person to use this weapon systematically was Gordon Reece in his advice to Margaret Thatcher on her TV appearances after she became Tory leader in 1975. Reece drew up a list of interviewers to be avoided as too hostile and likely to make Thatcher respond stridently. He also pushed her into appearing on lighter shows, such as the early evening *Nationwide* and Jimmy Young's radio programme. Along with the downmarket papers he also targeted, these reached many less politicised voters. Reece explained:[68] 'Everything was geared to the floating voter. Some Conservatives hated any use of the *Sun*, *News of the World* and light television and talk shows. But I was aiming at a particular type of audience that read those papers and watched those programmes.' Other politicians have followed suit. The more recent expansion of current affairs programming has also given politicians greater scope to choose between the political interviewers, sometimes to eschew tougher interviewers in favour of softer options.

And there is one other choice, which can be in the hands of parties rather than individual politicians – casting, or which people they put up for interviews. The party hierarchies naturally prefer to obtain maximum exposure for those they regard as the most effective performers, and minimum exposure for those they regard as the worst, although their preferences have often been contaminated by internal faction-fighting and personal jealousies.

It was easier for parties to regulate casting in the early television elections because of the power ceded to them by broadcasters. In the elections from 1959 to 1970, the broadcasters generally allowed the parties to nominate representatives for election programmes rather than demanding their own independent choice. During the 1970s, as the broadcasters became more assertive, the influence of party managers on which politicians were interviewed decreased. The pendulum swung back in the other direction from the mid-1980s, when party headquarters took greater care to run more tightly controlled media operations. Labour's press office under Peter Mandelson promoted selected politicians such as Tony Blair and Gordon Brown – derisively dubbed the 'beautiful people' by colleagues who felt excluded.

In the 1987 and 1992 elections, several leading figures judged not telegenic became noticeable by their absence from TV screens. This tactic backfired to some extent when their disappearance in itself became an issue. Some politicians who were annoyed by their exclusion (Nigel Lawson, the intellectual chancellor of the exchequer, on the Conservative side in 1987; John Prescott, rumbustious shadow transport secretary, on the Labour side in 1992) responded by dealing direct with the media to bypass the official party press offices. Others seemed happy to conform with the view that it would be best for their party if, as it was figuratively put, they locked themselves in a cupboard for the duration of the election.

## PRESSURISING THE BROADCASTERS

Unlike the press, television and radio stations have to be impartial in their political reporting.[69] This gives the parties

an extra lever to use in trying to influence the broadcasters
– they can complain about alleged unfairness.

Like most other individuals, politicians are usually ultra-
sensitive to instances of unfairness of which they are victims
and largely oblivious to injustices suffered by opponents. Some
have had genuine grievances which deserved rectification.
Some have managed to convince themselves that the broadcasters, or usually at least the BBC, are systematically biased.
For other politicians and party managers, making complaints
is simply a move in the party political game – a conscious
and deliberate tactic to put pressure on broadcasters. But
whatever the motives, complaining to broadcasters has become
an increasingly routine and intense feature of campaigning
since the mid-1980s.

Nevertheless, the practice of politicians protesting to the
BBC about its programmes is just about as old as the BBC
itself. In the 1920s and 1930s, Conservative Central Office
frequently bombarded the BBC hierarchy with objections
to the 'tendentious socialist propaganda', which was allegedly being transmitted to the nation's radio listeners. In 1929,
Central Office persuaded the corporation to postpone a talk
on 'the human effects of trade depression in the industrial
North' until after the general election.[70]

After the war the process continued. Churchill thought
the BBC was 'honeycombed with socialists, probably with
communists'.[71] He protested vehemently to the BBC when
a radio broadcast of his in 1950 was followed by an unconnected programme called *We Beg to Differ*.[72] Conservative
Central Office's first head of broadcasting, John Profumo,
set up a monitoring operation to back up the party's complaints. He paid long-term hospital patients, recruited through
an advertisement in the *Daily Telegraph*, a small fee to listen
to radio programmes in search of left-wing bias. Profumo
reckoned that with the help of the evidence thus collected
he 'made a great deal of headway with the BBC'.[73] Labour
also had its conflicts with the BBC. In 1950 its protests led to
the cancellation of the proposed repeat of a TV comedy which
questioned the principles of fictitious left-wing politicians.[74]

Once broadcast reporting of elections started, it was inevitable that parties would respond to coverage to which
they objected. In the 1959 election Labour found that 'on

several occasions it was necessary to make informal representations to the BBC and ITN about the contents of news bulletins'.[75] In the following election in 1964, the party's general secretary noted with approval how a complaint made to the BBC about a news bulletin which 'gave substantially greater coverage to the Conservatives' ensured that 'the imbalance had been corrected by the time of the late night bulletin'.[76] Within Conservative Central Office, however, there was a feeling that the Tories had failed to put the broadcasters under sufficient pressure during the 1964 campaign. One post-election internal memo noted:[77] 'We must resolve to be far more robust in complaining at infringements of the "impartiality" principle. Continued complaints often bring results, even if there is no sanction to back them up.'

Over the next ten years the continued complaints did flow, although they mainly emanated not from the Tories but from Harold Wilson and the Labour Party. This was partly due to the supreme importance Wilson attached to television. As leader of the opposition facing a government in difficulty, he had been on good terms with broadcasters whom he had cultivated keenly. But after he was elected prime minister in 1964 and his actions were examined with greater scrutiny, he decided that the BBC was in conspiracy against him. Wilson proved to be more obsessed with BBC bias than any other party leader before or since.

Labour's earlier complaints about television's political reporting had concerned what it felt to be isolated injustices against a satisfactory background of general impartiality. Wilson and his entourage, however, believed that the BBC was systematically and overwhelmingly biased against the party. Their many grievances ranged widely: from alleged impropriety in reporting of party conferences, through the claims that BBC interviewers were blatantly pro-Tory, and that at election time it consistently concentrated on campaign issues helpful to the Conservatives, to the charge that it carefully edited election coverage to show high quality film of the Tories putting over their case successfully, while scrappy reporting of Labour often consisted of shots of Wilson getting on or off trains.[78]

All this led to a constant battery of complaints from Labour. During the 1966 campaign, leading BBC producers 'perceived themselves to be the targets of a sustained campaign of pressure from the Labour party'.[79] It was a new feeling, but one to which they were to become accustomed. The Labour leader's personal staff became assiduous monitors of BBC programmes, detectors of bias and lodgers of protests, both inside and outside election periods. Wilson's other retaliatory measures included deriding the BBC at party conferences and refusing to give certain key interviews to BBC programmes. He even moved Lord Hill from running the Independent Television Authority to the chairmanship of the BBC governors, in the vain hope that this would tame the corporation.

Wilson's adversary, Edward Heath, and his successor, James Callaghan, adopted a different approach. Although not as suspiciously minded as Wilson, both were touchy and easily annoyed individuals who found plenty to feel vexed about in programmes they watched and heard. Nevertheless, neither felt they would gain by being seen to wage the kind of intense campaign against the BBC that Wilson did.

The next major public assaults by politicians on the broadcasters' overall record of impartiality occurred in the mid-1980s. The SDP leader David Owen was angry about what he regarded as the unfairly small proportion of airtime given to his party by television news. The Conservative Party chairman Norman Tebbit felt equally aggrieved, although in his case the cause was naturally the BBC's alleged anti-Tory bias. The importance Tebbit attached to tackling the BBC pugnaciously was reflected in a letter his secretary had published in the official Conservative Party newspaper in 1986. It stated:[80] 'Television in particular can win or lose the next election for us because it brings into everyone's home the biased and distorted views of the Left. . . . Unless these channels are hammered consistently and with absolute determination by us all then we shall carry as great a responsibility as the presenters themselves.'

Owen and Tebbit both faced the same problem in pursuing their party's interests. The broadcasters dealt with isolated protests by arguing there was no injustice when the overall picture was considered. Owen's response was to commission independent research to time the breakdown of coverage over a period of several weeks, and use this as a basis for a complaint to the Broadcasting Complaints Commission and then legal action (both unsuccessful). Tebbit's tactic was to try to combine his generalised and ferocious condemnations of the BBC with finding 'an example where the "we'll redress it next time" response would be clearly invalid'.[81] He announced he was setting up a media monitoring unit at Central Office, and then chose to launch a well-publicised attack on BBC reporting of the American bombing of Libya in 1986.

Whereas 15 years previously Wilson and his staff had felt that their persistent challenges to the BBC made frustratingly little difference to the corporation's self-confident behaviour, both Owen and Tebbit thought their aggression paid off. This was not to do with the outcome of their specific claims, but rather in terms of the knock-on impact on television journalism. Owen said that his court case 'led to a marked change for the better' in the way the SDP/Liberal Alliance was treated by television news, adding that 'politics is no longer presented simply as a two-horse race'.[82] Tebbit's view was that his action meant that 'members of the [BBC's] editorial staff began to look more critically at their own work'.[83] They certainly looked at it more cautiously.

In the run-up to and during the 1987 campaign, the broadcasters felt they were under constant scrutiny from all the parties. Like the Tories and the Alliance, Labour also thought it essential to keep TV journalists 'on their toes' by making it clear that programmes were being closely checked.[84] Peter Mandelson was an especially frequent, astute and belligerent complainant. 'There were occasions when I had to make an informal representation to the broadcasters about the treatment of the Labour Party in particular news bulletins,' Mandelson once told a TV programme.[85] He then managed to maintain a completely straight face as he added: 'But that was always conducted in a polite and civilised way. I deplore the actions of politicians and party managers who ring up and bully or seek to browbeat broadcasters into reporting in a favourable way.' ITN's editor-in-chief, Stewart Purvis, noted in the same programme: 'The calls from Peter Mandelson are more memorable than those from most people because of their vehemence.'

This kind of activity intensified in the run-up to the following election in 1992. Tebbit's high-profile assault on the

BBC and Mandelson's style of operating paved the way for a 'culture of complaint' – party officials felt they were not properly doing their job of attempting to maximise good publicity and minimise bad unless they were imposing judicious pressure on broadcasters. Each party had to ensure it was at least as forceful as the others, otherwise it thought it might lose out.

This process was encouraged by wider developments: the ever-increasing importance of the television battleground; the growth in the quantity of broadcast political coverage; the faster speed at which parties responded to events; and their determination not to miss any opportunity for enhancing their case. It was also fostered by the parties' greater understanding of broadcasting and their employment of former broadcast journalists as press officers. This meant that parties had staff who could make relevant, intelligent and detailed criticisms, and direct them to the places in broadcasting organisations where they would be most effective.

Thus during 1991–2, as the election approached, the parties regularly besieged the broadcasters in a quite unprecedented manner. Contact did not always take the form of complaint – it could be anything from a gentle steer through forceful argument to formal protest. But it related to just about every aspect of broadcast output, such as the placing of stories in bulletin running orders, the amount of coverage devoted to the different parties, phraseology of headlines, the angle taken by reports, the interpretation presented of party policy, and choice of interviewees, soundbites and shots. Labour's communications director, David Hill, proclaimed that there were some days when he telephoned the BBC and ITN to protest after every single news programme, and that it was a rare day which passed without any complaint.[86] The other parties were similarly assiduous.

There is an important distinction between this and the traditional forms of pressures which the parties used to apply to broadcasters. In the past, politicians generally relied on making their complaints to senior figures in the BBC and ITN hierarchies, backed up at times by public criticism. This has not been abandoned. Well-publicised attacks on alleged bias are frequent, particularly on the part of the Conservatives, but sometimes Labour too, while the Liberal Democrats fuss persistently over the level of coverage given to the third force. But the parties now also try to intervene more directly in the editorial process, making their detailed points to broadcasting staff who are actually taking day-to-day decisions. In this way they hope they are more likely to influence the next bulletin. As a technique it is often effective, but when particularly annoying to those on the receiving end it can be counter-productive. Its over-use has also meant that the currency of complaint is being gradually devalued – most broadcast journalists have developed thicker skins.

During the 1992 election itself the pressure actually dropped off. Complaints were still made, but the party spin doctors were too busy with their many other campaign tasks to maintain them at the same level of intensity.

It is now an established aspect of campaigning for parties to put pressure on the broadcasters through every means – the lodging of protests at all levels, public denunciations of bias and encouraging supporters to flood the companies with complaints. All this has made the broadcasters warier in their political coverage, and even more careful to ensure that they can justify judgements and programming which they think may be challenged.

The parties will clearly increase the pressure as the next election approaches, although the broadcasters are also planning more carefully how to organise resistance. The thinking behind party tactics is explained by Tony Blair's press secretary, Alastair Campbell:[87] 'Quiet life merchants exist at every level of every walk of life, and they know the best way to lead that quiet life is to avoid situations that provoke wrath.' For political parties, the price of good television coverage is eternal vigilance – and belligerence.

## ELECTION PRESS CONFERENCES

Daily press conferences are today a central feature of election campaigns. The parties use them to try to set the agenda, get good coverage and put their own gloss on campaign events.

Their origin goes back to 1959, when they were introduced largely by accident. Prior to this, campaign press briefings had been routine affairs, in which journalists were provided with speakers' itineraries and copies of leaflets. But in 1959, Labour politicians who wanted the party general secretary, Morgan Phillips, out of the way during the election allowed him to run formal daily press conferences. He used them to deliver well-prepared, highly quotable summaries of policy and attacks on the Tories. In their first week the new Labour press conferences scored over ten times as much coverage in the national papers as the conventional Tory briefings obtained.[88]

The tactic was so effective that the Conservatives were obliged to fight back by instituting their own rival press conferences. For the journalists these events generated a reliable daily flow of good stories. In fact, the hacks were so pleased to have this new source of easy copy that at the last press conference of the election they gave Phillips an ovation.

This constituted a powerful early demonstration in party politics of how an artificial event arranged by a few individuals simply for the purpose of generating substantial national publicity could do just that. The battle of the press conferences has continued ever since. They assumed greater importance in the following election in 1964, when they were televised for the first time and the Labour ones were attended by the party leader, Harold Wilson. Since 1970 their prominence in general elections has been guaranteed, since they have generally been taken by the party leaders.

As television became increasingly crucial, the parties focused the press conferences more on providing appealing footage for TV news bulletins. The growth of broadcast coverage of the campaign meant that the morning conferences were old news by the next day, and by 1970 there was little straight reporting of them in the dailies.[89] But they still featured strongly in the lunchtime and early evening news bulletins and the evening press.

Politicians, therefore, used the events to deliver brief statements on their chosen theme which were sufficient to provide enough material for TV news. The focus on television also meant that the parties became more concerned about the visual appearance of the conferences. In the 1960s and 1970s they began to use posters and placards with slogans behind the speakers to emphasise their message in the TV coverage. By today's standards the resulting pictures tended to be jumbled and cluttered. But the basic idea still remains, although it is used more circumspectly. In 1992 the Conservatives had posters behind the main desk in all their press conferences. 'The visual poster image was carried into everyone's home for every television news bulletin whenever the report used pictures from the day's press conference,' according to Shaun Woodward, the Tory director of communications. 'To some extent we were appealing over the heads of the media, directly to the voters.'[90]

From the 1970s the parties started to use charts and props to help reinforce their points. Ironically, the first party which regularly exploited the potential of visual aids for increasing the quantity and impact of TV coverage was Labour in its much derided (and indeed in many ways derisory) campaign in 1983. In 1987 the use of graphics and props became common and more ingenious. The best were those that provided simple visual dramatisation of the political point, such as Labour's 'crimeometer', ticking up additional crimes being committed, and a Conservative map of Britain with flashing lights to illustrate the hospital building programme. But the incautious use of visual devices can also have its drawbacks: the Alliance health spokesman Simon Hughes was severely embarrassed when it turned out that a huge pile of computer printouts were not, as he claimed, lengthy hospital waiting lists but in fact party membership details.

Now that most people had colour television, the parties also started paying more attention to the colour of the backdrops to ensure they were television-friendly. The Conservatives are lucky – blue looks good on TV. Red does not. Labour used it in 1983, but on television it bled into Michael Foot's white hair. The backcloth eventually had to be supplemented by a softer pink and orange strip.[91] Since then Labour has usually favoured light grey. It gives a nice, sharp TV image, appearing white without dazzling. The party has also experimented with other colours. These included a garish pistachio green used in 1994, discarded by the incoming director of communications, Joy Johnson, as a 'hideous' colour which 'did not combine well with human flesh'.[92]

Since the mid-1980s the parties have taken to constructing much more stylish and complex sets, with carefully designed colour patterns, lighting arrangements and sound systems. This provides a stark contrast with the past, when politicians made do with a table on a raised platform, covered in simple material. The aim now is to ensure that the television pictures convey the values with which the party wishes to be associated. Thus the purpose-built set employed by the Liberal Democrats in 1992 featured a shiny steel framework and TV screens. The point, according to party leader Paddy Ashdown, was to appear 'modern and urgent'.[93]

Some important press conferences have also become increasingly theatrical, especially those held at the start of the campaign to launch the manifesto, with musical fanfares and highly contrived entrances by party leaders. These can provide television with excellent action pictures, but involve much careful timing, rehearsals and thought about camera angles.

The leading example of this was the launch of the Labour manifesto in 1987 at the plush new Queen Elizabeth II conference centre in London. Neil Kinnock and his deputy, Roy Hattersley, marched down the central aisle to the sound of Brahms (the party's campaign anthem), split left and right to go up the steps, joined their colleagues on the platform as their names were announced over the loudspeakers, and then stood together at the main lectern. The event was famously described in the *Guardian* as seeming like a 'gay wedding'. But it worked well on TV, and (along with the Kinnock biographical party political broadcast) it symbolised Labour's new-found glossy professionalism.

The creation of the daily press conferences contributed greatly to the 'nationalisation' of election campaigns. By giving the media a national focal point, it encouraged them to concentrate their reporting on the activities of national leaders and party managers rather than electioneering around the country. And the public was given a single, central message as the party's point for that day.

In several elections the press conferences have also promoted debate or cut-and-thrust between the parties. (The rapid growth in broadcast coverage has also had this effect.) Before 1959 the rival party campaigns rarely impacted on each other. Since then, politicians have varied in their tactical willingness to devote time to the rebuttal of claims from the other side. But when they have done so, the press conferences have been one means by which charge and counter-charge has been transmitted from one camp to the other. In the early 1970s they thus helped to foster the widespread feeling, which boosted the Liberal revival, that the two main parties indulged in too much point-scoring and mud-slinging against each other.

Over the years the daily election press conferences have tended to get earlier and earlier. This has been partly driven by the need for party leaders to set off on their trip for the day, and (since 1983) the opportunity presented by breakfast television. But it is also due to the desire of parties to go first in an attempt to set the agenda. Politicians have generally regarded it as more important to launch their own attacks and get opponents on the defensive, rather than refute the allegations of their rivals. In 1979, the squabbling over times was such that Labour and the Conservatives ended up holding their conferences simultaneously at 9.30 am. By 1992, the Conservative proceedings started at 8.30, Labour's at 7.45 and the Liberal Democrats at 7.15. The early start did not please the journalists from the dailies. 'It was good for breakfast news', says the Liberal Democrats' campaigns director Chris Rennard, 'but it was rather too early for the columnists.'[94]

Regular press conferences have now become features not only of general elections, but also (usually on a daily basis) of the campaigns for European elections, local elections and by-elections. As well as this, they were the main vehicle the parties used to fight the 'long campaign' in the pre-election period in 1991/2.

For the parties they do have risks. This is sometimes due to poor physical presentation. The Conservatives notoriously botched the launch of their 1987 manifesto, when Margaret Thatcher and her senior ministers sat shoulder to shoulder, badly cramped on a platform far too small for them. According to Thatcher herself, 'the television shots of the conference looked truly awful'.[95] But more often this is due to their potential for gaffes. Election press conferences have resulted in numerous famous blunders – from the statement by Quintin Hogg (then Tory education secretary) in 1964 that anyone who fell for Labour policy was 'stark, staring bonkers'; to Labour's general secretary, Jim Mortimer, announcing in 1983 that the campaign committee were 'all insistent that Michael Foot is the leader of the Labour Party', as if that morning they had seriously considered trying to ditch him.

The parties have tried to reduce the likelihood of gaffes by asserting fuller control of the proceedings: taking up time with their own statements, trying to concentrate questioning on their chosen topic of the day and preventing journalists from firing supplementary questions. This was taken particularly far in 1992, much to the annoyance of the assembled media.

Parties have at times discussed internally the idea of abandoning the press conferences,[96] but this would open them up to the charge they are trying to avoid awkward questions, and they have decided that their advantages outweigh the downside. As a platform for launching initiatives and commenting on campaign events, they enable politicians to seek to structure the campaign and influence reporting. They are a key element in projecting the parties' 'themes for the day' in conjunction with other campaign activities such as walkabouts, photo opportunities and rallies.

Although their influence on the national press is still limited,[97] they make a substantial contribution to television coverage. In 1992, 13 per cent of the stories on the main TV evening news bulletins stemmed from party press conferences.[98] The figure would have been much higher for the lunchtime bulletins, at which stage little else has generally happened in the campaign day.

Indeed, the increasing demand of round-the-clock television coverage for new angles and new stories during the day has even meant that in 1992 press conferences had to be held more than daily. Labour organised 43 in the three and a half weeks of the campaign.[99]


CONCLUSION

Media work has increased in importance more than any other aspect of party political campaigning over the past 50 years. This is reflected not only in the level of resources allocated to it, which has increased enormously, but also in its strategic relationship to other facets of party operations – it is now primary instead of secondary. The transformation is largely due to the domination of television as a communications medium and the consequent need to influence it, but contact with the press is also now given a higher priority.

There are two parts to media work: the handling of relations with the media; and the creation and management of news events or stories.

In terms of party–media relations, the most significant broad development is that parties have become much more vigorous – proactive, opportunistic and assertive. This is especially true at the base, where contact between party officials and journalists has grown in significance more than long-established high-level communication between senior politicians and media hierarchies.

As for relations between the parties and television in particular, that can be divided into the following stages. Initially there was a kind of stand-off – politicians and broadcasters alike were wary of political TV, and neither side sought to get the most out of it. The broadcasters were the first to acquire confidence and presented the parties with difficult challenges. The parties then became more confident and effective in turn, and the relationship between the two became more confrontational as they both asserted themselves. And now there are times when the broadcasters give the impression of having been pushed back into wariness on their part, as the politicians have grown in confidence.

The creation and management of news events have also changed dramatically. In the early post-war period publicity in the media was generally thought of by the parties as a by-product of their other activities, such as speechmaking, party political broadcasts, policy development and manifesto publication. Today, electioneering is geared to maximising media impact, and it is usually the media thinking which drives the rest of the planning.

Thus rallies, conferences, policy announcements and so on – the regular enterprises of a political party – are now arranged in such a way as to derive the best possible media coverage. But the search for good publicity also pushes parties into other endeavours, things which they would not do at all if they did not get reported – 'pseudo-events', as they

were famously labelled by Daniel Boorstin.[100] These constitute a major portion of the activities of a contemporary
political party – the press conferences, photo opportunities,
poster unveilings, 'campaign launches', 'research surveys',
and all the rest.

And there is another kind of pseudo-event – those that
involve pure fakery, when TV misses out on the real happening and gets pictures of pretence instead. On one occasion in 1974, Harold Wilson discovered that ITN would not
be able to get film of his election meeting later that night
to the studio in time for the news. Wilson therefore arranged
for his portable rostrum to be set up in the hotel room
where he was staying, and he delivered the most newsworthy
extract of his speech there and then in front of an ITN
camera as if he was speaking at the meeting.[101] During the
1987 campaign Margaret Thatcher took a telephone call on
her 'battlebus' while TV cameras were filming. She pretended
that she was learning that a British diplomat kidnapped in
Iran had been released. In fact she already knew this. The
scene was a fraud, but the footage of her apparently receiving the good news led the television news bulletins that
evening.[102]

# 5 Rallies and Conferences

*People want to have a good time when they come and listen to a political speech.*

Margaret Thatcher, 1987[1]

*Tonight's rally is the last before election day and we need your help to ensure its success. This envelope contains a skip hat, Union Jack and party popper. Please keep this with you and do not use any of the contents until the end of the rally. Immediately after the prime minister's speech he will be joined on stage by Mrs Major. By this time you will very likely be on your feet applauding and at this stage please put on your hat, wave your flag and explode your party popper.*

Instructions to audience placed on each seat at
Conservative election rally, 1992[2]

*I was sitting next to Robin Cook and . . . Robin said, 'I don't think this is going to work.' I said, 'It did in Nazi Germany.'*
John Prescott on Labour's 1992 Sheffield rally[3]

Political rallies were an early form of mass communication. As the electorate grew in the nineteenth century due to the extension of the franchise, and as election campaigns evolved from individual local battles into a coherent nationwide conflict, political leaders found they had to take their case to growing numbers of voters. The efficient way to do this was to gather them together in one place. Large public meetings, both indoors and outdoors, became a crucial means of electioneering, attended often by thousands and sometimes by tens of thousands of people.

Audiences of this size were once thought huge, but are now tiny – given the millions who can simultaneously receive a political message via television or radio. Rallies and meetings have become much less important in terms of direct communication to those present. Their role has increasingly depended on how they communicate indirectly to those who are absent. Big speeches are still used by politicians to set out themes and policy, but they matter primarily as media events.

This change has meant that different skills are required of both politicians and party managers. At one time the most important communications talent for political leaders was platform oratory. Today, compared to a flair for television, it is immaterial. Indeed, the kind of fervent rhetoric which can enthrall and inspire a large crowd often comes across as over the top when seen in close-up on TV. Moreover, in the past the impact of a rally (or a party conference) hinged on the personal oratorical abilities of the politicians speaking. Today it relies just as much, if not more so, on the way the event is planned and stage-managed by party officials. This is not only thoroughly TV-oriented, but also a far more complex task than it once was, involving vastly superior equipment and resources – sound, lighting, stage-sets, and so on.

Over the past 15 years or so, the style of political speechifying has also been influenced by some aspects of technological advance. Video recordings of televised speeches have made possible the systematic study of which rhetorical tricks generate applause in the hall and also get reported on the TV news. Academic research in this field was pioneered in the early 1980s by Max Atkinson of Oxford University's Centre for Socio-Legal Studies. Atkinson's most publicised conclusion was that a successful 'claptrap' (the word originally meant a device to elicit applause) often involved specific verbal formats: a two-part contrast or a three-part list.[4] This is exemplified by numerous celebrated instances of political oratory, such as the two-part contrast of Margaret Thatcher's 'You turn if you want to/The lady's not for turning', and the list of three in Hugh Gaitskell's 'There are some of us who will fight and fight and fight again to save the party we love'.

Atkinson's book (first published in 1984) was read at the time by many politicians, but has not affected political rhetoric quite as much as some commentators predicted. Plenty of politicians are natural orators who, in any case, use these and other effective devices instinctively. Others are poor speakers who persist in paying little attention to tricks of the trade which could assist them (nor are they helped by speechwriters, who often specialise in knowledge of policy rather than phrase-making). Nevertheless, there is a third group of the keen to learn, such as Labour's shadow chancellor Gordon Brown, a particularly assiduous character. He has become especially fond of peppering his speeches with contrastive pairs, like 'Young people don't want opportunities to beg, they do need opportunities to work'.[5] Atkinson himself has trained Liberal Democrat speechwriters and contributed to Paddy Ashdown's major speeches. The party's campaigns director, Chris Rennard says:[6] 'For a party leader, Atkinson's work is important. A good conference speech can bind the party together.'

A second and more important technical development has been the autocue or speech-prompting device, sometimes nicknamed 'the sincerity machine'. With this equipment the text of a speech is scrolled over two discreetly placed transparent reflecting screens in front of the speaker at eye level, one to the left and one to the right. It can be read by the speaker, but is not visible to those in the body of the hall or watching on TV. This means that instead of frequently looking down at notes or text, the speaker can maintain constant eye contact with the audience, shifting gaze from left to right and back. The concept is similar to the television autocue, which enables broadcasters to talk straight to camera.

Politicians had used the television equivalent for many years, but only adopted the technology for speeches a long time after it had been widely used for presentations in the business world. The gadget was introduced into British politics by Ronald Reagan, when he delivered a special address to Parliament in 1982. Margaret Thatcher congratulated him afterwards on speaking so fluently off the cuff. She had assumed that the two screens in front of him were some kind of state-of-the-art security device.[7] Thatcher was sufficiently impressed to borrow the idea, first employing it at the Conservative conference later that year after much practice in private. 'I taught Mrs Thatcher how to use it,' says Chris Lawson,[8] the Conservative director of marketing at that time. 'She was terrible at first. She kept moving her eyes from side to side, and she looked so shifty. I had to tell her to move her head and shoulders. But she learnt very quickly and became an expert.' Thatcher went on to use the apparatus for virtually all her important speeches. She was always a script-bound speaker, and in Cecil Parkinson's view,[9] 'it was a remarkable improvement for her.'

Many leading politicians have taken to the autocue for their set-piece speeches with similar enthusiasm. Others consider it an encumbrance to be avoided. The advantages are several. It gives speaker and audience a better view of each other, which should enable a more direct relationship. By disguising the fact that a speech is being read, it may create an entirely false impression of spontaneity. It can give an air of authority to an unconfident speaker. And, not least, it results in much better TV shots than the sight of politicians with their heads down glancing at their notes.

On the other hand, reading a script always makes delivery more stilted. Practice and skill are required to use the machinery naturally. Politicians who cannot manage it come across as uneasy, glassy-eyed automata, with less rather than more contact with the audience. And the autocue cramps the style of talented orators, as a prepared text is difficult to combine with large gestures and ad-libbing. Many politicians also have horror stories about the equipment malfunctioning, whether due to mechanical breakdown, operator error or TV lighting, which can easily interfere. John Major was never keen and abandoned it after the 1992 Tory conference, when one of his screens faded out in mid-speech.[10]

However, changes in the form of political oratory are small compared to the transformation which has affected the staging of election rallies and party conferences.

## RALLIES

By the second world war the heyday of the public meeting was passing, thanks to competition from the rival attractions of radio and cinema. This trend intensified after 1945, particularly in due course because of the growth of television. Nevertheless, in the early post-war period rallies still consumed much of the effort involved in national electioneering. Senior party figures traversed the country addressing meetings, so they were directly seen and heard by a fair

number of voters. Reports of their speeches reached many
more people – they constituted a good proportion of newspaper coverage of the campaign. During the 1950 election
Clement Attlee spoke to a cumulative total of over 100 000
people at 34 meetings,[11] even though his low-key manner
hardly made him a charismatic, crowd-pulling speaker. His
adversary ,Winston Churchill, a far more gifted orator, made
fewer speeches but often to larger audiences, addressing a
gathering of 20 000 at one open-air event in Cardiff.[12]

Although such rallies featuring leading politicians were
focal points of the national campaign, they tended to be
basic, even spartan, affairs. Speakers generally addressed the
multitude from a simple, drab platform. There were often
some rudimentary extra ingredients – perhaps organ music
and/or singing; the display of posters, flags, flowers or portraits of party leaders; the wearing of rosettes; the distribution of literature. But only limited attention was paid to
visual presentation or maximising the theatricality of the
proceedings. The drama of the occasion came mainly from
the speeches themselves, the fervour of the crowd and the
combat with hecklers (which, especially at open-air meetings, occasionally degenerated from verbal to physical).

The first major attempt to introduce a different style of
election rally which combined politics with show business
was made by Labour at the 1964 election. The party launched
its campaign with a 10 000-strong gathering at Wembley. The
programme featured not only political speeches, but also a
colliery brass band, a Welsh male voice choir, Pakistani danc-
ers, African drummers, the Humphrey Lyttleton jazz group,
readings by the actress Vanessa Redgrave and a comic monologue by Harry H. Corbett, the younger half in the immensely
popular TV series, *Steptoe and Son.* Steptoe junior reassured
his father in a mock telephone call that they had nothing
to fear from a Labour government. He had checked in the
party manifesto, and their struggling rag'n'bone business
was not on the list of major industries to be nationalised.[13]

The event helped to enthuse party workers, and associated Labour with enjoyment and popular culture. With its
similarities to the razzmatazz of American presidential con-
ventions, it also fitted with Harold Wilson's strategy to identify himself with the youthful, progressive, modernising spirit

of the recently assassinated John F. Kennedy. Labour, however, did not continue with such events at future elections.
Such showbiz productions then remained absent from British elections until the idea was revived by the Conservatives
in 1979.

But there was another change in approach that did stick.
From the 1960s the organisation of rallies became increasingly driven by the demands of television, which now reported them. The way was led initially by Labour under
Wilson, then by the Conservatives under Edward Heath.

In the 1964 election the BBC and ITN ran live extracts
from party leaders' meetings during their evening news programmes. In the case of the guileless Tory leader Sir Alec
Douglas-Home, television viewers heard whatever he happened to be telling his immediate audience at the time.
But Wilson, wily as ever, had prepared special soundbite-
packed passages to which he would suddenly turn when live
filming started. These portions of his speeches contained
the key themes and phrases that he particularly wanted to
convey to the mass of voters. He delivered them with particular care, looking at the cameras. After this election there
was a shift from live to recorded coverage. The incoming
Conservative leader Edward Heath joined Wilson in using a
similar technique. Both men included in their standard
speeches, which were largely repeated from one venue to
the next, a brief self-contained fresh section on each occasion. This was intended to be newsworthy, quotable and
reproduced by TV news bulletins.

The presence of TV cameras also led eventually to the
prevention of heckling, which had traditionally been a common and generally accepted feature of political meetings.
At first, the impact of television was simply to affect the way
heckling was handled by politicians like Wilson, a master of
quick-witted repartee. He soon grasped that for his crush-
ing rejoinders to make sense to the TV audience he first
had to repeat the heckle, which would have been audible
in the hall but not picked up by the broadcasters' microphones.

But gradually the parties started to believe that, while
heckling might help a meeting to come alive, they were better
off without it being televised. Many politicians claimed an-

grily that TV greatly encouraged the practice, as the cameras and lights would swing towards the hecklers at their first intervention. The broadcasters certainly liked showing it, for its drama and unpredictability. The parties found that, however effectively heckling was dealt with, the resulting broadcast exchanges rarely featured the key political points for which they wanted maximum publicity. And the subliminal message was to undermine the authority and dignity of the politicians on the receiving end.

The worst outcome was when the politician failed to dominate the hecklers. The most notorious instance occurred at a rowdy meeting in Birmingham in 1964 when Douglas-Home, appearing strained and defensive, was completely unable to make himself heard above determined chanting from opponents located in the audience. His experience may have attracted sympathy, but it did nothing to make him seem commanding. This kind of humiliation, which previously would have been witnessed by the thousands present, was now seen by millions watching at home. Many Conservatives, including Douglas-Home himself,[14] regarded it as a turning point in his loss of the election. Party managers resolved that such a nightmare must never be allowed to recur. Their worries were increased by the growth of militant student protest in the late 1960s.

In 1970 the Conservatives decided to make Edward Heath's meetings all-ticket, question-free affairs, although this policy was relaxed to some extent during the campaign. Wilson derided it at every opportunity, even though the threat of televised heckling was one reason why Labour decided in this election not to hold conventional leader's rallies at all[15] (Wilson instead devoted his time to the new idea of walkabouts). By 1974 the norm was for leaders to address all-ticket rallies of party loyalists. This tendency was reinforced at the following election. At the start of the 1979 campaign, the Conservative Northern Ireland spokesman Airey Neave was murdered by the Irish National Liberation Army. The police recommended ticket-only meetings as part of the greatly increased security for politicians which resulted. Since the 1970s heckling has more or less ceased at indoor meetings and, indeed, has come to be regarded as an illegitimate and disruptive activity. Anyone who today attempts verbal sparring with a politician of the kind considered routine 40 years ago is likely to be promptly ejected.

Edward Heath's meetings in 1970 were innovative for much more positive reasons. As well as being located and scheduled to suit the convenience of television newsgathering, the events themselves were planned to be telegenic above all else and to an unprecedented extent. Heath's publicity team (led by Geoffrey Tucker) devoted much care to lighting, sound arrangements and camera positions and angles, to ensure he was filmed in the most flattering way. They also commissioned a mobile backdrop which was put up behind Heath wherever he was speaking. It featured a series of concentric blue circles, with the slogan 'A better tomorrow'. This design was created to look good on TV, whether in black-and-white or the new technology of colour (the same symbol was used at press conferences and in party political broadcasts). Wilson's riposte was to describe it as looking like a vortex which would swallow up the unfortunate Heath shortly before polling day.[16]

The portable backdrop was criticised by some for making it seem as if Heath was always in the same place, fostering the impression that he did not get about and mix with people. But it was greatly superior to what had previously been the main visual interest surrounding an orating politician – a platform party of individuals liable to fidget, whisper and yawn. And it had one particularly important group of admirers – Harold Wilson's staff. 'The visual impact of the 1970 platform presentation of Edward Heath had impressed us enormously,' recorded Wilson's aide, Marcia Williams (later Baroness Falkender).[17] She felt that its 'look of efficient simplicity' tied in well with Heath's straightforward but punchy campaign message.

So in the 1974 elections Labour constructed portable backdrops for use at Wilson's rallies, as well as at press conferences and meetings addressed by other top party figures. The February election was fought at a time of national crisis and bitter conflict due to the miners' strike; the backdrop featured a Union Flag-based pattern with its connotations of national unity. The October version sported a large red rosette and the slogan 'Britain will win with Labour'. Wilson's entourage were now determined to locate TV cameras in the most advantageous spots, even when they blocked the view of some of the audience. Williams thought that 'the resultant shots were consequently more flattering – [Wilson] looked decidedly less sinister and weary' than in 1970.[18]

Labour's rally organisers also wanted the events to be more dramatic, particularly for the leader's entrance. Previously Wilson had often slipped quietly onto the platform while another speaker was addressing the meeting. Now his arrival became a key feature of the proceedings. The warm-up speaker would be abruptly interrupted by a grandiloquent loudspeaker announcement: 'Ladies and gentlemen, the next prime minister: the right honourable Harold Wilson.' Spotlights, cameras and eyes would swivel towards the incoming Wilson, who would march up the central aisle of the hall to his place on the platform. In October a recorded musical fanfare was added. To the tune of 'Hello, Dolly', Labour produced 'Hello, Harold . . . It's so good to have you there where you belong'.[19] (This tune obviously appeals to political lyricists – at the next election the Tories hit back with 'Hello, Maggie . . . Now you're really on the road to Number Ten'.[20])

Thus the Conservatives in 1970 and then Labour in 1974 had fundamentally altered the basis on which leaders' rallies were organised. The priority in planning them was how they would seem to the millions who saw short extracts on television, not to the thousands or hundreds actually present. In achieving this the officials responsible in both parties had faced considerable opposition from more traditionally-minded elements.

Since then major election rallies have become much more theatrical, complex and expensive productions, a remarkable contrast with the straightforward speech-making of the past. The key individual responsible for this transformation was Harvey Thomas, who worked for the Tories from 1978 to 1991. Thomas had previously spent 15 years organising huge evangelical meetings for Billy Graham. During this time he had acquired technical expertise in stage-managing large gatherings which was well ahead of that possessed by Conservative Central Office. He had learnt how to focus a crowd's attention on the central individual at an event. Above all, he had developed a shrewd grasp of how to manage an audience's emotions.

The Tory election rallies organised by Thomas involved having a good time, loud and rhythmic music, imposing stage-sets, and parades of stars from sport and show business. The crowd was encouraged into singing along with familiar tunes, waving Union Flags and party flags, throwing streamers, brandishing placards, and cheering as if it were a sporting or entertainment event. Since these were all-ticket affairs limited to party enthusiasts, the audience was usually only too happy to oblige. The exuberant atmosphere would guarantee a rapturous ovation for Margaret Thatcher when she triumphantly marched out after all the excitement to deliver her political message.

The rallies gradually became more extravagant, as Thomas was given increasing scope by the satisfied party hierarchy and his success undermined opposition from those who regarded it all as vulgar and undignified. From the mid-1980s more costly technology was deployed, including laser displays, dry ice and giant TV screens or video walls above the stage. These screens have a number of uses – they can play video clips, say as preparation for the arrival of the main speaker; they give everyone present, however far back they are sitting, a clear view of the speaker; by showing the speaker in dramatic close-up, they demand attention and enhance the speaker's impact; and via closed-circuit TV cameras directed at the crowd, they can play the audience reaction back to itself as it happens, reinforcing applause and cheering.

'The principle behind the rallies is that at first you give people fun and get them excited with lots of music, singing, flag-waving and crowd involvement,' says Thomas.[21] 'Then you switch the mood and calm them down, so they are open-mouthed, slightly exhausted, feeling they've enjoyed themselves, and are now ready to listen when the politician comes onto the platform.'

This approach was exemplified by the rallies organised in 1979, 1983 and 1987, at Wembley on the final Sunday of the campaign. These were the flagship Conservative events of each election, intended to provide a headline-winning, morale-boosting climax in the last week.

The 1979 production was a rally of Tory trade unionists. Following the union militancy of 'the winter of discontent', the party wanted to demonstrate it had support from many ordinary union members. Thatcher walked onstage to the sound of the pop singer Lulu, plus audience, belting out 'Hello, Maggie' at top volume. The 1983 version was a youth rally – this time the Conservatives wanted to show that the party appealed to the young as well as their elders. Celebrities were given an even greater role than in 1979. The occasion was compèred by comedians Jimmy Tarbuck and Bob Monkhouse. The crowd sported 'I love Maggie' T-shirts, and thunderously chanted 'Maggie, Maggie, Maggie, in, in, in' when the object of their affections appeared. The 1987 event was billed as a family rally. The audience was less uproarious than at the previous election, but greater technical resources were now employed. Lasers flashed slogans such as 'Five more years'. The giant screens on the stage played images of Thatcher as world leader, to the accompaniment of suitably thrilling music.

The 1983 event provides an excellent illustration of the media-friendly nature of such occasions. (This is despite the fact it was marred by Kenny Everett joking 'Let's bomb Russia! Let's kick Michael Foot's stick away!' – and Conservative embarrassment was increased because these remarks induced raucous shouts of approval from the hyped-up, youthful audience). On the same day the People's March for Jobs, a union-backed demonstration by unemployed workers which had set off some weeks previously in Glasgow, culminated in a rally in Hyde Park addressed by Michael Foot. The numbers present were several times the 2500 young Tories at Wembley. But it was the lively and colourful telegenic pictures of celebrity participation and crowd enthusiasm at the Conservative event which ensured it got far more good publicity than the old-style demonstration.

Michael Foot's speaking tour in 1983 paid less regard to the needs of television than previous Labour campaigns had. It was the last fling of unadorned oratory delivered to traditional public meetings as a major political party's means of electioneering. Foot sometimes even failed to deliver the brief pre-scripted passage which had been intended as that speech's news story.[22]

As soon as Foot was succeeded as Labour leader by Neil Kinnock, the party started to catch up with the techniques

employed by the Conservatives. Its rallies for the 1984 European elections mixed entertainment and serious political
speeches. During the 1987 general election the party redis-
covered the importance of planning for TV coverage – all
major Labour rallies were presided over by celebrities, platforms were constructed in a way which maximised the prominence of the speaker, and Kinnock made flamboyant spotlit
entrances to the sound of music. On the final Sunday of
the campaign, Labour copied the Tories in laying on a showbiz presentation with a carnival atmosphere. Presented as a
family day out, this rally in Islington featured Glenda Jackson,
a brass band, gospel singers, balloon releases, children's
activities and much flag-waving and cheering by the 3000
party activists present.

Rallies like this boost the morale of both politicians and
supporters, and enable the party to borrow the popularity
and glamour of the celebrities involved. More importantly,
they look good on TV. Television loves the movement, the
colour, the excitement, the star-studded cast-lists of these
events. The resulting pictures communicate cheerfulness,
warmth and confidence. If striking enough, they may get
repeated so often that they become treated as symbolic of
the party's attitude.

By the late 1980s both parties had the same carefully
planned approach to ensuring the most desirable TV coverage. According to Harvey Thomas:[23] 'It is very important to
get the 90 seconds that you want into the news, and the
way that you do that is by trying to put . . . the television
companies in a position where the very best television comes
in the 90 seconds you want to go out.' Or, as the point is
put by Jim Parish, the campaigns officer who coordinated
the presentation of Labour rallies:[24] 'You present the TV
cameras with pictures so good they can't really refuse to
use them.'

While the greatest spectacles are reserved for the most
important events, even the standard electioneering rally
organised by any of the three main parties is now a highly
theatrical performance. It relies on professional design and
meticulous planning. Basic ingredients include the grandiose stage-sets, elaborate lighting, dramatic entrances accompanied by stirring theme tunes and a gaggle of celebrities.

Add to this an audience of party enthusiasts which knows it is itself part of the show and is keen to fulfil its responsibility of flag-waving, applauding, cheering adulation in front of the cameras. Extra effects are added as required for the more significant occasions.

John Major's formal rallies in 1992 (the informal 'Meet John Major' sessions which were also organised are described below) were held in an intimate, circular setting, in which he felt more comfortable. He performed on a well-lit blue stage in the middle, while a high-tech backdrop with large TV screens encircled the audience. The equipment was extremely expensive, and the rallies were produced with verve by Andrew Lloyd Webber, who also composed the theme tune to which Major made his tightly stage-managed entrances.

However, by far the greatest extravaganza mounted as a campaign rally was laid on by Labour in 1992. The most striking and memorable feature of the entire election, in retrospect it was blamed by many for contributing to the party's failure. The event was held at the Sheffield Arena eight days before polling. Labour strategists hoped to invigorate the last week's campaigning (which had lacked energy in 1987), and create the impression of a bandwagon of support starting to roll. Despite much internal opposition to the idea, they also wanted to give the party the prestige of organising the most spectacular political occasion Britain had ever seen.

The crowd of 10 000 was huge for an election rally by recent standards. Their mood was euphoric – three opinion polls in the previous 24 hours had appeared to reveal a Labour breakthrough (they did not know that polls already conducted for the following day's papers were much less favourable). In his opening speech, deputy leader Roy Hattersley talked as if Labour had already won the election. Musical performances ranged from pop to opera. Above the stage six large flags fluttered in an artificial breeze. A gigantic screen relayed a succession of celebrity endorsements, and, as the sense of expectation grew, showed live film of Neil and Glenys Kinnock arriving nearby in a helicopter. Labour even hired a satellite link so that it could provide broadcasters with pictures shot by its own camera units, which were located at special vantage points.[25]

In a manoeuvre copied from a French Socialist Party rally, the entire shadow cabinet paraded the length of the hall through the audience and onto the vast podium. 'It was an extraordinary experience', wrote Bryan Gould later,[26] 'with all the lights, music, cheering, to walk what seemed hundreds of yards through a forest of clutching hands and rosettes, a cacophony of noise in our ears, with people in tears of excitement, shouting and waving and slapping us on our backs.'

Kinnock's reception was even more ecstatic. For the calmest of people it would have been exhilarating. For Kinnock, an emotional man at the best of times, the effect was overwhelming. He bounded onto the platform and, jerking his head, roared three times, 'We're all right', following up with 'We'd better get some talking done here, serious talking.' To the elated crowd it seemed perfectly appropriate behaviour. On television – and the scene was shown repeatedly – it did not come over well. Not only did it overshadow the powerful speech he went on to make, in one undisciplined moment he had undermined the statesmanlike image he had been desperately trying to cultivate for years.

Since the election the Sheffield rally has been widely criticised, both for its generally triumphalist ethos of certain victory and for Kinnock's loss of self-control. Labour officially described it as 'a serious mistake',[27] and Kinnock himself has publicly regretted his conduct in several interviews. On the other hand, the event's supporters argue that if Labour had won, the rally would now be regarded as a trailblazing masterpiece of electioneering.

What is clear is that some of the difficulty stemmed not from the fundamental concept, but from its execution. First, Labour was ironically unlucky that it coincided with the most optimistic polls of the campaign. Second, long walk-ons through the crowd are liked by television (reporters can use them for scene-setting), but they do run the risk of disturbing the speaker's concentration. Kinnock's blunder would probably have been averted if he had been brought on at the back of the stage and, only after the speech, out through the audience. (Alternatively, his entrance might have been more stately if, as in the French Socialist rally from which the idea was taken, a wider aisle had separated him from the crowd). Third, late running due to organisational hiccups meant that the highlights of Kinnock's speech did not come at the best time for TV news.

The occasion was also condemned by political opponents on grounds of morality rather than effectiveness, as an exercise in mass manipulation akin to a Nuremberg rally. In fact, Sheffield was only different in degree rather than fundamentals to other election events. It simply extended the same techniques which all major parties had already used. Most large political meetings are and always have been about motivating crowds through the grip of emotion, and are just as vulnerable to the same principled if idealistic criticism.

Thus most election rallies have become much grander, more imposing and rousing affairs over recent years. But there has also been one different, though less important, strand. Party managers have sometimes been faced with leaders who are not suited to formal, tub-thumping oratory, and they have tried to create less majestic settings to play to their strengths. This tactic has met with one persistent and overriding problem – the resulting meetings appear dull and unspirited on television.

Edward Heath's publicity team believed that formal settings held two disadvantages for him. First, such settings reinforced his tendency to appear stiff and stilted in public. Second, in February 1974 the televised extracts focusing on his attacks on Labour meant he came across as confrontational and aggressive, at 'a time when the surge in Liberal support suggested that the public was tiring of adversary politics. For the October 1974 election Tory strategists came up with the idea of 'talk-ins' as a solution. These were informal, smaller gatherings of voters (not necessarily Conservatives – although, naturally, most were), where Heath would be seen to listen, and could speak and answer questions in a conversational manner which his advisers felt showed him to best advantage. However, while the meetings themselves went well, they were poorly reported. Unlike set speeches, they were not regarded by the media as a reliable source of news stories. Furthermore, they lacked the drama and sense of occasion to make good TV.

A similar concept was employed by the Liberal/SDP Alliance in both the 1983 and 1987 elections. Meetings took the form of 'Ask the Alliance' rallies, in which questions were put to leading figures from the two parties by supposedly uncommitted audiences. This plan was adopted initially because it was hoped these open-style gatherings would convey accessibility and responsiveness in an appealing contrast to the other parties' all-ticket affairs limited to the faithful. It was continued for 1987, since both David Owen and David Steel felt more comfortable with this conversational approach than set-piece speeches, and the format had also been successful in recent by-elections.

As in Heath's case, these sessions often worked well in the hall, but not on the screen. This problem was much worse in 1987 now that Labour as well as the Conservative Party was organising highly televisual events. In comparison, the Alliance rallies were short of passion and compelling visuals, and failed to impart the impression of popularity created by rapturous receptions from cheering supporters. Television reports described the meetings as dreary. Alliance strategists regarded them as a failure, and the formula was abandoned for the Liberal Democrat campaign in 1992.

The third attempt to conduct election rallies as informal, question-and-answer occasions was the 'Meet John Major' affairs run by the Conservatives in 1992. With his low-key style and monotonous delivery, Major is ill-suited to platform oratory. His advisers thought that if he was placed in a more relaxed setting, then his persuasiveness in ordinary conversation could be effectively demonstrated to the public. Major told his campaign strategists he had felt particularly comfortable when visiting British troops in Saudi Arabia and he had chatted with them in small circles. This had also been a big publicity success. So the plan was to develop a format which recreated this kind of atmosphere. Party managers were especially influenced by folksy group discussions held by George Bush in his victorious 1988 US presidential campaign, in which Bush sat on a stool amidst a group of voters.

So, whereas 18 years previously Edward Heath had taken off his jacket and sat in a swivel chair to take questions, in 1992 John Major took off his jacket and sat on a high stool. The audience was seated all around him in a plain hall. To avoid the risks of assassination or of brief television reports concentrating on hostile questioning, it consisted of known Tory supporters. This decision backfired badly, because it meant that the media dismissed the rallies as artificial and sterile. Of course, they were actually no more contrived than many other campaign activities, but unlike the others they purported to be less controlled and were presented by Tory press officers as 'high-wire campaigning'.[28] While some nice press photographs did result, most comment was derisive. The events were nicknamed Major's 'Val Doonican sessions'. They were no better at generating good TV coverage than the similar efforts by Heath and the Alliance. The first one of the campaign was described on BBC TV news as 'desperately tame'. Major's frustration at the reaction to these rallies was instrumental in his impulsive decision in the second half of the campaign to address outdoor crowds from a soapbox with the aid of a loudhailer.

## PARTY CONFERENCES

These autumnal seaside gatherings are the most important occasions in the annual calendar of the main political parties. Throughout the post-war period, party conferences have fulfilled a number of basic functions: they inform and inspire activists, allow for the venting of grass-roots opinion, and provide good opportunities for major national publicity. Over the decades the balance between these roles has changed substantially. The Conservative conference was largely a non-contentious rally to enthuse the loyal party workers who attended, while Labour's acted as a resolution-passing, policy-making body. Today party managers (although not necessarily all the rank and file) prefer to treat their conferences as a public relations exercise – a form of extremely long party political broadcast, with edited highlights shown during the news and reported in the press.

Conferences are thus no longer events primarily internal to the party, whether morale-boosting or decision-making. Instead, they are increasingly performances for the benefit of external observers – the voting public. (A similar although weaker trend has also affected sectional and regional conferences, especially when addressed by the party leader.)

And conferences do often give a boost, even if temporary, to the standing of parties in the polls and the satisfaction ratings of their leaders.

The first crucial factor behind this development was the televising of party conferences which started in the 1950s. This meant conferences would eventually become showcases for presenting the party to the electorate, and that politicians could use them to speak to the country as well as, or instead of, the party. Following a series of approaches from the BBC to both parties, the Conservatives agreed to their conference being televised in 1954. Labour, however, generally slower in adapting to the new medium, refused to let the TV cameras in.[29] A few leading Labour politicians backed the BBC's idea, but most were opposed. Some feared the public exposure that would be given to the party's internal conflicts, others (according to Richard Crossman)[30] to the system of trade union block voting. Nevertheless, the coverage of the Conservative conference was regarded as such a success that Labour was reluctantly forced to follow suit the following year.

Television soon made a small mark on the appearance of party conferences, as politicians and party managers responded to the presence of the cameras. At the very first televised conference, Conservative officials arranged for attractive women to sit behind Churchill during his leader's speech. Unfortunately, they included a cabinet minister's wife who appeared to fall asleep.[31] One downside of televising was that it subjected those sitting on the platform to the intense and uncomfortable glare of early TV lighting. Many Labour politicians in particular (even including party leader Hugh Gaitskell) responded by wearing dark glasses, making this political assembly look more like a convention of gangsters.

Television also influenced the timing of conference business. In 1958 the Conservatives scheduled a debate on flogging for a slot when (in those cumbersome days) it would be too late for film to be flown to London and developed in time for the nightly conference programme.[32] This was an early instance of party managers manipulating conference agendas to minimise TV coverage of rank-and-file attitudes which the leadership found embarrassing. In later years this was achieved by arranging awkward debates at times when live reporting was interrupted by children's programmes. Tory conference organisers planned for Enoch Powell's speeches to coincide with *Play School*,[33] while their Labour counterparts dealt similarly with sessions on lesbian and gay rights, Northern Ireland and the Gulf crisis.

More importantly, television coverage made it vital for the parties to exploit their conferences fully as a vehicle for the projection of their leader. During the 1960s Labour gradually converted the customary and often contentious debate on the annual activities of the Parliamentary Labour Party into merely a formal peg for the main speech from the party leader, to be followed by the ritual adulation of a standing ovation.[34] Thus the leader was now not so much participating in internal discussion as ceremoniously addressing the party and the nation.

As for the Conservatives, Sir Alec Douglas-Home and his predecessors as party leader had not even deigned to attend conference. Instead, they arrived grandly on the last day simply to deliver their message from on high to a respectful post-conference rally. In 1965 the newly-elected Edward Heath set the pattern for a different approach. He turned up for the entire event, both to demonstrate a fresh style of less remote leadership and to maximise his TV exposure through speaking in debate and being seen on the platform. Later, in 1975, the Tories shifted the duration of conference from Wednesday–Saturday to Tuesday–Friday, to get better television coverage for the leader's speech on the final day.

In some other respects changes were less far-reaching than had been expected. When televising was first considered, it had been widely predicted that party conferences would automatically become anodyne affairs, and that honest disagreement and open discussion would soon cease.[35] The party leaderships certainly became more desperate for a public demonstration of party unity, whether real or fake, especially if an election was due in the next year or so. But (particularly in the case of Labour and Liberal conferences) other elements still often proved unruly and demanded to have their say.

And it was a long time before there was much change in the visual presentation of conferences. The dominant physical

feature of conference halls was invariably the raised platform for the party hierarchy. In the 1960s and 1970s, the
average platform consisted of politicians crowded onto serried
rows of tables draped in cloth (blue, red or other, as politically appropriate) and cluttered with microphones, carafes
and papers. Television shots of a platform speaker would
show the people sitting behind and their distracting habits,
such as chatting, smoking or putting on facial expressions
to indicate disagreement with the speaker's argument; alternatively the shots might show empty chairs occupied by
discarded teacups. Similarly for the audience watching in
the hall, the platform offered no real focal point to concentrate on but plenty of diversions to flit between. Television
started to avoid the intrusive backgrounds by filming speakers with 'up the nostrils' shots from below (an angle not
available to many members of the audience). Platforms were
sometimes decorated with flower displays, flags, large slogans, a proscenium arch or a cloth backdrop. Nevertheless,
the overall effect of the staging of the event did little if
anything to reinforce the party message.

Since the 1970s the presentation of conferences has been
transformed. The leading individual responsible was again
Harvey Thomas. To create the right atmosphere in the hall,
boost the impact of the speeches and provide much better
TV pictures, he applied the same increasingly elaborate techniques to Conservative party conferences as he did to election rallies (and had to combat the same conservatism from
those who objected). These included the grandiose sets, giant
screens or video walls, complex lighting, the autocue, dramatic entrances and (particularly for the leader's speech)
the management of audience emotions through music, flag-
waving, and so on.

This was combined with other changes specific to conference. Thomas fought a running battle with the Tory hierarchy to have the size of the platform party cut back, on the
basis that the fewer people on the platform then the fewer
distractions for the representatives to gawp at. This impinged
on the self-importance of party dignitaries, and he was only
partly successful. 'We didn't need any of these people there,'
says Thomas,[36] 'but their pride was the problem.' However,
at least he managed to create a separate speaker's rostrum

as a visual focal point, and to clear the area around and directly behind this to provide a cleaner TV image.

Thomas also aimed to construct sets whose design chimed in with the party's political messages. The 1982 conference took place in the wake of the Falklands War, when the Conservative strategy for exploiting the electoral benefits of military victory relied on frequent indirect references to it. The conference slogan was 'The Resolute Approach', a war hero's widow sat on the platform, Margaret Thatcher entered to the sound of 'Land of Hope and Glory', and the backdrop resembled a grey battleship. In 1990 (before Major succeeded Thatcher) the Tories wanted to emphasise the theme of strength of leadership. The slogan was 'The Strength to Succeed', and the backdrop featured a main central pillar intended as a symbol of the notion of strength.

Thomas summarises his changes in the visual presentation of the leader's conference speech from 1979 to 1990 as follows:[37] 'In 1979 there was no focal point for the audience to look at, there were lots of distractions, there was just one spotlight on Thatcher, and she looked down at her text. In 1990 Thatcher was the focus of attention, there were no distractions, the two big screens increased the impact of the message considerably, there was sophisticated modern lighting, and because of the autocue she looked up. Everything was integrated to make it as easy as possible for her to communicate.'

The presentation of conference has been further developed since Thomas left Central Office in 1991, notably in the special arrangement now used for Major's speeches. In recent years John Major has spoken from a low peninsula, built forward and down from the main stage and extending into the main conference area, so that he is almost among the audience. This reinforces his image as accessible 'man of the people' rather than a grand and aloof figure.

However, the Conservative conference which was most successful as a communications exercise involved much more than technical stage-management. Early in 1986, private Tory polling had indicated that the government was losing popularity because it was widely perceived to be running out of steam. Party strategists decided to use that year's conference – probably the last before an election would be called

– to package the government as full of practical ideas for the future. Speeches and literature were all coordinated to fit in with one integrated message encapsulated in the conference slogan, 'The next move forward'. Party chairman Norman Tebbit pressed ministers into revealing a battery of specific new initiatives across all departments. This had been trailed in advance in unprecedented pre-conference newspaper advertising.

Well-received in the media, the conference was followed by the Conservatives taking a lead in the polls which they maintained until the election took place the following June. The same slogan was then used for this campaign. In retrospect, many party managers and politicians regarded the 1986 conference as the springboard for their 1987 victory. But the party has never since been able to reproduce the same all-encompassing, single-minded emphasis on one meaningful and coherent theme.

The Labour party conference has changed over the years even more than the Conservative one. The Tory gathering has always been tightly controlled by party managers. Most topics for debate, motions and speakers are fixed to suit the leadership. Many 'debates' consist simply of a succession of loyalists obsequiously backing a tame motion before the hall listens reverentially to the frontbench politician who winds up. This is the ideal which the Labour hierarchy would jealously like to emulate, and it has recently come a long way towards doing so.

Of course, the Labour leadership always tried to arrange things in its favour behind the scenes, but it often failed. The leader could not be sure that his will would prevail on the party's national executive committee (NEC), or with the trade unions whose block votes dominated conference. Leaders frequently suffered the humiliation of losing important votes, while vigorous debates highlighted bitter internal divisions. Senior frontbenchers, if not on the NEC, possessed no speaking privileges over ordinary delegates. This may have been a more democratic way to run a political party, but it was not a more effective way to convey the party's message to the voting public.

Then from the mid-1980s the balance of power within Labour shifted away from the left and towards the leadership. Neil Kinnock developed an increasingly tight grip on the party machine. The results of votes could still not be guaranteed, but the leadership now controlled the planning and running of conference. 'Totally unashamedly, we have used the conference to project the party to make an impact on the public,' said Peter Mandelson,[38] Labour's director of communications, in 1990. Shadow cabinet members spoke from the platform and not the ordinary delegates' microphone, whether or not they were on the NEC. Their speeches were scheduled to suit TV news coverage. Other speakers were also carefully pre-selected in a concern for effective external communication rather than open internal discussion – increasing the proportion of time given to frontbench MPs and neatly dressed candidates from marginal seats. And as the left gradually lost influence among the party's grass roots, more delegates became happy to see their primary tasks as applause and cheering instead of discussing and voting.

The visual presentation of conference was also reformed. In the 1970s the only planned element was the slogan, and even this was a haphazard affair, according to the long-serving campaigns officer Jim Parish:[39] 'The whole publicity department would meet in September, and Percy Clark, the head of publicity, would say "Has anyone got any ideas for a slogan?" We would all chip in, including the typists, and at the end of the meeting Clark would ring the banner maker with a slogan. And that was that. There was no input from politicians.'

The first time that Labour had a custom-built set for the platform instead of the tables, chairs and lecterns supplied by the venue was at Brighton in 1983. Kinnock wanted a proper set for what would be his first conference as leader. Labour's publicity team had no idea who to get to build it. So Parish phoned Conservative Central Office to obtain the details of the company which had constructed the Tory conference set in Brighton the previous year.[40]

Labour's conference presentation became more professional from then on, with slick organisation and good visuals. The next major step came in 1986, when the backdrop featured TV-friendly pastel shades of cream and pink, and the party's newly launched logo, the red rose. The conference ended with a soprano singing the 'Red Flag', and telegenic scenes of Neil and Glenys tossing roses randomly into the excited crowd.

In the following years, the party moved into yet more imposing sets and fancier lighting. Conference organisers established an isolated off-centre rostrum, designed to help focus audience attention and ensure uncluttered TV pictures. They also tried to rework the musical finale, which traditionally consisted of the 'Red Flag' and 'Auld Lang Syne', but with less success. In 1989 these old favourites were supplemented by a specially commissioned pop song 'Meet the Challenge, Make the Change'. In 1991 the shadow cabinet was forced into the ridiculous spectacle of holding hands, swaying and singing along to the sound of Queen's 'We are the Champions'. This was an experience which many of them clearly found extremely embarrassing. It was a bad idea poorly implemented, and a good illustration of how presentational excess can be counter-productive.

# 6 Opinion Research

*Several politicians in all parties sampled opinion by talking to as many strangers of all sorts as possible: railway porters, taxi drivers, barbers and news vendors.*
David Butler and Anthony King, 1965[1]

*I'm not talking about packaging soapflakes or breakfast cereal; I'm talking about talking to the British electors in the language they respond to and [that] best communicates to them the favourable face of Labour's policies. If you don't want to do that you're daft.*
Memo from Bob Worcester of MORI, Labour's polling company, to the Labour Party, 1983[2]

Politicians have always been keen to know what would attract voters and what would repel them. Armed with such knowledge, they can try to modify their campaigning to maximise its effectiveness. Forty years ago they relied on little more than informed guesswork. Today, systematic opinion research is an important tool of political communication, and a key influence on the content, style and means of delivery of party propaganda.

Before political polling became widespread, politicians who sought to discern public opinion depended on various unreliable sources: the attitudes of the untypical people they actually met (from party activists to troubled constituents), what they read in the papers, their correspondence, canvass returns, audience reaction at meetings, reports from constituency agents, and so on. All these things still count – no politician is uninfluenced by them. Indeed, in plenty of cases sensitivity and experience can provide helpful insights into the views of the electorate, but in many others these channels are so unrepresentative as to be worse than useless. For the senior figures and strategists who control party presentation, the importance of other indications of public opinion has dwindled as that of polling has increased.

Properly conducted opinion research is by no means a perfect guide to the behaviour of the electorate, as its failure

147

to predict the 1992 general election result demonstrated. However, it is much better than any alternative and certainly good enough to be worth exploiting. Ever since published polls first appeared, party officials and politicians have studied their results. Presentation and policy are also influenced by parties' own private opinion research, to which the Conservatives and Labour have devoted large sums of money, and the Liberal Democrats and their predecessors smaller sums. This chapter examines how the parties have developed and exploited private research to assist campaigning. Private polls are not only used to influence party communications. They also affect, for example, prime ministerial choices of election dates. Their main purpose, however, is as a communications tool to inform propaganda.

Opinion research generally comes in two forms: quantitative and qualitative.

Quantitative research involves putting set questions to a (hopefully) representative sample of a population, and extrapolating from the results to estimate findings for the whole population.

Sub-divisions of quantitative work include:

(1) 'tracking' surveys, in which the same questions are repeated at different times to different samples, to track overall shifts in attitudes or behaviour;

(2) 'panel' studies, in which the same individuals are re-interviewed to see how many people who previously did or thought one thing are now doing or thinking something else, and why. The initial survey may be called the 'baseline', the later ones 'recalls'. Panels provide valuable information which is otherwise unobtainable, but have disadvantages such as a tendency to become unrepresentative. The less cooperative interviewees drop out, while those who tolerate being regularly quizzed on which party they support end up being more likely to vote than the general public – although not necessarily for any particular party. (A panel can be run in conjunction with tracking polls to check that its overall pattern of party preference is not becoming unrepresentative.)

Qualitative research most commonly consists of 'focus groups'. These are small discussion groups, typically of six to ten people, steered around relevant topics by a researcher. Such groups allow open-ended expression of opinion and

associations, and enable deeper probing of the factors underlying people's attitudes than quantitative surveys do. They
are highly dependent on the skills and impartiality of those
who guide and report the discussions. Sessions are often
recorded on video so that tapes of extracts can be compiled. Results can later be subjected to more rigorous quantitative testing.

BEGINNINGS

Private polling by British political parties started in a limited way during the 1945–50 Parliament. Its introduction
stemmed from the polling industry's inaugural triumph in
1945, when published surveys by Gallup predicted Labour's
otherwise unanticipated overwhelming victory. This was the
first general election since national voting intention polling
began in Britain in 1939.[3] Its result convincingly demonstrated the merits of systematic sample surveys – and the
drawbacks of whatever methods for assessing public opinion were used by the politicians and journalists who maintained the voters would not humiliate their war hero, Winston
Churchill.

The impact of the initial private polls on party strategy
was minimal. The Conservatives were encouraged in their
use by Colman, Prentis and Varley (CPV), the advertising
agency they appointed in 1948 and which was already accustomed to commercial market research. The party's polling programme included a survey of over 5000 interviewees
(a very large sample by today's standards) to study characteristics of floating voters.[4] But the agency's head of research
was not impressed by his client's disregard for survey results. 'The research was wasted,' he said.[5] 'Talking to them
was more infuriating than talking to a small-minded provincial manufacturer of shoelaces.'

But there was one finding which did interest the Tory
hierarchy. A confidential poll commissioned from Gallup
showed that the party would not gain or lose votes by replacing Churchill as leader.[6] And politicians did exploit
publicly one minor use of private polling before the 1950
election – the disclosure of selective favourable items of data.

The Conservatives claimed a survey showed 38 per cent of trade unionists were Tories. And in a numerical coincidence, the Liberals announced that 38 per cent of the electorate said they would 'vote Liberal if they thought they could really have a Liberal Government', a theme the party has doggedly pursued ever since.[7]

During the 1950s party officials devoted increasing effort to analysis of published polls, trying to identify favourable issues and attributes of undecided voters. But the information made little difference at first to the behaviour of their political masters. Politicians took it no more seriously than their other, less scientific, sources of insight into the public mind. However, the authority of polling was gradually becoming established, and in the second half of the decade the parties began to appreciate properly the potential benefits of private surveys.

The unprecedented advertising campaign run by the Conservatives in 1957–9 was informed by opinion research. On its own initiative CPV commissioned polls about public recall of and reaction to its poster and press advertisements. When one survey showed that the intended audience were particularly anxious to get grammar school places for their children, ads on the theme of opportunity were revised to feature teenagers in school uniform rather than toddlers.[8]

Starting with the 1958 Rochdale by-election, the Conservatives also commissioned their own more general surveys, using Nielsen, the market research firm, and National Opinion Polls (NOP). The findings confirmed the CPV strategy of targeting publicity at the more prosperous working class – reasonably paid skilled manual and clerical workers who had young families and were starting to acquire consumer durables. The polls indicated that many no longer wanted to identify themselves with the working class and therefore the Labour Party.[9] However Oliver Poole, party deputy chairman and key strategist behind the CPV campaign, was only partly committed to rigorous methods of research. He also sought to improve his understanding of the prosperous working class by regularly spending Saturday afternoons watching them shopping in Watford.

Labour made restricted use of private polling before the 1959 election. In 1956, the new Labour leader, Hugh Gaitskell, authorised a small, 400-strong survey of voter attitudes to issues and the party's image. This was organised by Mark Abrams, managing director of Research Services Ltd and a prominent figure in the growing market research industry. Abrams then wanted to conduct a study into the perceived strengths and weaknesses of Gaitskell personally, an idea rejected by the party leader.[10] In 1957, another survey was carried out into views on education, but research then ceased. The use of commercial techniques was frowned on by some other senior Labour politicians, notably Aneurin Bevan who famously described polls as taking 'the poetry out of politics'. Although Gaitskell was keen himself, he bowed to their opposition.

After 1959, however, Labour was the first party to move from isolated surveys to a systematic research programme. The death of Bevan removed an important obstacle, while the party was spurred on by the successful Tory use of modern communications (principally advertising) for the 1959 election and by the impact of some opinion research produced by Abrams in 1960. Published in the right-wing Labour magazine *Socialist Commentary*,[11] it suggested that Labour's image was outdated and unappealing to young people and the expanding middle class. This work was dismissed by some who regarded Abrams as a committed Gaitskellite rather than an impartial investigator of public opinion, but it impressed many in the party hierarchy. During 1962–4 extensive polling was commissioned from Abrams, and results influenced party presentation.

Abrams' first aim was to identify uncommitted electors in marginal constituencies (whom he was probably the first to call 'target voters') and discover their concerns. His research concluded that Labour should appeal to them on education, housing, pensions, town planning and managerial efficiency, while avoiding nationalisation, defence and foreign affairs. He then established several panels of target voters who were regularly sent questionnaires about key issues, Labour politicians, party slogans, advertisements and political broadcasts.[12] Individual ads were also tested with small groups of voters. The results were central to the work of the party's publicity team.

Labour's professional advertising advisers, such as David

Kingsley, supported a research-based creative strategy. 'Advertising is a reinforcing agent,' says[13] Kingsley. 'It can't change people's minds, but it can strengthen and build on attitudes already there. So research was important to know what those attitudes were. The 1964 campaign drew very heavily on our knowledge and understanding of what people felt.'

The research was used both to help determine which issues to focus on, and also to influence the approach of particular advertising campaigns. The party's first national press ads in May 1963 featured large photographs of the new leader, Harold Wilson, as a direct consequence of surveys showing his popularity. On the other hand, ads discarded after testing included one with an attractive young woman. Its intended audience of women voters thought she looked as if she should be advertising toothpaste or false eyelashes.[14] Overall imagery was researched as well – the thumbs-up logo adopted for the 1964 campaign was tested to make sure it had no undesirable overtones.[15]

Labour's planned and innovatory use of research reflected three factors: the skills of Mark Abrams, the professionalism of advertising advisers who were keen and able to implement its results, and the interest and support of party leaders – first Gaitskell, then Wilson. However, while advertising, slogans and the prioritisation of issues were tied in to research, large parts of Labour campaigning (such as party political broadcasts) fell outside the remit of the publicity committee and were still largely uninfluenced by polling.

In the 1959–64 period the Tories continued to commission some research, mainly from NOP, including postmortem polls after disappointing by-election results. In 1963 the party sponsored a massive survey with 10 000 interviewees. The largest political poll to have then been carried out in Britain, it was big enough to allow reliable study of small subsamples such as young working-class voters. The aim was to discover how to win support from Tory defectors and 1959 abstainers.[16] CPV also copy-tested ads with small groups of voters. This led, for example, to the use of 'standard of living' rather than 'prosperity', since the former term apparently meant more to the ordinary voter.[17]

But there was nothing like the close relationship between research and major elements of presentation which Labour achieved. George Hutchinson, the Tory chief publicity officer appointed in 1961, was a former journalist who favoured instinct rather than surveys in determining political strategy. He took hardly any notice of the research. Even the findings of the huge 1963 study were mainly ignored.

Thus in 1964 Labour was leading the Conservatives in the productive exploitation of private polling. In the second half of the decade, however, this was reversed. After its 1964 victory, Labour failed to advance its opinion research. Little was commissioned from Abrams during the 1964–6 Parliament. Party managers felt they had learnt all they needed to know from the work before 1964.[18] Campaign planning was also hindered by the more distant relationship between party officials and politicians, now that the latter had affairs of state to busy themselves with.

Some research resumed in 1968, when Labour was doing desperately badly in the published polls and by-elections. Work commissioned from Abrams' company included a survey of young voters, prompted by the reduction of the voting age to 18. In early 1970 the party had to find a new pollster quickly, when Abrams became a civil servant at the Social Science Research Council. It picked Bob Worcester, who had recently set up Market & Opinion Research International (MORI) and went on to poll for Labour for the next 20 years. Like others working for Labour, MORI was encouraged to anticipate an October 1970 election. Its plans were disrupted by Wilson's decision to go for June. The firm only had time to carry out two surveys during the campaign itself. In 1970 Labour was making less use of polling than it had in 1964.

In contrast the Conservatives, prodded by defeat in 1964 and publicity about Abrams' role, leapfrogged ahead. Private polling was given an unprecedented central role in party strategy in the second half of the 1960s. A key influence was Sir Michael Fraser, the Tory deputy chairman and one of many senior figures who felt the party had lost touch with ordinary voters. Much thought was put into how best to exploit opinion research – and in particular how to use it systematically, rather than the ad hoc approach employed previously (for example, in seeking retrospective explanations of by-election disasters). As a result, in 1965 the party set in

motion two ambitious new research initiatives. Their purposes were to reveal to the party its public image, to identify target voters and how to sway them, and to educate senior
Tories about voting behaviour.

In the first innovation the Conservatives used the British
Market Research Bureau (BMRB), a leading market research
company, to establish a long-term panel, initially of 4500
electors first interviewed in 1965. Every seven months about
700 were re-interviewed. By going back to the same people
to see how their views had changed, it was possible to monitor
the complex flows of support in and out of different parties
and the don't knows, rather than just comparing the overall level of support with the previous poll to get the net
swing.

The BMRB panel found (as panels always do) that the
net figures masked an enormous amount of churning. The
net swing from Conservative to Labour between the 1964
and 1966 elections was 2.7 per cent, but according to the
panel data over 30 per cent of the electorate changed their
voting intention in some way during this period. Women,
C2s and under-35s tended to be more volatile.

The second initiative was even more far-reaching. It involved the creation of a new research firm, the Opinion
Research Centre (ORC). In its various guises this remained
the main Tory polling organisation until after the 1992
election.

ORC was established in November 1965 on the basis it
would do monthly private polling for the Conservatives. The
two key individuals were Humphrey Taylor and Tommy
Thompson, who both left Central Office to start the company. Taylor was a former NOP executive who had worked
on polls sponsored by the Tories; Thompson was familiar
with polling from a previous job as the *Daily Mail*'s political
editor. Both had been disappointed by the party's failure to
take research sufficiently seriously at the 1964 election.

Their aim was to provide Central Office with a continuous flow of information about public attitudes. The monthly
polls usually covered a different area each time, such as
education, tax, industrial relations or nationalised industries.
ORC also did quick reaction polls after party political broadcasts, to be ready by lunchtime the next day, as well as studies

to test the appeal of various slogans and words and the impact of particular speeches.

Some limited results of this work were in evidence by the 1966 election. The perception was revealed that the party was out of date, stale, and still associated with the Profumo scandal and other unhappy events of 1961–4. This led it to discard defence of its old record and concentrate instead on its new leaders and policies.[19]

The main impact came afterwards. Taylor regarded the 1967–70 period as the peak of ORC influence on the Conservatives during the ten years that he conducted party polling.[20] In a foretaste of the future, support for the sale of council houses was stressed in the 1967 Greater London Council campaign because research clearly demonstrated its popularity. Taylor's work also encouraged the party to support higher pensions and accept comprehensivisation of secondary schools, policies which it later implemented in government. And for the successful 1970 Tory campaign, ORC polling was important in determining the focus on two issues: inflation and tax. Surveys suggested that working-class women in particular were concerned about price rises, and some were moving to the Tories. The party's publicity advisers came up with the slogan 'the shopping basket election', and their work emphasised rising prices at every opportunity. Due to the BMRB panel evidence on voter volatility, the Conservatives also took care not to offend C2s when designing their tax proposals.

As for the Liberals, throughout the period up to 1970 they could only afford a little private polling. This was usually aimed at contributing to local success. A survey was commissioned before the 1963 Colne Valley by-election, partly to try to show that while the Tories could not beat Labour, the Liberals could (they narrowly failed). Another study into perceptions of candidates and policies was conducted for the 1969 Birmingham Ladywood by-election, which the party did win. The Liberals also used local polls to help decide which constituencies were winnable and therefore merited extra resources. At a national level some publicity material was copy-tested, and some irregular issue research was done, for example on attitudes to comprehensive schools.[21]

SINCE 1970

The 1970 election was an embarrassing setback for the polling industry generally, since (probably due to late swing) most of the published polls failed to predict the Tory victory. However, this did nothing to impede the uptake of private polling. After the 1970 election Labour renewed its interest in opinion research, so that for the first time both parties simultaneously treated it as an important political tool. The rest of this chapter first examines the overall development of private polling since 1970, and then looks at three specific aspects – campaign polling, psychographics and people-metering – which are distinct from the bulk of political opinion research.

**Overall developments**

After their 1970 victory the Conservatives continued to employ ORC and BMRB. Recalls of the BMRB panel were commissioned periodically, while the main source of information remained ORC. As before, its monitoring included the changing salience of issues and reaction to party broadcasts. However, now they were in office, the Tories did not pay their pollsters quite as much attention or money as in opposition. They cut back particularly on research into popularity of policy options. The elections of 1974 then led to a reassertion of the pollsters' influence. By indicating public dislike of inter-party slanging and preference for coalition over polarisation, ORC work helped bring about the 'government of national unity' platform on which Edward Heath unsuccessfully fought the October 1974 campaign.

In 1975 the Tories dropped the BMRB panel. Due to doubts about lasting representativeness, they have never since mounted a similar long-term panel exercise. They continued to make full use of ORC, where in 1976 Humphrey Taylor was succeeded as managing director by John Hanvey, who became the key Conservative pollster. In the run-up to the 1979 election, ORC research made important contributions to Tory campaigning. Survey results stressed the popularity of lower taxation and selling council houses, and encouraged the high profile given to these policies.[22] They also pinpointed the skilled working class, especially women, as swayable voters. As in 1970, party publicity was targeted in this direction.

Research was also used to improve Margaret Thatcher's television performance, thanks to her publicity adviser, Gordon Reece. He carefully studied polls of audience reactions to her early TV broadcasts as leader. 'The poll we commissioned after her first party political broadcast as leader became very important. We went back to it frequently,' says Keith Britto,[23] the Conservative official in charge of polling. Focus group discussions also informed Reece's advice to Thatcher. Viewers were often impressed by strength of character, but tended to find her style hectoring, her appearance austere and her voice shrill and upper-class.[24]

When the Conservatives appointed Saatchi and Saatchi as their advertising agency in 1978, the agency brought to the task the research approach it used for ordinary clients. Saatchis relied more on qualitative rather than quantitative work in guiding the content, tone and phraseology of party advertising and broadcasts in the approach to the 1979 election. It paid heed to focus groups which suggested attacking the Labour government on unemployment and the economy, and the use of simple, clear language, such as 'prices' rather than 'inflation'.

During the 1980s the Conservatives continued to commission most of their work from ORC, which in 1983 was renamed the Harris Research Centre and where in 1986 John Hanvey was joined by Robert Waller as in charge of Tory polling. ORC/Harris material was augmented with information from other firms. This included the employment of specialist qualitative research companies, and the purchase of data from regular Gallup surveys which were large enough to provide useful demographic and regional breakdowns of political attitudes.

The nature of the party's private polling altered in emphasis. As the number of polls reported in the media increased, it made sense to do work which supplemented rather than duplicated published information. Greater use was made of qualitative work, while quantitative work shifted from polls intended to be representative of the national population to specialised studies of particular categories of voters and marginal constituencies. In the run up to the 1987 election, for example, Harris conducted fortnightly tracking polls in groups of marginals.

In the 1987–92 electoral cycle, the party's major polling effort went on an innovative and expensive programme which was ultimately of limited impact (it is described below under 'Psychographics'). But the Tories still bought regular data from Gallup and commissioned surveys of marginals from Harris, particularly as the election approached. The focus on tax and trust as campaign themes in 1992 was partly due to polling. Surveys demonstrated that, while voters were less likely to believe the powerful old lines that Labour was soft on defence and union-dominated, they were still convinced it would raise taxes. And research also revealed that the Tories did better when interviewees were asked which party they most trusted to handle a particular issue such as the economy, as opposed to which they thought would handle it best.

While the quantitative work influenced the party, Saatchi and Saatchi paid more attention to qualitative research for the 1983, 1987 and 1992 elections, just as it had done for 1979.

The most important finding from qualitative research in 1979–83 was highly reassuring for the Conservatives. Although published quantitative studies universally showed that voters thought unemployment the most important issue facing the country, focus groups in 1981 indicated that the public did not blame the Tory government for its high level, nor did they believe that Labour could reduce it dramatically. The Conservatives then seized every chance to blame unemployment on the world recession and high wages, and to repeat that no Labour government had reduced unemployment.

'The real thing we learnt from research', says Jeremy Sinclair, creative director of Saatchi and Saatchi,[24] 'was that we didn't have to worry about unemployment. Unemployment had shot up, but it was not seen as a consequence of the government's actions. That was very good intelligence. It meant we didn't have to try to justify it.'

In 1985–6 Saatchi and Saatchi again used a major qualitative exercise to guide advertising strategy. It showed people felt the government had run out of steam and lacked a sense of direction. Thatcher was perceived as the least forward-looking of all the party leaders, stubborn without purpose. The Conservative response was a series of radical new policy initiatives, along with the slogan 'The next move forward', which was successfully deployed at the 1986 party conference and in the election the following year. The research may not have determined individual policies, but it inspired the overall theme within which those policies were presented. After the election John Sharkey, joint managing director of Saatchis, claimed that these focus groups 'led directly to the turn in the party's fortunes'.[26]

Whatever the benefits of the research for the party's presentation, it did no good at all for the relationship between Thatcher and Saatchis. Excerpts from recordings of the groups were played to a grim-faced prime minister at an election strategy meeting in April 1986. She was not pleased to be told that she was bossy, uncaring and incapable of listening – or, at least, so people thought. This badly undermined her relationship with the agency and fostered the bitter internal conflicts of the 1987 Tory campaign. Nevertheless, it did prompt attempts to soften her image. In a speech the following month to the Scottish Conservative party conference she used the word 'caring' eight times in one minute.[27]

Saatchis also relied heavily on qualitative research in producing its work for the 1992 election, such as the widely displayed posters stating 'You can't trust Labour', in which the 'L' in 'Labour' was a red learner driver symbol. 'We chose the learner symbol after the most comprehensive research ever undertaken for a political slogan,' said Maurice Saatchi.[28] 'Our focus groups concluded that Labour were inexperienced, incompetent, unqualified and had never passed the test.' For this election there was also a move towards more research into pre-testing rough advertisements and ideas for party political broadcasts (which, however, were finished too late for the final product to be tested).

After the 1992 election the Conservatives cut back sharply on private polling, especially quantitative work, because of financial pressures. They terminated their contract with the Harris Research Centre, but continued to receive advice from Robert Waller, who left Harris to join a new company,

Wirthlin Europe. In 1996 the party appointed ICM as its polling company.

In the period since 1970, Labour's commitment to private polling has waxed, waned and waxed again. The first period of enthusiasm was 1972–4. In 1972 the party decided to employ MORI on a regular basis. Harold Wilson's entourage had been stunned by the result of the 1970 election, believed Edward Heath had benefited from his regular supply of private polling data, and wanted similar information for themselves. The party's publicity advisers also pressed for a proper polling programme.

MORI set up a large panel to model the electorate in a similar way to the BMRB panel used by the Tories at the same time. The baseline survey, conducted in February 1973, involved 2100 respondents. Recalls were done in February and July 1974. The interviews concentrated on issue salience, party identification with these issues and party images. MORI used the data to try to identify which groups of voters could be swayed and by what issues or aspects of party image. Voters were classified in a 'psychographic' as well as the traditional demographic manner (see below). This was supplemented by fortnightly tracking surveys, which MORI carried out in the run-up to each of the 1974 campaigns.[29] Labour also commissioned several by-election studies and three special surveys in Scotland.

Together with the campaign polling (described below) which was carried out during the two 1974 elections, this represented a substantial and wide-ranging exercise in opinion research which was valued by party leaders. Wilson was a former statistician and took a close interest in MORI's work. Indeed, Bob Worcester regards 1974 as the high point of his polling career for Labour, even though it was to continue for another fifteen years. He says:[30] 'February 1974 was the best election. It was well-grounded work, done for a clever politician who had a better memory for my data than I did. He had an excellent team, and we all worked well together. The results were used strategically and tactically.'

Over the next ten years the balance of political forces within the party meant Labour's polling was cut back, and any that did occur was not planned as part of a proper communications strategy. The left grew in strength, becoming increasingly powerful on the national executive committee (NEC) which controlled party expenditure. Most of the left were highly suspicious of polling as a device that led the party to seek to be all things to all people and weakened Labour's ideological commitment. Powerful opponents of polling included Norman Atkinson MP, party treasurer, 1976–81, who told the NEC that consulting his constituency's general management committee provided an equally good guide to public opinion, but was much cheaper.[31]

So, after 1974 Labour spent virtually nothing on polls (apart from a few by-election studies) until 1978. James Callaghan, who succeeded Wilson as prime minister in 1976, was not a polling enthusiast like his predecessor, but eventually announced that he wanted surveys 'to tackle the problem of Scotland and of women'.[32] Labour faced problems in Scotland due to the rise of the Scottish National Party. Callaghan also feared women were being alienated from Labour by trade union militancy. The proposal was narrowly endorsed by the NEC. MORI's pre-campaign polling consisted mainly of a Scottish survey and a panel covering marginal seats.[33] The results went to Labour politicians, but did not reach the party's advertising advisers, who were forced to conduct their advance planning on the basis of publicly available data.[34]

Campaign polls were then conducted during the 1979 election, but for nearly four years afterwards the power of the left meant that Labour commissioned no polling at all. The absence of private research annoyed leading members of the shadow cabinet. As the election approached, the NEC was again persuaded to relent and in February 1983 Labour unleashed a private polling blitz: it commissioned MORI to do £150 000 worth of work. This turned out to be more than the company could spend sensibly before polling day in June. The first stage consisted of 14 focus groups on party images and motivations for voting. The work was used by Labour's advertising agency, Wright and Partners. It suggested avoiding personal attacks on Thatcher, and concentrating on unemployment and social services but not disarmament. This was followed by a panel survey in April, and a battery of polls during the campaign itself in May/June 1983.

After Neil Kinnock became Labour leader in October 1983, the party adopted a very different approach to the process of winning votes. Its deployment of modern communications methods, including polling, was transformed. The first indication came with the European elections of 1984. The party's campaign planning took full account of quantitative and qualitative work conducted by MORI. This suggested building up Kinnock's image and concentrating on domestic rather than European themes.[35] The same attitude to research applied to Labour's mid-term campaigning. The 1985 'Jobs and Industry' campaign was developed in the light of focus group discussions,[36] and the 1986 'Freedom and Fairness' campaign was, according to director of communications Peter Mandelson, 'rooted in extensive quantitative and qualitative research'.[37] The new approach was also reflected in the most conspicuous symbol of Labour's new style – the adoption of the red rose logo. Prototypes were tested exhaustively in focus groups (see Chapter 8).

Unlike the two previous electoral cycles, work with MORI was planned well in advance of the forthcoming election. During the pre-campaign period it included surveys of target groups and marginal seats, along with by-election studies. In February 1986 MORI established a panel which was regularly re-interviewed over the next 12 months to detect shifts in voter attitudes.[38] The research influenced the party line of adding to its well-established but unpopular policy of unilateral nuclear disarmament the 'strengthening of Britain's real defences'. It also identified health and education as more important issues to target voters than jobs.[39]

But the most important feature of Labour's research, before and after the 1987 election, was a huge programme of qualitative work. This was mainly conducted through its new network of professional volunteers, the Shadow Communications Agency (SCA), established in early 1986. The key individuals were Philip Gould and Deborah Mattinson. Leading figures of the SCA felt qualitative research was crucial to dig deep into understanding negative public perceptions of the party and the motivations of voters who might, but didn't, vote Labour. They believed that the numbers provided by quantitative surveys revealed little not already known.

It was only the qualitative work which would extract new truths – the 'why' behind the raw figures. Such was their sense of mission that they were dragging the Labour Party into the second half of the twentieth century, that some thought focus groups had never previously been used by Labour, which was far from the case. By the end of the 1987 campaign, SCA volunteers had conducted over 200 focus groups, mainly involving lapsed Labour voters.[40]

After the 1987 election, SCA qualitative work figured heavily in the party's postmortem on the reasons for defeat. It also formed the backdrop to Labour's wide-ranging policy review during 1987–90, in which several unpopular policies were abandoned, especially in the areas of nuclear disarmament, nationalisation and trade union law. Research identified widespread barriers to voting Labour, reinforced the need for change and spelt out a broad direction in which to head. While some specific proposed policies were tested for their popularity,[41] overall the research was an important background influence rather than the determinant of detailed policy.

Qualitative work was also deployed as a key weapon in the internal party battle by those who, with Neil Kinnock, wanted to remodel Labour. Responses from focus group participants provided them with a rich source of one-liners which conveniently illustrated their case: that Labour was regarded as outmoded, untrustworthy, extreme, weak on defence, union-dominated, associated with minorities and out of touch with the aspirations of 'middle Britain'.

In 1989 Labour switched its quantitative polling from MORI to NOP, which was now part of the commercial empire of Clive Hollick, a Labour-supporting businessman who became closely involved in party strategy. The decision reflected poor working relationships between MORI's Bob Worcester and some party managers. Under Nick Moon, NOP operated more closely with the Shadow Agency than MORI. This meant its quantitative work was better coordinated with the agency's qualitative work than MORI's had been (for example, in the use of focus groups to test questions for surveys, and the use of quantitative surveys to identify productive kinds of electors for qualitative research). NOP's work included polls on the electorate's values and perceptions of Labour's weaknesses and strengths, which were carried out every three months or so, as well as by-election studies.[42]

As the 1992 election approached, Labour continued to pay close attention to polling. Qualitative research informed a series of SCA strategy documents, which stressed the need to persuade floating voters that Labour was trustworthy and economically competent. Labour highlighted its charge that the Tories would privatise the NHS because surveys showed people believed that to be the case. Focus groups were employed to test campaign themes, phrases, rough-cuts of party political broadcasts and policy packages such as the 'shadow budget' launched just before the 1992 election. Polling also encouraged Kinnock's ill-fated plan to appear more open to the introduction of proportional representation in the manifesto and in the last week of the campaign. This backfired due to his reluctance to make clear his own position on the issue he himself had raised.

Since the 1992 election Labour has continued to use NOP for quantitative research. The Shadow Communications Agency has been disbanded, but focus groups have been arranged by the party's advertising agencies (first Butterfield Day Devito Hockney, then BMP DDB Needham), and also by Philip Gould and Deborah Mattinson.

During the 1970s the Liberals still felt that their financial constraints made private opinion research prohibitively expensive. However, their allies in the Social Democratic Party, set up in 1981, were keener on modern communications and devoted considerable sums to research. The SDP used Gallup omnibus surveys, commissioned their own qualitative work, and ran an innovative exercise in telephone polling during the 1983 campaign (see below). Following the 1983 election, the SDP continued to use private polling while the Liberals did not. The SDP's research included by-election surveys (for example, at Greenwich in 1987, where the party won a famous victory), some qualitative work, and polls in target seats.

After the merger of the two centre parties in 1988, the Liberal Democrats sponsored a limited amount of research prior to the 1992 election. The new party logo of a bird (see Chapter 8) was thoroughly tested in focus groups. A professional survey was carried out for just one by-election, at Kincardine and Deeside in 1991, which the Liberal Democrats won. Party strategists felt it was invaluable in identifying attitudes in different geographic areas and among different demographic groups.[43] In the run-up to the 1992 campaign, the party arranged small-scale telephone surveys in 17 target seats, although these were not conducted by a recognised polling company. Some results were publicised to foster tactical voting. Since 1992 the Liberal Democrats have commissioned work from MORI.

## Campaign polling

The previous section dealt with the opinion research that parties conduct outside the four weeks or so of the election campaign itself. Once the campaign starts, the parties launch a very different and intense polling programme, aimed at much quicker monitoring of public opinion through rapid collection and analysis of data.

Up to the mid-1960s, parties had primarily tried to keep track of public opinion during elections by making sense as best they could of the unreliable information gathered from local canvass returns. The earliest attempt at private polling during the campaign was in 1964, when Labour's pollster Mark Abrams tried to check on reaction to party broadcasts through informal surveys.[44] But the history of party campaign polling really begins in 1970, when the Conservatives became the first party to research public opinion seriously during the election itself. They used ORC to carry out three separate daily polls. These covered the previous night's party broadcast, attitudes on issues and the impact of the mass media. Some use was made of this thrice-daily flow of information. The high approval rating achieved by shadow chancellor Iain Macleod in one broadcast led to his also appearing in the next. The party was also confirmed in its backing for a large pay rise for doctors, an issue which arose during the campaign.[45] In the next two elections in 1974, ORC also supplied daily polling on issues and reactions to broadcasts.

Labour arranged only two polls during the 1970 campaign, conducted by MORI which had just recently been appointed. The first was to identify switchers and campaign issues, the second to report on leaders' television performances and voters' contact with canvassers. The party began to carry out proper campaign polling in 1974. During both elections in this year MORI conducted a programme of daily polls. Subjects covered included party images, issue salience, tactical voting, and reaction to party broadcasts.

These polls helped reassure Labour leaders during the February election, called by Edward Heath because of the miners' strike. This was despite the fact that the Tories were in the lead throughout. By tracking issue salience, MORI showed that Labour was slowly but surely succeeding in shifting the election agenda away from the Tory territory of 'who governs Britain?' onto its desired ground, notably inflation. Labour stuck to its strategy, and the election resulted in a hung parliament and a Labour government. In October the campaign polls helped Labour cope with a startling pledge from Margaret Thatcher, then shadow environment secretary, that the Conservatives would introduce a 9.5 per cent ceiling for mortgage rates by Christmas. This worried Labour, which contemplated counter-moves, until MORI's polling revealed the main impact on public opinion was a 20 per cent jump in those who thought the Tories were making promises the country could not afford.[46]

On top of the daily surveys MORI introduced a new element to campaign polling. During the February 1974 campaign it organised a recall study of the panel established in the previous year. This identified key issues for the swayable voters as wages and salaries, house prices, poverty and unemployment; and the need for the party to represent all classes and keep promises.[47] These themes were emphasised by Labour in the last days of the campaign. (The panel was again recalled in July, but not during the October campaign.)

Thus during the 1974 campaigns both parties were monitoring public opinion on a more or less daily basis. In elections since then Labour has largely continued to do so, preferring to have data which is as up to date as possible, while the Conservatives have found an alternative approach more useful for informing decision-making.

'The problem we had when we ran daily polls was information overload,' says Keith Britto,[48] the party official who supervised Tory polling for 20 years. 'We were generating too much information, and the pressure on everybody during the campaign meant that the huge majority of it was not being used.' So in 1979, instead of a continuous programme of small daily 'quickie' polls with results available the day after fieldwork, the major Conservative effort went into four larger and more detailed surveys carried out at weekends. These were supplemented by mid-week quickies, broadcast reaction surveys, and special studies in certain kinds of constituencies, including marginals.[49]

In the three elections since then the Tories have stuck to this pattern of using Harris to conduct larger, 2000-strong polls each weekend, combined with smaller, 1000-strong, mid-week quickies. The party has also arranged additional polling which has varied in each election.

In 1983 the main extra element was 'fast feedback', an innovation devised by Chris Lawson, the director of marketing. Two hundred 'opinion leaders' (doctors, publicans, teachers, journalists and Rotarians, but not necessarily Tories) responded each night to a standard set of questions on their reactions to campaign events of the day, the parties' activities and television coverage. The results were easy to digest and often influenced the party line taken at press conferences the following morning. The system was appreciated by Margaret Thatcher and other leading Tories.

A similar operation involving 150 opinion leaders was organised in 1987, but was found less useful. Fast feedback was abandoned for the 1992 campaign. Instead, the party ran focus groups for the first time during an election. These were mainly devoted to testing ideas for broadcasts and advertisements. It also continued its pre-campaign surveys of groups of marginals.

Labour's campaign polling has expanded considerably over the last four elections. In 1979 the budget was sufficient for only ten quickie polls in a lengthy 36-day campaign, compared to 17 in the 23-day campaign of October 1974. Bob Worcester was not as close to party strategists as in 1974, and his polls had less influence on Labour's electioneering.

In 1983 the bigger budget meant that 20 quickies were carried out, and there was a recall of the panel which had been first interviewed during the previous month. But although the flow of information was greater than in 1979, it was just as politically redundant. Party leader Michael Foot seemed more impressed by his enthusiastic reception at meetings and walkabouts than by the gloomy tidings of representative surveys. For those who believed the data, its main effect was to reinforce low morale.

In the 1987 campaign, MORI again conducted 20 quickie polls. Due to advances in information technology, the full analysis of the results was available that evening rather than the next morning as in previous elections.[50] In an innovation for Labour, they also reported verbatim answers to open-ended questions about campaign events. This was a form of 'fast feedback' similar to that initiated by the Tories, except the Tories interviewed opinion leaders while Labour relied on the normal representative samples. For the first time, focus groups were also arranged during the campaign.

In 1992, when NOP had taken over from MORI, the daily surveys continued and were augmented by greater additional campaign polling. Twenty-eight quickies were combined with surveys in six marginals and a panel (initially 700-strong) of Labour inclined floaters who were interviewed each weekend. Fifty focus groups of floating voters in marginal seats were also organised. Neil Kinnock made a point of reading a selection of verbatim quotes from these groups.[51]

The main contribution by a centre party to campaign polling techniques was in 1983, when the SDP commissioned a series of telephone polls from Audience Selection. An initial survey was followed by nine tracking polls involving around 750 interviewees and covering issues, tactical voting, reactions to broadcasts, and so on.[52] These showed an increase in Alliance support, which not surprisingly was leaked to the media.

This was the first time a political party had depended so heavily on telephone polling. It has important advantages such as speed, better supervision of interviewers and unclustered sampling, but a key drawback: the need to correct for the substantial minority of the population not on the phone or ex-directory. Audience Selection's private and published polls in 1983 consistently gave higher Alliance ratings than in surveys conducted by traditional face-to-face interviews and the election result itself. This problem has inhibited the uptake of telephone polling, although both main parties have used it for certain pieces of research.

**Psychographics**

Most polling and market research, whether political or commercial, divides the population demographically (usually by sex, age and class, and sometimes by other criteria such as form of housing tenure) and analyses its results in terms of these groupings. However, it is also possible to view the population according to psychological characteristics, such as values, motivations, personality and attitude to life. Advocates of 'values research' or 'psychographics' believe that through this approach people's behaviour can be better explained and influenced. Such methods were fashionable in commercial marketing in the 1960s, lost popularity, and then came back in the 1980s. While the vast majority of political polling has been demographically based, by far the most ambitious and expensive exercise in opinion research carried out by a British political party was founded on psychographics.

The first significant party polling to use what could be called psychographic classification was MORI's major early piece of work for Labour – the panel it ran in 1973–4. This identified 13 clusters of political values ('old-style Labour' – nicknamed 'old Fred'; 'new-style Labour' – nicknamed 'Jack'; 'floating left'; 'authoritarian'; 'apathetic', etc.) and categorised voters according to these groups. The aim was to identify issues and aspects of party image which most concerned each group and would swing voters to Labour. As noted above, the results influenced the party's themes in the February 1974 campaign. It relied on recent advances in computing, which facilitated cumbersome mathematical operations like cluster analysis. MORI wanted to continue with the panel after 1974, but because of the party's move away from polling this did not happen.

Psychographics then left politics untouched until the mid-1980s when it aroused the attention of Margaret Thatcher. This was due to the advertising agency Young and Rubicam (Y&R), which had developed a psychographic system called 'CCCC' (Cross-Cultural Consumer Characterisation) or '4Cs'. It derived from 'VALs', a means of classification based on values and lifestyles (hence the acronym) developed by the Stanford Research Institute, California. Based on in-depth interviews about individuals' goals and values, the Y&R methodology partitioned the population into three main groups and then seven subgroups: (1) 'the middle majority', divided into (a) 'mainstreamers' (mainly motivated by responsibility), (b) 'aspirers' (envy) and (c) 'succeeders' (ambition); (2) 'innovators', divided into (a) 'reformers' (moral certitude) and (b) 'transitionals' (self-assertion); and (3) 'the constrained', divided into (a) 'survivors' (resignation) and (b) 'sustainers' (desperation).

Y&R regarded this system as providing a unique competitive edge. From 1984 it tried to persuade the Conservatives of the advantages of 4Cs over conventional polling. 'For politics the socioeconomic classification is bunkum,' says John Banks,[53] then chairman of Y&R. 'It doesn't discriminate at all between different voting motives. People vote on the basis of their hopes, fears and dreams, their motivations in life and their personal values.'

Thatcher became interested following a secret meeting in early 1986. The Y&R research showed that the Conservatives were holding on to support from the achievement-oriented 'succeeders', but losing support to the Alliance among the solid, unadventurous, home-loving 'mainstreamers'. This was worrying because these conventional-minded folk constituted 40 per cent of the electorate and an even higher proportion of Tory voters. They were particularly concerned about education, crime and the NHS.[54] This message had something in common with the depressing view coming at the same time from Saatchi and Saatchi, but with at least one crucial difference: 'Saatchi and Saatchi said Thatcher was the problem,' says Geoffrey Tucker,[55] the former Tory director of publicity and a consultant to Y&R. 'Our research showed she should stay.'

Thatcher asked for the information flow from Y&R to continue, so that she was receiving her own supply of polling data separate from that officially commissioned by the party and its appointed ad agency, Saatchis. There is no clear evidence that the research influenced the way in which policy was presented. But it may have helped to restore Thatcher's confidence in the troubled wake of the Westland affair of January 1986, when conflict over her style of leadership led to Michael Heseltine's resignation from the cabinet.

During the 1987 campaign the Y&R work contributed to what was in due course called 'Wobbly Thursday' (see Chapter 2). John Banks told Downing Street on the Wednesday night eight days before the election – when a conventional published poll also showed a dip in the Tory lead – that his surveys revealed mainstreamers were drifting to Labour and needed reassurance. His and Tucker's analysis had some influence over the phrasing of Thatcher's remaining speeches in the campaign, but quite how much is uncertain.[56] Y&R's intervention did not impress their commercial rival, Saatchi and Saatchi, who after the success of polling day issued a press statement stating: 'The result of the election demonstrates with startling clarity the complete uselessness of [Y&R's] research methods.'[57] After the election and until her downfall, Thatcher continued personally to obtain information from Y&R, including the tracking of attitudes to possible military action following the Iraqi invasion of Kuwait in 1990.[58]

After 1987 the Conservatives embarked on a much more sophisticated and expensive exercise in psychographic research. However, the work was not completed and was largely unused. Opinions within the party varied from some who thought it a decisive advance in political campaigning, through those who believed it had merit but was poor value for money, to others who regarded it as simply a complete waste of a million pounds. Certainly, a British political party had never before embarked on such an ambitious attempt to work out why people vote the way they do.

This programme was based on the work of Richard Wirthlin, an American pollster who was a key adviser to Ronald Reagan in the 1970s and 1980s. Wirthlin had devised a sophisticated process for exploring the links between people's deeply held core values, shallower attitudes and voting behaviour. His system had important advantages over VALs/4Cs. First, VALs/4Cs imposed on politics a psychographic classification which had been developed for commercial marketing. Wirthlin's approach was to construct his model specifically for British politics on the basis of interviews conducted for this purpose. Second, this meant that he dealt in values. VALs/4Cs, however, was also about lifestyles. These are relevant to commercial brand-buying, but values are more central to political choice.

The role of core values was not a unique insight. Labour as well as Conservative strategists have often stressed their importance. However, the hard work – and trade secrets – lie in the means of discovering and classifying underlying values, and relating them to voting behaviour. Wirthlin's approach relies on probing and carefully structured one-to-one interviews, in which voters talk about the important features of their lives and reasons for their beliefs or decisions. They are continually pressed by highly trained interviewers for deeper motives. Wirthlin's work is also notable for its use of modern computing power to manipulate many attitudinal variables to establish the connections between values and other beliefs.

Conservative strategists were keen to learn from the man who had helped bring to power a US president in tune with Thatcher's free-market ideology. Wirthlin discussed his work with leading Tories during the 1983–7 Parliament, but it was not until Kenneth Baker became party chairman in 1989 that he was formally employed by the party. Director of communications Brendan Bruce was an ardent enthusiast, along with Baker.

Under Wirthlin's guidance the Tories' regular polling firm, Harris, carried out the expensive and detailed interviews into the electorate's values and fundamental aspirations, and then tested the outcomes quantitatively. Bob Worcester was also employed as a consultant on the project, after he had ceased to work for Labour. The results suggested that voters' most important values were 'hope', 'security' and 'peace of mind', in that order. 'Opportunity' figured high as well. At a strategy meeting in January 1990, senior Central Office personnel agreed that their first strategic imperative was to 'Reinforce the perception of Hope tied to the Future, upheld by Peace of Mind and Opportunity.'[59]

This informed speeches delivered by Kenneth Baker[60] and party political broadcasts controlled by Brendan Bruce (for example, a film about the environment downplayed scientific arguments and sought to tap into the value of 'peace of mind' with soft-focus pictures of parents and children).[6] But sceptics thought the practical implications of the research were unclear. Its impact on party propaganda was limited before it was overtaken by unexpected events –

Thatcher's fall and Major's rise. Had Thatcher stayed as leader, Baker as chairman and Bruce as director of communications (a keen Thatcherite, he departed soon after her downfall), then the party would have developed and exploited Wirthlin's work further. But Chris Patten, the chairman appointed by John Major, regarded it as unlikely to be of use for the forthcoming election and ended Wirthlin's contract.

This decision pleased those who believed the enormous expense outweighed the benefits. In 1990–1, when most of the work was conducted, the exercise cost £965 000.[62] (For comparison, the Tories spent about £100 000 a year on polling in 1983–7.)[63] But it angered adherents of the research, some of whom describe Patten's decision as 'mad' or 'foolish ignorance'. Bruce's enthusiasm remains unrestrained: 'Wirthlin's research methodology represents the most important advance in political communications of the last two decades. . . . The party that first grasps the true importance of Wirthlin's work and applies it to the British political process will win an enormous advantage over their opponents and greatly increase their chances of gaining power.'[64]

**People-metering**

Prior to the 1992 election both main parties experimented with an innovatory method of political opinion research which fits neither the traditional quantitative nor qualitative mould – instant audience response measurement systems, often referred to as 'people-metering', 'voter-metering' or 'pulsing'.

A group of voters (usually 50–100, probably a representative cross-section or members of a particular target group) sit in an auditorium to watch a TV screen. They are provided with electronic handsets on which they register instantaneous and continuous reaction to a speech, broadcast, interview or anything else as it is played. These responses are fed into a computer for analysis. This is the only way to measure second-by-second responses to a piece of communication, and identify exactly which visual, verbal or thematic components score and which are counter-productive. The analysis can indicate the differential reactions of demographic, political or other subgroups. The participants can also be questioned before, during and after the sessions to gain further understanding of their responses. Simplified versions of this technique were in use academically and commercially in the US as far back as the 1930s, and it has been employed commercially in the UK for some time, but its value for political communication was only really appreciated in the US in the 1980s.

It was imported to British politics by Richard Wirthlin, who introduced the Conservatives to the technology in 1989. He had used it in the US to identify 'power phrases' – those which get an immediate large positive response. These were then employed prominently and repetitively in future campaigning. While Brendan Bruce was director of communications, the Tories employed people-metering retrospectively, testing speeches and broadcasts which had already occurred as a guide for the content of future ones. The party used it occasionally afterwards, but Shaun Woodward (Bruce's successor, appointed early in 1991) thought it an expensive way of confirming known truths. Nor did the apparatus impress Saatchi and Saatchi, reappointed by Woodward as the party's ad agency. Saatchis regarded it as particularly unreliable in assessing negative communication, their favourite form of political advertising. By the time of the election it had been abandoned.

Labour, however, found people-metering more helpful. It used the technique initially in 1990 with assistance from Mellman and Lazarus, a US Democrat political consultancy, and continued right up to the election. Party political broadcasts were tested retrospectively. Unlike the Tories, Labour also employed the system to pre-test rough-cuts of broadcasts before transmission so that they could be modified if necessary. The sessions involved groups of 60 floating voters, with results analysed separately for men and women.[65] Labour has used people-metering again since the 1992 election.

CONCLUSION

In 1960 David Butler and Richard Rose wrote:[66] 'Anyone talking to political organisers must be struck by their lack of knowledge about the nature of their market; although they may offer elaborate theories about the social changes that are taking place and about the efficacy of different types of propaganda, they can quote surprisingly little hard evidence for their judgments. Almost no systematic testing of electioneering has been tried.'

1959 was the last election about which such generalisations could be made. Ever since, the development of private party polling has meant that those whose sell politics have possessed a method to become increasingly well informed about their market and to test campaign techniques and political platforms.

Most early party research in the 1960s and 1970s consisted of quantitative surveys with national samples that concentrated on attitudes to issues, comparative salience of issues, satisfaction with leaders and perceptions of party images. The main use was to help decide which issues to highlight or play down, and which aspects of the party and policies to maintain or modify. However, for many years now this kind of information has often been available in public polls (although parties still need to pay for it sometimes to ensure the latest data is available at the right time for their decision-making processes). Parties have therefore sought to complement rather than duplicate the material published in the media.

The most important development in private polling since then has been the growth of qualitative research. Even in the early years parties commissioned some qualitative work, mainly for testing reactions to specific advertisements and slogans. Focus groups are still used for these purposes, and more so now than before. But today they also play a central role in determining party communications strategies and campaign themes.

In the case of the Conservatives, this stems from the appointment of Saatchi and Saatchi as their ad agency in 1978. Modern advertising practice generally draws more inspiration and guidance from the verbal outcomes of focus groups than the statistical results of quantitative surveys, and the approach of Saatchis reflected this. Labour's commitment to qualitative work came later but went further. Although MORI conducted focus groups for the party in the 1970s and 1983–6, it was following the formation of the Shadow

Communications Agency in early 1986 that qualitative research by Labour really took off.

The nature of quantitative work has also changed over the years. There has been a shift away from national samples and towards more sophisticated and specialised surveys, such as those of marginal seats and particular categories of target voters (whether defined demographically or by political affiliation). Quantitative work has also operated increasingly in tandem with qualitative work, such as testing hypotheses which emerge from focus groups. And advances in computing power have meant that the analysis of results is easier and quicker (especially important during the campaign), and that some more complex mathematical operations which were previously unfeasible can now be carried out to provide additional information.

On the whole both main parties have favoured the same polling methods. But there have been two consistent differences. First, Labour's pollsters have made more use of panels, which the Conservatives have avoided since the mid-1970s, partly because of methodological doubts about their long-term validity. Second, Labour has generally tried to maintain a fairly continuous flow of information during the campaign, while for the last four elections the Tories have directed most attention to large polls carried out at weekly intervals.

Opinion research is only one of a number of factors affecting political strategy, policy and presentation. It is often an influence, but rarely a determinant. Its conclusions may be outweighed by the policy or presentation preferences of leading politicians, their own feelings or prejudices about public opinion, feedback from constituencies and internal party pressures. Sometimes it reassures the party in what it would be doing anyway. Frequently it is one of several factors which together are taking the party in a particular direction.

Nor is opinion research some kind of infallible basis for winning elections. But it is a very useful tool which today helps parties to do the following:

1. tap into and build on beliefs which the electorate already holds, whether about issues, parties or politicians;
2. ensure they talk to voters in language voters understand about things which really matter to them;

3. discover what aspects of their policies, images and leaders are popular or unpopular – and thus what they should emphasise or play down, and what might be electorally profitable to maintain or change;
4. identify what kind of people are target voters, and what concerns them most;
5. make political points or encourage tactical voting by leaking helpful findings to the media (accuracy in findings is generally desirable except in this case, where inaccuracy may be more useful – in particular, constituency-level 'polls' leaked to promote tactical voting are often methodologically spurious);
6. monitor which of their messages, and which of their opponents', are becoming more or less widely believed;
7. monitor the impact of party political broadcasts, advertising and other forms of campaigning;
8. test reaction to possible strategic concepts, themes, policies, lines of argument, slogans, phrases, words, symbols, advertisements, broadcasts and creative ideas.

# 7 Personal Image

*It will be an unfortunate day if it should come about that an election in this country is decided not by what either side says, but by the way they looked while saying it.*
Times editorial about the dangers of television, 1955[1]

*Unfortunately, because of [Neil Kinnock's] physical appearance on TV a lot of people, especially women, did not think he would make a prime minister.*
Denis Healey, 1992[2]

*Gordon [Reece] was absolutely terrific . . . he understood that it wasn't enough to have the right policies, one had to look good in putting them over, and he said my hair had to be changed and we'd better have a look at the make-up and we'd better have a look at the clothes and see how they looked on television, and so on.*
Margaret Thatcher, 1995[3]

*Pipes, in politics, are extremely useful: they can be filled, lit, tamped down or sucked in while the owner is thinking out a reply to a tricky question; they can be waved about for emphasis, or they can be sucked slowly to give a reassuring, thoughtful and trustworthy effect.*
Baroness Falkender (Marcia Williams), former private and political secretary to Harold Wilson, 1983[4]

*The more Wilson appears to be contrived and the more he concentrates on his 'image', the more you will – and should – appear to come over naturally and spontaneously. The bane of Wilson's life has been the interference of PR men and gimmickry. In contrast you should appear to eschew all the tricks. . . . Therefore, we must make certain that we get no stunts, no tricks and that no-one for a moment thinks that the PR men are getting at you!*
Publicity advice to Edward Heath from his PR man, Geoffrey Tucker, 1969[5]

The personal image of politicians – the set of characteristics associated with them in the public mind – is a central element in modern democratic politics.

One of the most common goals of politicians, for example, is to seem authoritative and experienced. Those already in power have a major advantage in trying to achieve this. Since Harold Macmillan's pathbreaking prime ministerial visit to Moscow in 1959, which was followed by his televised informal chat with US President Eisenhower a few months later, and then shortly afterwards by his calling a general election, incumbents have sought to maximise the electoral dividend from their rubbing of shoulders with world leaders on the international stage. Margaret Thatcher was especially good at this. As well as her visit to Moscow (which was highly successful in terms of publicity) shortly before the 1987 campaign, she attended summits of the Group of Seven, the world's leading industrial countries, during both the 1983 and 1987 elections. Of the 1987 summit she later noted: 'My role as "international statesman" was a more important element in our election campaign this time; so there were even stronger political arguments for making the visit.'[6]

Opposition leaders have often tried their own international trips, but usually with less impact. They have had to resort to other devices to boost their status and depict themselves as heading a 'government in waiting'. Tony Benn's plans for presenting Hugh Gaitskell in Labour's 1959 party political broadcasts epitomise this. 'The desk, the table lamp, the crystal ashtray, the globe, the bust of Keir Hardie, the wallpaper and so on will all create the image of a prime minister waiting to take office,' argued Benn, who also firmly instructed his colleagues that 'only the leader himself must ever appear on the leader's set.'[7] Years later, Labour also went to great lengths to counter the perception of Neil Kinnock as a lightweight and portray him as prime ministerial material. As well as trying to dissuade him from the exuberant behaviour to which he was naturally inclined, his advisers sought to cultivate gravitas through periodic emphasis on big, serious speeches, and transporting him in a chauffeur-driven Daimler in the 1992 election.

This is only one aspect of the image battle constantly fought by today's political leaders. A politician's image is partly forged via his or her political actions, ranging from international diplomacy through running the country and electioneering to internal party faction fighting. But it is also profoundly affected by other factors which are not overtly political.

## APPEARANCE

In the Sherlock Holmes story, *The Adventure of the Norwood Builder,* Holmes is visited by an agitated young man in search of assistance. Before the young man can tell Holmes about himself, the famous sleuth looks at him and says: 'Beyond the obvious facts that you are a bachelor, a solicitor, a Freemason, and an asthmatic, I know nothing whatever about you.' The rest of us may not possess the same powers of deduction as Sherlock Holmes, but nevertheless we are all in our own way amateur detectives, subconsciously inferring from their appearance characteristics of people we come across.

We have all acquired the habit of associating aspects of personality with various physical attributes, forms of posture, mannerisms, gestures, clothes, accessories, hairstyles, and so on. These associations are generally made automatically without conscious thought, and are reinforced by powerful cultural stereotypes. Naturally, therefore, our thought processes ascribe to politicians important qualities such as competence, compassion, likeability, authority, sincerity and strength of purpose, partly on the basis of how they look. Appearances may well be deceptive, but unfortunately that does not stop them being influential.[8]

Few voters meet many politicians, but they do see visual representations of them. At one time, before and immediately after the second world war, these generally took the form of photographs in newspapers or party posters, and films for cinema newsreels. The visual images involved could be managed, to help make the right impressions or avoid the wrong ones. Pictures of the post-war party leaders illustrate nicely the connotations of different methods of consuming tobacco. Winston Churchill's favourite prop when photographed was his cigar, icon of power and authority; Clement Attlee was shown in Labour posters clasping his pipe, symbol of solid dependability, alongside the reassuring slogan 'You can trust Mr Attlee'. Similarly, newsreels also involved presentational artifice, even when the participant being filmed was Attlee, an individual who spurned affectation. He submitted to having his face powdered and hair combed, but found it difficult to cope with conflicting advice on whether he needed to lighten his dour demeanour by smiling more often.[9]

Today, however, voters see politicians on television. And TV has made the appearance of politicians much more important than it ever was before. Still pictures lack the impact and memorability of their moving counterparts, while, in contrast to TV, newsreels never gave audiences lengthy close-up views of their leaders on a screen just a few feet away.

This consequence of television was clear from the start, not least to those who regretted its incipient role in political communication. In 1948 Churchill refused to appear on TV, explaining why it would be even worse than radio:[10] 'When I was very young, if one said something at Oldham [Churchill's first constituency] that might have led to trouble if it was spread abroad, nothing happened. But now one has to weigh every word, knowing all the time that people will be listening all over the country. It would be an intolerable burden if one had to consider how one would appear, what one would look like, all over the land.'

While for Churchill going on television was an option he could reject, for his successors as prime minister and their rivals it was a necessity – and one which did indeed mean they had to consider what they would look like all over the land. The next man in, Sir Anthony Eden, was mainly concerned not to be seen wearing glasses, despite resulting difficulties in reading his script for ministerial broadcasts. This was especially true at the time of the Suez conflict, when he felt it essential to be perceived as tough and energetic rather than as giving ground to the ravages of time.[11] Eden turned out to be the first in a long line. Other politicians who later proved similarly averse to wearing their glasses on TV include Macmillan, Wilson and Thatcher, as well as many lesser figures. Eden's successor, Harold Macmillan, underwent a thorough make-over. He abandoned baggy trousers in favour of spruce new suits from Savile Row, pruned his moustache and fixed his disarrayed teeth.[12] When he did a party political broadcast without wearing a waistcoat under his jacket, his press secretary was pleased by the 'image of informality and youthful indifference to clothes and weather'.[13]

Other politicians found that their faces did not suit the new medium. When the Labour leader Hugh Gaitskell did a TV interview in 1958, his advisers had to ensure that the make-up artist 'took tremendous care to obliterate his double chin and remove the bags and even to shorten that long upper lip'. This was recorded in his diary by the party's broadcasting expert, Tony Benn, who added:[14] 'It was quite a new thing, but I think it was right.'

An even greater challenge to telegenicity was presented by Sir Alec Douglas-Home, the reluctant prime minister who never felt at ease with techniques of modern communication. Prior to one TV appearance in 1963, he had the following dispiriting conversation with a make-up artist: 'Can you not make me look better than I do on television? I look rather scraggy, like a ghost.' 'No.' 'Why not?' 'Because you have a head like a skull.' 'Does not everyone have a head like a skull?' 'No.'[15] Sir Alec's favourite joke on the stump was to tell his audience that he had come to show them that 'I don't really look as I'm made to look on television'.[16]

By the mid-1960s television had given many politicians a greater interest in personal grooming. Harold Wilson then showed, after he became Labour leader in 1963, that how politicians looked on TV was actually about much more than this – it was really an exercise in image-building.

Wilson attached enormous importance to his television image. 'TV had one great advantage for the Labour Party,' he said in retrospect.[17] 'Most of the press were against us. And if the right-wing press were tempted to say about me – "This is a terrible man, looks like an ogre, his voice is terrible", then you go on television and the people say – "Oh look, he is an ordinary chap like the rest of us."'

And Wilson, an extraordinary man who had already (in 1947) been the youngest cabinet minister since 1806, believed it vital to ensure that voters did indeed see him as an 'ordinary chap' they could feel at ease with. A former Oxford economics lecturer himself, he criticised his predecessor Gaitskell, whose middle-class Hampstead intellectualism Wilson had always scorned, for 'adopting more the manner of an Oxford don explaining economic theory than seeking to identify himself in homely terms with the electorate'.[18]

Wilson set out to be seen as the homely, unaffected man with the common touch. He employed two distinctive accessories to his appearance to help promote his desired image (as well as using his family, roots and interests outside politics; see below). One was his unpretentious, mass-market Gannex raincoat, manufactured by his friend, Joseph Kagan, who later became a peer of the realm (thanks to Wilson) and after that a convicted fraudster. 'The Gannex raincoat... seemed to epitomise everything [Wilson] represented,' according to his influential aide, Marcia Williams. 'It stood out because it was different from anything they had ever seen a leading politician wear.'[19]

However, Wilson's most important prop was his ever-present pipe. He was also a keen cigar smoker, but this rich man's indulgence was kept hidden from the public. It was his pipe which Wilson puffed during press conferences, lit during TV interviews, posed with in photographs, and brandished as he went from place to place. As an apparently classless smoking implement, it fostered his image as an everyday man of the people.

The pipe had an important, additional advantage. It conveyed, as it had previously for Attlee (and before the war for another pipe-smoker, Stanley Baldwin) a relaxed, comfortable, reassuring impression. This too was an important part of Wilson's strategy. He once told Irish prime minister Sean Lemass that 'a political leader should try to look, particularly on television, like a family doctor – the kind of man who inspires trust by his appearance as well as by his soothing words', and that he (Wilson) measured his success on TV 'by the extent to which he projects his family doctor image'.[20]

The role of personal appearance in politics achieved much greater recognition from the second half of the 1970s. This was because a major party now had a woman leader. The appearance of women is a more important factor in their image, usually involves more planning and effort, and is subject to greater scrutiny and interest than that of men. Margaret Thatcher was not the only top politician to have cosmetic dentistry – others include Macmillan, Wilson, Heath and Major[21] – but much more fuss was made in the media over her teeth jobs than over anyone else's. Newspapers devoted entire articles to topics like her preferred brand of electric rollers for her hair. Once the televising of the House of Commons started in 1989, she would receive letters from eagle-eyed viewers pointing out she had worn the same suit on successive occasions.[22]

However, the focus on Thatcher's looks was not simply due to gender. It was also because of her attitudes. Unlike some other leading female politicians, such as Shirley Williams, who had little interest in clothes or cosmetics, Thatcher took her appearance very seriously. And she was happy to have that appearance transformed in the search for votes – or, as the point was put by her speechwriter, Sir Ronnie Millar, 'she used high fashion . . . as a political weapon'.[23]

Thatcher had always attached priority to ensuring she looked immaculate and carefully groomed, well before she became party leader. When she was a junior minister in the early 1960s, her department's top civil servant thought 'she would turn up looking as if she had spent the whole morning with the coiffeur and the whole afternoon with the couturier'.[24] By the mid-1970s the main result of all the effort she devoted to how she looked was to solidify the public impression of her as remote and snobbish. Conservative private polling showed that people thought she seemed austere and school-marmish.[25] The most distinctive feature of her appearance were her elaborate and much ridiculed hats, which associated her with a kind of uppercrust stuffiness.

The person primarily responsible for changing her style was Gordon Reece. A former television producer who had worked on numerous Conservative party political broadcasts since the late 1960s, he ran the publicity side of Thatcher's successful leadership challenge in 1975, and then became her full-time publicity adviser and later (in 1978) the party's director of publicity. Thatcher liked and trusted Reece, regarding him as possessing 'an almost uncanny insight'[26] into television presentation. While she was leader of the opposition, he advised her to adopt a simpler, more relaxed appearance – less fussy clothes, no frills, less jewellery, softer hairstyle and make-up. She considered this advice an 'invaluable service . . . quite an education'.[27]

From then on her choice of clothes was regulated by the endeavour to create the right media impact. 'You have to think – what's it going to look like in black and white on the front page of the *Sun*? or what's it going to look like on the news on television?' she said in a 1981 TV interview.[28] Cabinet colleagues admired her professionalism – Kenneth Baker noted how 'in both party conference and television appearances she used her clothes, style and manner to convey the strength and vitality of her character, employing with devastating effect the fact that she was a woman'.[29]

During her time as prime minister she gradually assumed a more glamorous look, but there were also particular points when her style distinctly changed. During the Falklands affair she wore darker, sombre clothes, appropriate to a period of war and death (her Falklands attire was described in the *Daily Mail*[30] as 'crisis chic'). In early 1987 her image was revamped, thanks to a new adviser on personal presentation and clothing. She abandoned matronly outfits and bows, adopting darker blues and more fashionable power-dressing square-cut suits with large shoulder pads.[31] The new look was first tried out on her highly successful trip to Moscow in March, which generated much excellent and useful news coverage in the run-up to the 1987 election. Later, the televising of the House of Commons from 1989 forced changes in her parliamentary apparel – she had to drop the stripe and check patterns which dazzled on TV.[32]

Thatcher cared not just about the political impact of her own appearance but also about that of her less fussy cabinet colleagues. While causes for her concern included sightings on television of Kenneth Clarke's yellow waistcoat and Nicholas Ridley's old cardigan,[33] her pet peeve was the length of Nigel Lawson's hair. The long-running disagreements between Thatcher and Lawson involved not only exchange rate policy and relations with Europe, but also the management of hairstyles as a tool of political communication. Thatcher was decidedly interventionist, devoting a good chunk of each week to having her hair seen to in one way or another – the hairdresser's visit was often her first appointment of the day.[34] Lawson preferred a more laissez-faire approach, complaining that Thatcher's 'admirable radicalism ... stopped short with matters of personal deportment'.[35] When she promoted him from energy secretary to chancellor of the exchequer in 1983, she told him to get his hair trimmed. Lawson later recounted:[36] 'She obviously thought that ... if you're going to be a responsible figure, with the world's financial community hanging on your every word, you have to have your hair cut.' Four years later during the 1987 election, when the country's voters might be hanging on Lawson's words, she again proclaimed that a haircut was needed to rectify his 'appalling' appearance.[37]

While the attention paid to the appearance of politicians greatly increased due to the alterations undergone by Margaret Thatcher, it also received an additional boost from the contrasting experiences of a much less image-conscious politician, whose favourite quotations included Thoreau's maxim, 'Beware of all enterprises which require new clothes'.[38] Michael Foot, who led Labour from 1980 to 1983, sported thick glasses, long white hair, crumpled suits and a walking stick. None of these characteristics is necessarily an impediment to being a good prime minister, but they contributed to an overall impression that he was old, doddery and eccentric. His appearance was ruthlessly pilloried in Conservative-supporting newspapers, which compared him unfavourably to television's walking scarecrow, Worzel Gummidge. At the Cenotaph remembrance service in 1981, Foot wore a short green overcoat which stood out among the black coats worn by others. The claim that he had worn a duffel coat or donkey jacket became part of political folklore, and was exploited by his opponents – both inside and outside the Labour Party – to allege that his manner of dress 'dishonoured the dead'. Foot was undoubtedly damaged by this incident and the more general attacks on his physical appearance.

Since then most party leaders have ended up having to make concessions to the politics of personal appearance. Neil Kinnock's appearance changed quite dramatically fairly soon after he became Labour leader in 1983. He had his hair cut short and 'came out' as bald, in place of the easily ridiculed 'Bobby Charlton' hairstyle in which hair on one side is grown long and combed over the bald patch. He wore darker, more formal and statesmanlike suits to help parry the Conservative charge that he was a lightweight lacking in gravitas. On the day he was elected party leader he wore his Transport and General Workers' Union tie.[39] This was rarely seen again, however, as the party leadership tried to distance itself from the unions and Kinnock moved into regimental-style ties, which connote respectable manhood.

The Liberal Democrat leader, Paddy Ashdown, who has been advised by the image consultant Mary Spillane, also changed his style, adopting more sober, better-cut suits, and casual gear at weekends. His hair is kept short in an echo of his military past, and he has always tried to avoid being pictured while smoking, a habit which conflicts with his 'Action Man' image. Kinnock's successor, John Smith, did not need making over in the same way, but he was not completely immune to considerations of appearance – he preferred to avoid interview settings which emphasised his short, stocky build.[40]

As for John Major, soon after he became prime minister he said that he would not submit to the 'tutelage' of the image-makers and that he was content to remain as 'plug-ugly' as he always had been, adding, 'I am what I am and people will have to take me for what I am.' This proclamation fitted nicely with his established down-to-earth, unassuming image. In fact, Major is not really so disdainful of such matters. 'John Major has always been extremely pernickety about checking in a mirror before an interview, much more so than most other politicians, even before he became prime minister,' according to someone who has witnessed many TV appearances by him[41] – this is partly due to his anxiety about his five o'clock shadow.[42] Whether tutored by image-makers or not, within a year of becoming prime minister Major was parading more expensive double-breasted suits, different colour shirts (pink as well as blue), a smarter, hairspray-drenched haircut and new glasses.

This greater interest in appearance also infected many less senior politicians. Some MPs have always been more worried than others about how they look, but in the late 1980s there was an overall shift (especially after the Commons was televised in 1989) towards greater concern about appearance. The trend was particularly noticeable among Labour MPs and candidates, an increasing number of whom (men and women) opted for more conservative, business executive-type clothing, as the party itself sought to make its image more respectable and move towards the centre in its desperate drive to be seen to be 'fit to govern'. The greater emphasis on personal appearance also reflected the style-conscious culture of the time, and the rapid growth of the 'image consultancy' industry, which claims to base stylistic guidance on a systematic process rather than just personal taste. Generally, its methods mainly focus on the use of colour, but also take into account the shape of clothes, hairstyles, glasses, make-up and accessories. (The more sophisticated consultants cover other aspects of self-presentation as well, from how to make small talk to how to present your partner.)

Politicians from all three parties have used image consultants. Over 150 MPs and many candidates have sought instruction from Britain's leading consultancy, Color Me Beautiful.[43] Its managing director, Mary Spillane, has made a specialism out of advising politicians. She has addressed Conservative and Liberal Democrat training seminars. The Liberal Democrats in particular have pressed all their MPs and candidates with a chance of winning to join Paddy Ashdown in seeking her guidance.

Numerous Labour frontbenchers, including Robin Cook and Harriet Harman, altered their appearance following advice from Barbara Follett, a party activist and media trainer, who extended her work into image consultancy and ended up giving her name to a new term in the political lexicon, 'to follett'. At one period all the party's by-election candidates were sent for a session with Follett, before she abandoned image consultancy after the 1992 election.

VOICE

Politicians spend a lot of time talking. Whether they are addressing the House of Commons, a meeting in their constituency or a television audience, their voice is a vital means through which they conduct their attempts to persuade. And voice, like appearance, is a powerful (but not necessarily reliable) conveyor of associations or impressions about character and background. These can stem from accent, mispronunciation, loudness, pitch, monotony, timbre, nasality, articulation, pace, rhythm, breathing patterns, hesitancy, and so on.

Many politicians have had voice coaching. Many too have altered their speaking habits through their own efforts, often to lose a regional accent or to preserve enough of it to maintain a flavour of authenticity and roots. Particularly notable attempts to modify the way they talked were made by two politicians whose voices represented a serious handicap – Edward Heath and Margaret Thatcher. This provides an interesting illustration of their different attitudes towards the communications imperative.

Heath's publicity advisers distinguished between what they called his 'private' voice and his 'public' voice. The private voice he used in ordinary conversation with people he knew well was relaxed, pleasant and carried conviction. The public voice he used at rallies, on television and for similar events was stilted, plummy and off-putting, a voice used for talking at people rather than to them. His advisers fought a constant struggle to get him to use his private voice on political occasions, especially TV appearances. But Heath never took to such presentational tactics with enthusiasm, especially once he became prime minister. Success was intermittent – if he managed it one time, then he often relapsed at the next.

This proved to be a stark contrast with his successor's willingness and ability to modify her manner of speaking. Margaret Thatcher possessed a naturally high-pitched voice, which easily sounded strident and grating, especially when she needed to make herself heard above the din of the House of Commons. It was unpleasant to listen to, and had the wrong connotations in a culture which associates low pitch with calm authority and high pitch with emotional outbursts. The Conservative Party's private polling showed that voters found her voice too shrill. Her advisers recognised it as a problem. 'The main disadvantage Margaret Thatcher faced as a woman party leader in a male-dominated society was her voice,' says Sir Tim Bell.[44] 'Until then no one ever commented on a politician's voice. The Labour Party tried to build her up as a harridan bitch with a shrill voice.'

Thatcher herself had been aware of the problem for some time. She had tried to lower the tone of her voice before becoming party leader, but this had usually resulted in a sore throat.[45] Gordon Reece arranged for her to see a voice tutor from the National Theatre who gave her humming exercises, taught her to modify her breathing and explained how to talk from the front of the mouth, not the back of the throat. In the ten years up to 1983, Thatcher reduced the pitch of her voice by 46 Hz, about half the average difference between male and female voices.[46] This was a remarkable achievement, especially since at her age women's voices tend naturally to rise as time passes. The pitch reduction was accompanied by a slower, steadier pace of speaking.

Despite all this, Thatcher's voice never became a mellifluous boon to her campaigning. One poll on the tenth anniversary of her becoming prime minister found that 24 per cent of people thought her voice was the most annoying thing about her. It was objected to more than any other feature, such as her policies or alleged personality characteristics like her 'uncaring nature'.[47] No one knows, of course, what this figure would have been without the humming exercises.

## FAMILY

One useful asset for a politician is a happy and photogenic family. Family life can be a valuable tool for getting many voters to see their leaders as reasonably normal human beings, who are capable of ordinary human relationships, share some important experiences of the average citizen, and understand the everyday concerns and hopes of most people. It can also help counter any suspicions lurking in the minds of homophobics. This applies at all levels of politics – that is why election addresses of local candidates often include 'family album' pictures. But it is particularly important for politicians at the top, who are most likely to seem remote from the electorate.

The central ingredient in the portrayal of family life is, of course, the spouse. The spouses of party leaders now play an increasingly prominent role in electioneering, but the basic idea has been around for some time. Back in the 1955 election, for example, both Violet Attlee and Clarissa Eden played bit-parts in their husbands' publicity campaigns. Mrs Attlee appeared alongside Clement in a Labour party political broadcast set in a studio replica of the cosy sitting room of their family home. She also fulfilled an important functional task in her husband's election tour – she drove their car. Clarissa Eden, however, who was much younger than her husband, performed a decorative role during their election tour, which was highly valued by the Conservative Party chairman, Lord Woolton. He later wrote:[48] 'Lady Eden, who went everywhere with [Sir Anthony Eden], looking young and charming, served by her presence to emphasize this conception that I was anxious to put forward of the new "young" Prime Minister.'

The presentational advantages of being married can make things difficult for those politicians who aren't. The most notable example was Edward Heath. 'Our continual worry was that as Ted was not married he was seen as lofty and out of touch,' says Geoffrey Tucker,[49] Heath's publicity adviser. Tucker and his colleagues attempted to counter this through party political broadcasts which showed Heath mixing easily with ordinary people (see Chapter 3). Other tactics employed at various times included Heath talking about children's enjoyment of Christmas in a new year message[50] and being pictured playing with the children of friends.[51] Conservative Central Office also tried various means of presenting him to the public in female company. At the start of the 1970 election campaign, the party organised a photo opportunity of Heath sailing on his yacht with a crew that included an attractive young woman. Heath himself slightly spoilt things, however, by telling the press that she was 'only the cook'.[52] During the October 1974 campaign he was joined on his tour by Sara Morrison, a party vice-chairman and personal friend, who had to deny to the media that she was there as a wife-substitute.[53]

Harold Wilson certainly regarded his marriage as an important source of competitive advantage over Edward Heath. He told his cabinet colleague Richard Crossman that Mary Wilson should be brought into Labour's election campaigning, because 'It's a positive advantage to us that I and Mary appear together and Heath has nothing.'[54] This view was shared by his staff – Marcia Williams described Mary as 'a political asset in publicity terms', recording that 'extra thought had to be given to her projection'.[55]

Mary herself was far from enthusiastic about the role of politician's wife. But she gave newspaper interviews and accompanied Harold prominently on his campaign tours. She also participated in television programmes showing domestic scenes of the Wilsons 'at home' at Downing Street and Chequers, in which the happy couple talked about how they first met and qualities they admired in each other. Harold was always keen to raise his wife's profile. In TV interviews he would deliberately put his left hand on his face so that his wedding ring was clearly visible. He described his family as 'an essential release, relief and inspiration'. And his litany of protests to the BBC hierarchy about anti-Labour bias even included a complaint that, to help Heath, the corporation had allegedly imposed a secret ban on Mary Wilson being shown on screen.[56]

Enoch Powell once referred to the Wilson–Heath battle, which dominated British politics during 1965–75, as a contest between 'a man with a pipe and a man with a boat'. Wilson was doubtless happy for his classless pipe smoking to be contrasted with the expensive pastime of yachting, but he wanted his personal duel with Heath to also be seen in another light – as family man against solitary bachelor.

Since then the spouses of party leaders have been forced into increasing prominence. Television has made them recognisable figures, often seen at their partners' sides. The growing personalisation of politics has boosted interest in the personal lives of politicians and thus of their families. During the 1992 general election, Norma Major and Glenys Kinnock were pictured more often in the national daily press than any politicians, except for the party leaders themselves and an ex-leader, Margaret Thatcher.[57] Senior advisers to John Major thought of Norma as 'a powerful vote-winner in her own right'.[58] Labour strategists certainly regarded Glenys as a boon to electioneering.

There are two minimum requirements for politicians' spouses to conduct themselves usefully. The first is to avoid

gaffes, whether through expressing discordant political opinions or revealing embarrassing details about domestic arrangements. One of Denis Thatcher's main virtues was the
fact that he was 'silent', according to Brendan Bruce, Conservative director of communications in the last phase of
the Thatcher premiership.[59]

The second is to be seen in the right place at the right
time. Thus spouses accompany party leaders on the platform at party conferences, at election rallies, on photo opportunities and at a host of other political engagements, as
a constant reminder of their partner's personal adherence
to conventional family values. And they have to look the
part. While as a man Denis Thatcher only needed to don a
suit and tie, wives such as Norma Major and Cherie Booth
(married to Tony Blair) have responded to press criticism
of their appearance by dressing more glamorously – and
have then sometimes been led into expensive overdressing.

## ROOTS, INTERESTS, PERSONALITY

Politicians have also tried to communicate a sympathetic image
to voters through other aspects of their personal lives, such
as their roots and previous occupations, interests, consumer
preferences and aspects of their personality.

Politicians can exploit their roots effectively, providing they
are at least reasonably humble. A childhood without privilege makes the point that, however high and mighty the
politician is now, he or she knows what life is like on 'the
wrong side of the tracks' (as John Major's supporters proudly
described his origins in the 1990 Tory leadership election).
It also emphasises personal achievement, proclaiming that
the politician has risen to the top through his or her own
efforts and merit.

The initial exponent of this strategy was Harold Wilson,
the first prime minister since MacDonald not to have been
educated at public school, and always determined to stress
his credentials as the common man. So, for example, Wilson
starred in a TV programme in which he revisited his childhood homes, schools and friends in Huddersfield.[60] Later
party leaders such as Thatcher, Kinnock and Major made

similar use of their past. This was partly done through party political broadcasts (see Chapter 3), but it was also pursued through other means.

Thatcher gave numerous interviews in which she talked about her early life as a grocer's daughter in Grantham – 'home really was very small and we had no mod cons', 'we hadn't very much money', 'it was years and years later that we actually had a vacuum cleaner... in my childhood we did it by dustpan and brush'. And thus she claimed that 'when people tell me about these things, I know about them'.[61] Brendan Bruce encouraged Thatcher to talk about her roots to persuade voters that 'she had not forgotten what it was like to look up the class mountain'. In his opinion this was a more effective way of conveying her views about opportunity than merely relying on 'the intellectual case', which was 'impeccable but cold'.[62] It is for exactly the same reason – namely, that personal experience impresses voters more than rational abstract argument – that Neil Kinnock famously described himself, during the 1987 election, as 'the first Kinnock in a thousand generations' to go to university, and that John Major from time to time reminds us that he was once unemployed.

Occasionally, some politicians have managed to squeeze some electoral benefit out of their previous occupations before becoming an MP. A Liberal Democrat party broadcast in 1992 contained some old film of a much younger Paddy Ashdown as a marine commando in the Borneo jungle. But Ashdown has resisted pressure from advisers to make more out of his military past, due to the undercover nature of operations he was involved in. 'We wanted to play that card more, but he doesn't want to,' says Alec McGivan,[6] the party's deputy campaign director in 1992.

There are many other facets of life which politicians have used to draw attention to a relaxed, human side to their characters – whether real, exaggerated or invented – in the hope that they avoid seeming remote and come across in a way ordinary people can relate to. Most human activities can be exploited in this way, ranging from a liking for eating in *Happy Eaters* (to demonstrate unpretentious tastes) to strategic church-going (based on the assumption that atheists are more tolerant of religion than the religious are of atheism). A few politicians have made displaying their personality on TV light entertainment shows into a frequent activity, ensuring they are noticed by many more viewers than watch current affairs output. A little humour goes a long way in humanising a politician's image.

This was another field in which Wilson led the way. Well-publicised details which contributed further towards his persona as a man of the people included his liking for watching *Coronation Street* and beach holidays on the Scilly Isles. The other politician who tried hardest was Thatcher, as at periodic intervals her advisers decided it was time to make another attempt to soften her image. Thanks to Gordon Reece she appeared on entertainment programmes like *Jim'll Fix It.* While Heath said of the 1974 coal crisis that 'I don't think a miners' strike is the time to come on television and ooze charm',[64] for Thatcher the 1984/5 miners' strike with its bitter confrontation was the ideal moment to become the first serving prime minister to take part in a TV chat show, cosily discussing with Michael Aspel what she had for breakfast. Some ploys were favoured by both Wilson and Thatcher – both liked to be pictured with dogs, and both allowed the television cameras into Downing Street to film their domestic routine.

One of the most common gambits is an interest in sport. Wilson made much of his concern for the fortunes of Huddersfield Town football club, and appeared on the television programme *Sportsnight with Coleman* to talk about his love of the game. Kinnock wrote reviews of rugby books, and was shown coaching his son's rugby team in a Labour party political broadcast. Major likes to be pictured in the crowd at football matches, and bats cricket balls for photo opportunities. Blair has retaliated by speaking about the state of the game of soccer at a dinner in honour of Sir Stanley Matthews, and heading a football back and forth with Kevin Keegan.

The party leader who devoted by far the most effort to sport was Heath, who took up competitive sailing and achieved remarkable success, winning international races. While motivated by enjoyment of the activity, he also hoped that patriotic triumphs in world-class sporting events would boost his image as a team leader and national standard-bearer. He obtained some adulatory publicity as a result, but there was a downside too: it led to him being identified with an exclusive amusement pursued by a wealthy few.

Music is another field favoured by politicians who want to demonstrate publicly that they do not live by politics alone. Wilson was determined to show he was in tune with young people in modern times. He presented entertainment industry awards to the Beatles on television in 1964, and then gave them his own award in the form of MBEs a year later. Heath conducted an annual Christmas carol concert in his home town of Broadstairs, and conducted the London Symphony Orchestra on one occasion while prime minister. Geoffrey Tucker told him: 'Your musical activity has worked beautifully and to your advantage.'[65] Kinnock appeared in a Tracey Ullman pop video, a gimmick unlikely to help a politician whose main image problem was a need to seem more authoritative. Blair confidently picked his favourite rock music during a Radio 1 interview, an event which certainly went down better with the youth vote than his predecessor's embarrassing appearance on the same network – John Smith had to admit he had never heard of either Take That or Sonic the Hedgehog.

Thatcher never professed any caring for sport or music, but for the benefit of the public she did display more traditionally feminine interests. She was pictured cooking and shopping, and in various interviews she discussed the contents of her freezer and her wardrobe, skin care and dress sizes, the shop from which she obtained her underwear, the wallpaper and curtains in Downing Street, and how to combine motherhood with a career.

## CONCLUSION

Image-making consumes much effort on the part of politicians and their advisers. The images constructed strongly influence both how the media covers politics and how individual voters think about politicians and their parties. The highly self-conscious and thorough cultivation of a particular personal image really started with the shrewd and calculating figure of Harold Wilson, who grasped that it was a facet of political communication particularly well suited to the age of the impressionistic medium of television. It has been an important part of our politics ever since. Image-building is now a crucial weapon in the armoury of the political campaigner. Like the other weapons, however, it can also sometimes misfire. The extent to which it succeeds depends on at least the following five factors.

1: How committed the politician is to the exercise. The sharpest contrast here is between Heath and Thatcher. Heath was a naturally reserved and serious-minded man, who had little patience for presentational considerations and thought the way to counterpose himself against the famously image-conscious Wilson was to avoid anything which could be regarded as image-building gimmickry. He had to be reluctantly cajoled into heeding principles of communication and trying to appear more relaxed, friendly and approachable. He would cooperate under protest and intermittently before relapsing. Heath and his advisers found the process equally frustrating. Geoffrey Tucker says:[66] 'You'd get him up to scratch and then he'd go back to his old ways. After the 1970 election I said to him: "I'm off. Frankly, I've had enough of you." And I added: "And I suppose you've had more than enough of me."'

In comparison, Thatcher was an image-maker's delight, for she was determined to convey her strongly-held beliefs as effectively as possible. As she herself put it:[67] 'Every politician has to decide how much he or she is prepared to change manner and appearance for the sake of the media. It may sound grittily honourable to refuse to make any concessions, but such an attitude in a public figure is most likely to betray a lack of seriousness about winning power.' Thatcher was certainly serious about winning and keeping power, and approached the task of personal presentation with her customary level of dedication and attention to detail.

'Thatcher began by being very bad on television,' says Barry Day,[68] a Heath publicity adviser who noticed Thatcher's professionalism while she was still one of Heath's subordinates. 'We cut her out of a party political in 1970 due to her posh voice and false smile. She was ill at ease and looked extremely out of touch. But of all that bunch, she was the most willing to learn and to ask for help. She would ask: "Was I too shrill? Shall we do it again?" She became good, and in October 1974 we used her in two of the five party broadcasts. She understood she had to find the right techniques and style.'

2: Whether the new image has the right connotations. Politicians who dress too smartly and formally in the search for status end up distancing themselves from potential supporters. Those who appear on too many light entertainment TV programmes may lose credibility and sometimes demean themselves. Those who publicise expensive or unusual interests may find themselves regarded as elitist or eccentric.

3: Whether the presentational artifice involved itself becomes the subject of attention. Opponents will naturally try to make it so. Wilson in particular was often attacked as a gimmick merchant. But this problem can also leave politicians with a dilemma. They may be damned if they don't change their image and damned if they do; and it can be difficult to work out which way they get damned the most. Many voters react (whether consciously or unconsciously) against politicians who have ugly teeth or shrill, high-pitched voices or not much hair. But if those politicians respond by having their teeth altered or lowering their voice or disguising their baldness, then many voters don't like that either, for it is seen as a sham. And, who knows, some of these voters may even be among those who objected to the teeth, voice or hair in the first place. The public may like its politicians to look good, but it doesn't want to think that it therefore makes sense for them to do so because it helps win votes. The biggest victim of this was Margaret Thatcher. She was persistently ridiculed for the extensive changes to her appearance and voice, and accused of patronising voters in assuming that it would improve her electoral popularity. In fact, Thatcher was merely reacting rationally to the irrationality of the electorate.

4: Whether the image change is too far-reaching to be plausible. Under the British political system politicians slither slowly up the greasy pole. By the time they achieve prominence they already possess established images. Such an image cannot be transformed overnight, and an attempt to do so is likely to be implausible and counter-productive. It is difficult to get away with anything that appears totally out of character. The most effective image-making consists of a little stretch, pulling the politician a step in the right direction. (In due course a little stretching maintained over a long period of time can drag someone a long way.) This is why it is easier for image-builders to exploit a politician's strength than remedy a weakness. The former usually requires only a little enhancement or exaggeration; the latter may need drastic action.

5: Whether the image change is too far-reaching for the politician to manage to stick to it consistently. A new image may require unnatural behaviour from the politician which it is difficult to always maintain, especially at times of stress. Occasionally, the mask slips and the old image is reinforced. The impact can be considerable, because these unintended deviations from the new image frequently receive a lot of publicity.

Factors 4 and 5 often combine. Thus, despite the immense effort Tory and Labour campaigners put over the years into trying to alter the images of Thatcher and Kinnock, at the end they were still left with many voters who persisted in believing the old story. Before she became party leader, Thatcher was already widely regarded as the hat-wearing, uncaring 'milk snatcher' (this nickname stemming from her abolition of free school milk while education secretary in 1971). And from early in his leadership, Kinnock had an image as the over-exuberant boyo from the valleys who had never had a proper job. Whatever the impact of her political actions, Thatcher's attempt to be seen as a more sympathetic figure was not helped by her habit of self-righteously haranguing interviewers, or by her contemptuous reference during the 1987 campaign to people who 'drool and drivel that they care'. Many voters thought that in this unguarded moment the true face of Thatcher had been sighted. Similarly, Kinnock's desperate struggle to appear statesmanlike suffered from his tendency to get involved in fisticuffs when provoked by aggressive youths, and from his notorious, almost frenzied, shout of 'We're all right' at Labour's massive Sheffield rally in 1992 (see Chapter 5). Of this incident Kinnock himself remarked: 'All of the years in which I'd attempted to build a fairly reserved, starchy persona – in a few seconds they all slipped away.'[69]

And that is the image-maker's nightmare.

# 8 Party Identity

*The people's rose in shades of pinks*
*Gets up my nostrils and it stinks,*
*But ere our limbs grow stiff and cold*
*Our old Red Flag we shall unfold.*
*With heads uncovered swear we all*
*To let rose petals fade and fall.*
*Though moderates flinch and media sneer*
*We'll keep the Red Flag flying here.*

Tony Benn's alternative version of 'The Red
Flag', marking Labour's adoption of the rose as
party symbol, 1986[1]

*I love roses. I grow them in my own garden. But I prefer them*
*in my garden rather than on my lapel.*

John Prescott, 1995[2]

In the 1992 general election, the heat from the torch of
freedom wilted the rose of humanity, while the bird of aspiration failed to take off. Or that anyway was the result in
terms of party logos and their supposed connotations.

These symbols are seen in party advertisements, leaflets
and broadcasts. They decorate stages and walls at meetings,
rallies and press conferences. They appear on posters, badges,
rosettes, headed notepaper and a host of political paraphernalia from mugs to umbrellas. They often represent the parties
in television and newspaper graphics. They are reproduced
in local literature by constituencies under strict instructions
from party headquarters to use exactly the right design,
colours and typeface. Carefully researched in focus groups
before adoption, they are today an important aspect of a
party's presentation and the key component of its corporate identity or 'party identity'.

Logos have two complementary purposes: they are intended
to encapsulate vote-winning political values, and to give a
unified tone to party propaganda, so that a party's electioneering efforts all convey the same desirable associations. To

work well they must be easily recognisable, adaptable to different media and appropriate to the party's image.

Until the 1980s the visual identity of parties had mainly been based on colour, with at a national level the Conservative use of blue, Labour of red, and the Liberals of yellow or orange. This was supplemented by a disparate array of occasional symbols for certain elections. In 1964, Labour's advertising team devised a thumbs-up emblem to accompany its slogan – 'Let's go with Labour and we'll get things done' – and convey a spirit of optimism and positive action. Later designs were blander – a simple red and black circular shape in 1966, a drawing of a rosette in October 1974. The Conservatives' recourse to campaign logos was rarer, but they fought the 1970 election with the aid of a symbol consisting of concentric blue circles. These devices featured variously in leaflets, posters, publications, ads, party political broadcasts and backdrops at meetings.

Locally, the use of bright colour on posters, stickers, leaflets, rosettes, badges, banners, and so on, could contribute to the impression of widespread activity and support in an area, and was therefore a factor in building morale and enthusiasm. However, party colours varied across the country. Before national campaigning became dominant, regions or constituencies had adopted their own colours according to individual tastes at different times and in light of those which had already been seized by opponents. These hues then became a matter of local tradition.

The confused pattern which resulted is exemplified by the 1950 general election. While the Conservatives usually adopted blue, in the north of England they generally favoured red, in Kent and Surrey they deployed orange and purple, and choices elsewhere included pink and yellow. In Scotland and Birmingham they emphasised their heritage as Unionists through the use of red, white and blue. Labour predominantly picked red, but in some places green or a combination of yellow and black. Liberals opted most often for green or yellow, but sometimes for blue, red or all sorts of combinations.[3] Since then, as electioneering became increasingly nationalised, the vast majority of constituencies have fallen in with their party's standard colour. However, in some areas the drive to national uniformity encountered fierce local resistance. There are still a few local parties which maintain their own idiosyncratic colour schemes.

The first party to adopt a rigorous approach to corporate identity were the Social Democrats, when they were formed in 1981. As a new party the SDP was free of the encumbrance of tradition. The organiser of the party's launch, Mike Thomas (a defecting Labour MP), was determined to ensure that it demonstrated an efficient, professional outlook. He commissioned a party logo from a leading design consultant, Dick Negus, who produced a simple symbol based on the letters SDP underlined, in blue and red on a white background. Party founders were keen on the patriotic association with the colours of the Union Flag.[4] Negus explained that he made the logo so simple to assist local activists. He wanted to ensure that 'enthusiastic amateurs in the field could handle it tolerably well without making a mess of it'.[5]

In the next few years the two main parties followed suit and adopted a permanent logo (see below). Meanwhile, the SDP symbol was coupled with the word 'Liberal' inside a diamond shape for their combined campaigns as the Alliance in the 1983 and 1987 general elections. On the second of these occasions the Alliance also adopted a new joint colour. It was officially described as 'prime gold', but could more prosaically and just as accurately be termed 'yellow'. The colour was the idea of the Alliance's professional ad-man David Abbott, who claimed it communicated 'a warm, sunny and cheerful image'.[6]

After the two Alliance parties had merged, the Liberal Democrats unveiled their new highly stylised, yellow 'soaring bird' logo in 1990. Created by the design company Fitch RS, it was intended to convey the notions of individual liberty, aspiration and breaking free from the past. After much research into 'bird meanings' the designers settled on this 'everybird'.[7] Critics commented that it looked just as much like a snake in the grass. It was famously derided by Margaret Thatcher at the Conservative conference soon afterwards as a 'dead parrot', although the prime minister knew little if anything about Monty Python, and the cultural reference – and its humour – had to be painstakingly explained to her by her speechwriters. Nevertheless, the bird was praised within the Liberal Democrats and has been a success for the party. It is modern, distinctive, memorable, and comes across clearly and well on television and in print.

The first systematically used Conservative logo was introduced in 1982 at the initiative of Chris Lawson, who had become the party's marketing director a year previously. With a background in commercial marketing, Lawson was appalled to discover that a bewildering variety of miscellaneous symbols was employed by different party sections and constituencies as if they were entirely unconnected organisations. He arranged research which found that constituency workers associated the party with values like loyalty, tradition, leadership and the will to win. This led to the concept of an Olympic-type torch as the party logo, coloured of course with due patriotism like the national flag in red, white and (mainly) blue. Care was taken to make sure the flame was seen not as threatening but as warm and friendly. 'I had an awful job getting it through the prime minister and members of the cabinet,' says Lawson.[8] 'They said they'd never had such a thing as a party logo. It also met a lot of resistance from the constituencies. It meant they had to drop their own.'

In due course the symbol was accepted throughout the party. But over the years it became dated, and in 1989 the Conservative director of communications Brendan Bruce decided to modernise it. Research showed that it had low recognition. Even worse, people thought it seemed old-fashioned and dull. It was compared to an ice cream cone or a Bulgarian conductor's cap badge.[9] Bruce did not want an entirely new symbol, in case the media interpreted it as heralding a shift in the party's ideological direction. So a more dynamic, flowing, up-to-date rendering of the torch, now carried by a hand, was produced by the design consultancy Michael Peters. This new version possesses carefully constructed visual overtones of the Statue of Liberty as well as the Olympic flame. The Conservatives proclaim that the symbol stands for traditional Tory themes of freedom and the individual pursuit of excellence. Bruce says:[10] 'We wanted to make it clear that the fundamental argument was between the Conservative belief in a minimalist state and Labour's belief in a powerful central state.'

204        *From Soapbox to Soundbite*

However, the party logo which has had by far the most
impact on British politics is Labour's red rose, which was
introduced in 1986 and powerfully signified a break with
the past. Labour had possessed an official symbol of sorts
since the early 1920s, when it organised a competition to
design a party emblem.[11] The winning entry featured a crossed
torch, spade and quill pen – to represent the flame of knowledge and the 'workers by hand or by brain' who were referred to in Clause 4 of the party constitution. This retained
official status for several decades. However, due to simplify-
ing redesign it started to resemble a collection of household cutlery, and became popularly known within the party
as the 'knife, fork and spoon'. At various times the device
appeared on publications, and party stalwarts liked to sport
it on badges and ties, but it was not used comprehensively
as an all-purpose party logo. By the 1960s it hardly featured
in electioneering. The archaic design and symbolism did
not fit the image of a modern party, nor would it come
over well in advertising or as a backdrop on television. In
the early 1980s Labour's publicity department, feeling the
need for a clear, stylistically modern emblem, began to use
a billowing red flag bearing the words 'Labour Party' on
leaflets, booklets and conference backdrops.

The billowing flag was disliked by Neil Kinnock, who became party leader in 1983. In his view it was redolent of
old-fashioned Labourism and appealed to activists rather than
voters. During the 1984 Euro-elections, party campaign
materials featured the European socialist symbol of a red
rose with its stem grasped in a clenched fist. In 1986 Kinnock
finally decided that Labour should also adopt a red rose as
the centrepiece of its corporate identity. With the assistance
of the leading designer Michael Wolff, Kinnock and party
strategists studied large numbers of possible rose logos and
commissioned research into the impressions they created.
'We tested big roses, small roses, pink roses, red roses, hy-
brid tea roses,' says Labour's pollster, Bob Worcester of MORI.
'Altogether we tested over 40 roses.'[12]

Labour eventually picked a naturalistic flower which was
softer and more elegant than the European socialist version – even though Kinnock himself thought the stem too
long. (The design has since undergone various minor modi-

fications, partly to make its reproduction easier.) Labour's
red rose was unveiled to immense publicity at the 1986 party
conference. The symbol dominated the platform backdrop,
and was soon seen sprouting throughout the gathering on
newly purchased badges and carrier bags. The conference
culminated in Neil and Glenys Kinnock tossing roses into
the excited audience.

The rose has one flaw – it doesn't work well when reproduced in black and white. But Labour soon discovered it
had numerous advantages. Not only could real roses be thrown
into crowds, they could decorate tables at rallies and press
conferences, and be worn in politicians' buttonholes (deputy
leader and hayfever sufferer Roy Hattersley required an artificial substitute). Buttonhole wearing was mandatory for
senior figures on media occasions for some time, a requirement many found increasingly irksome. These physical ap-
plications have boosted the symbol's prominence in ways
that the other parties cannot emulate with blazing torches
or live birds.

As for its connotations, it suggested a neat combination
of English heritage and international socialism. The design
was fresh and welcoming, and Labour declared that it projected 'a feeling of warmth and humanity'.[13] Above all, however, it projected change. For any organisation, whether
political party or commercial business, the greatest power
of a new logo is often simply as a public statement that the
organisation is reforming itself radically. This was exactly
what party strategists wanted. Communications director Peter
Mandelson had argued internally for a new corporate identity on the grounds that it was 'vital to reinforce the impression of an innovative party shedding old associations'.[14]
The rose became a symbol not just of the Labour Party, but
also of the party's metamorphosis. Kinnock's transformation
of Labour – in which the party became more disciplined
and efficient, campaigned with flair and razzmatazz, and
moved to the centre ground – was often nicknamed the
'red rose revolution'.

One word is conspicuous by its absence from all three
contemporary party logos – 'party'. This fashion started with
the formation of the SDP. Focus group research conducted
to assist its launch showed that people found the word 'party'

unappealing. So the logo said 'SDP' instead of spelling out 'Social Democratic Party', and the party referred to itself as 'the Social Democrats'. For the same reason the Liberal Democrats have always insisted on being just that, not the 'Liberal Democratic Party'. The two main parties have been driven in the same direction, not by similar opinion research, but by a modern preference for simplicity and economy of expression. Since the red rose was introduced it has always gone together with the lone word 'Labour', without 'Party' attached. And when the revamped Tory torch was unveiled in 1989, it was accompanied by the single word 'Conservative'.

The other key element of a party's identity is its name. In the post-war period the biggest fuss over a party's name was prompted by the merger in 1987–8 of the Liberals and the Social Democrats. Most Liberals wanted to ensure that their cherished name was maintained prominently in the identity of the combined party. They argued that this was necessary if the new party was to hold on to the public goodwill and recognition that already belonged to the name 'Liberal'. And naturally most Social Democrats argued exactly the same way about their own name. (In fact, many protagonists on both sides were motivated by sentimental attachment or internal power-struggling rather than pure electoral considerations.) Frantic last-minute horse-trading resulted in the new single party being called the 'Social and Liberal Democrats'. An official short title of 'Democrats' was added later, although the party's opponents preferred to give it the short nickname of 'SaLaDs'. The name proved unpopular with many former Liberals, who agitated for change. The party suffered a loss of identity in the public mind due to confusion over the name, until a postal ballot of the membership in 1989 finally settled on 'Liberal Democrats'.

The two major parties have not formally changed their names nationally in the period since 1945. In parts of Britain the Tories campaigned under the heading of 'Unionist' for some time after the war (in Scotland until 1965), but 'Conservative' is now used universally. (The constituency wing of the party is still officially titled the 'National Union of Conservative and Unionist Associations'.) Both parties have, however, faced occasional internal proposals to revise their names nationally – usually in the aftermath of electoral defeat when a dramatic break with the past might make sense.

After the traumatic 1945 election many Conservatives thought their party name a handicap, and numerous alternatives were advocated. Harold Macmillan favoured the 'New Democratic Party'. The Conservative chairman Lord Woolton preferred 'Union Party', but insisted a change should only be made later when the party was in a position of strength.

Woolton never managed to alter his own party's label, but he did his best to modify that of his enemies. He regarded Labour's self-designation as a masterful tactic of electioneering, writing in his memoirs: 'The man who first called the Socialist Party the "Labour Party" was a political genius, for indeed the word "labour" implied the party that would look after the best interests of "labour".'[15] Woolton believed that 'socialism', with its connotations of bureaucratic state control, was a more useful term for the beliefs of his opponents. He decreed that Conservative propaganda should always refer to Labour as 'the Socialists', a policy also followed for many years by right-wing newspapers such as the *Daily Express* and the *Daily Telegraph*.

By 1959 and three successive election losses, there were those on the Labour side who argued that its name needed revision. Douglas Jay, a leading figure on the Gaitskellite right of the party, thought 'Labour' was outmoded, too class-conscious, and alienating to the better off. He suggested 'Radical'. Gaitskell himself had grave doubts, which he expressed privately, about the appellation 'Labour'.[16] But having being forced to abandon his goal of persuading the party to drop its constitutional commitment to common ownership, he never attempted the harder task of changing its name.

Thirty-five years later Tony Blair succeeded where Gaitskell failed and amended Clause 4 of Labour's constitution, discarding the pledge on common ownership. He has also instituted a kind of unofficial name adjustment. Blair and his supporters frequently refer to the party as if it was called 'New Labour', a tag which to their pleasure is now sometimes used in the media too. (This title incidentally was among those the founders of the SDP considered and rejected when setting up their organisation.)[17] For the party's leading modernisers, this is one highly visible element in their

continuing project to distance Labour from its election-los-
ing past. 'It is an absolutely essential part of Tony Blair's
political mission not only for Labour to change, but also to
make it clear that Labour has changed,' explains Philip
Gould,[18] a strategic adviser to Blair and the former coordinator of the Shadow Communications Agency. 'Tony Blair
wants an abrupt and manifest change between a party of
the past and a party of the future.'

# 9 Campaign Materials and Direct Mail

*We always, as far as our means permitted, tried to make our printed documents as handsome as possible, and did our best to destroy the association between revolutionary literature and slovenly printing.*
George Bernard Shaw, quoted by Neil Kinnock at the launch of Labour's 'Investing in People' campaign, 1986[1]

In early post-war general elections the production and distribution of printed literature was the main party publicity operation at national level. Since then, other activities have become more important. Nevertheless, the parties have continued to issue a wide variety of national leaflets, broadsheets, pamphlets, posters and stickers – and in quantities of millions for each election, on top of the even larger numbers produced locally. Most has been intended for mass distribution to unspecified audiences. This remains the case, but parties have also devoted increasing effort to using direct mail to target selected messages at specific sections of the electorate. (Posters have been covered in Chapter 2, since they have generally been used primarily as advertisements. One important exception which must be mentioned is the famous 1945 Labour poster that consisted of a huge 'V' dominating an idealised town and was captioned, 'And now – win the peace.' Designed by John Armstrong, it cleverly exploited the wartime 'V for victory' symbol and was a powerful evocation of Labour's campaign message. It has become an icon of Labour history.)

Political propaganda is not limited to printed literature. The parties have employed audio-visual technologies – film, videotape and audiotape – to help convey their case as well. Over the years they have also distributed an expanding range of other materials, although these are of less significance for campaigning. They include all sorts of paraphernalia emblazoned with party names or slogans – rosettes, badges, banners, poster boards, balloons, T-shirts, mugs, ties, cufflinks, scarves, pens, carrier bags, umbrellas and beer mats.

The parties are also moving into electronic publishing. The Conservatives, Labour and the Liberal Democrats have all established their own web sites on the Internet, providing access to certain policy statements, reports, press releases and various other documents. This form of party political communication is growing fast, but is still experimental and so far of limited impact.


MANIFESTOS

In formal terms the most important publications produced by political parties are their manifestos. The basic idea involved – of an authoritative proclamation of party policy issued at election time – has hardly changed since 1945.

The concept originally stemmed from the constituency election addresses of party leaders. After the second world war, the Conservatives initially maintained the pre-war tradition of portraying their manifesto as a personal message from the leader. The 1945 version was called 'Mr Churchill's declaration of policy to the electors'. But the Tories soon switched to presenting the manifesto as a collective rather than an individual statement. It is now usual for the manifestos of all three parties to consist of a brief leader's introduction followed by the substantive corporate account of party policy. Additional, more imaginative, elements, are extremely rare. In one exception Labour's 1992 manifesto began with a poem by Adrian Henri. It was entitled 'Winter ending' and concluded 'the cold blue landscape of winter/suddenly alive with bright red roses'.

Even the design of manifestos has changed remarkably little in the past fifty years. They consisted virtually entirely of large blocks of straightforward text until 1987, when parties introduced a few limited design features. Labour produced a full colour glossy cover, while the Tories and Alliance had some (rather dull) illustrations. The three parties also deployed some basic techniques to highlight certain elements, such as boxes, different coloured type and brief summary phrases located in the margins. (The latter enabled Labour, which wanted to play down its policy of unilateral nuclear disarmament, to summarise it with the phrase 'Commitment to conventional defence'.) However, these devices did little to relieve the unremitting visual tedium of the text.

In 1992 the Conservative and Labour manifestos were no better, but the Liberal Democrats produced a striking publication – the first party manifesto which looked as if it had been designed as well as written. Its bold use of dramatic photography, large type, colour, reversing out and diagrams gave it much more visual impact than any other manifesto has had. This style was maintained in the party's manifesto for the 1994 European elections. Labour's manifesto for these elections was also glossy and well-illustrated, a major improvement on its predecessors, while the Tory one still made little attempt to please the eye.

But although manifestos have changed little in format and style, they have altered substantially in other respects – notably their length and the numbers printed and distributed (their actual policy content is outside the remit of this book).

Since 1945 there has been a powerful trend towards policy inflation. This is for several reasons: the business of government has expanded; policy gaps are increasingly focused on and criticised by interest groups and the media; and politicians now make greater use of policy to target selected groups of voters. Thus, as parties have taken to adopting more policies and expressing them in greater detail and complexity, manifestos have generally got longer and longer. There have been deviations from this in certain individual elections, but on a decade-by-decade basis all three parties have consistently produced documents of increasing size. The average length of Conservative manifestos over the 1983–92 period was about four times the average from 1945–59. The same comparative ratio also applies for Labour, while for the Liberal Democrats/Alliance/Liberals it is around six.[2] (This trend has been present throughout the century – the 1945–59 manifestos were significantly longer than their pre-war predecessors.)

The longest party manifesto of all was the 1992 Conservative one, which ran to 29 800 words, compared to the 6100 words of its 1945 equivalent. Labour's longest manifesto was produced in 1983. Amounting to 22 600 words, it was famously described by Labour frontbencher Gerald Kaufman, who was appalled by its radical and electorally unpopular contents, as 'the longest suicide note in history'. Labour manifestos since then have been shorter (9100 words in 1987; 12 600 in 1992), but these are still much longer than the party's early post-war manifestos – its 1945 version was only 5000 words.[3]

The increasing length of Labour manifestos has been accompanied by an immense reduction in the number issued. For the 1945 to 1959 elections the party distributed enormous quantities, ranging between 920 000 (in 1950)[4] and 2 700 000 (in 1951).[5] But there was a dramatically reduced print-run in 1964 – only 130 000[6] – when the manifesto was roughly twice the length of the 1959 one, of which nearly 1.5 million[7] had been issued. Instead, in 1964, Labour produced hundreds of thousands of leaflets summarising the main points. From then until 1983 the print-run for the manifesto itself was generally in the 100 000–150 000 range. It increased to 195 000 in 1987[8] and 250 000 in 1992.[9] The fall in the number of copies of the Conservative manifesto has been much less stark. Average sales in the elections from 1951 to 1970 were 126 000;[10] in 1992 the party sold 70 000 copies (and distributed another 10 000 free).[11]

In any case the impact of a manifesto is not based on the numbers who directly read it. For its campaigning impact what counts is the reporting and discussion of it in the media. Manifesto launches have now become major media events of the campaign, with increasingly grandiose and elaborate press conferences.

Occasionally, a party's manifesto has become a campaigning tool for the other side. In 1983 Conservative Central Office bought 5000 copies of Labour's left-wing manifesto (Labour rather generously gave Central Office a bulk-order discount, charging 40p per copy instead of 60p).[12] During the campaign Margaret Thatcher brandished the Labour manifesto at her election rallies, while the Conservative treasurer Alistair McAlpine circulated it to wealthy donors to frighten them into giving more.

OTHER LITERATURE

While manifestos are not necessarily intended to be widely read, in contrast leaflets, broadsheets and pamphlets are aimed at ordinary electors. The main challenge parties have faced is how to make these materials attractive and accessible to voters whose interest in politics is limited, without losing or undermining the key political messages.

This challenge often proved too difficult. One academic study of the 1950 election[13] castigated national electioneering literature, especially pamphlets, stating that 'much of the printed publicity at this election fell very far below the average standards set by commercial printing of a similar nature'. While commending certain exceptions, it criticised the output of all three parties for lack of illustration, poor layout and the 'vast extent of close-set type, frequently set in far smaller letters than are normally encountered'. The need for improvement was acknowledged by Conservative Central Office. Its internal report on the 1950 campaign noted that for future printed literature, 'brightness of colour, simplicity of design and directness of language must be sought'.[14]

This sensible edict has been heeded only intermittently by all the parties. The quality of literature has fluctuated enormously over the years, ranging from the excellent to the nearly unreadable. However, advances in printing technology, such as in the use of colour, have generally helped to improve the appearance of campaign materials. Their impact has also been strengthened by greater integration of campaigning, as the content and design of leaflets and posters has been better coordinated with other aspects of party communications. This is particularly true since Saatchi and Saatchi started work for the Conservatives in 1978 and the Shadow Communications Agency was set up by Labour in 1986.

The clearest systematic shift in the quality of party publications was made by Labour between the 1983 and 1987 elections. The whole range of materials produced for its mid-term campaigns, first 'Jobs and Industry' and then even more so for 'Freedom and Fairness', were much more attractive, well designed and digestible than the party's previous literature. The 1987 election was the first for which most Labour leaflets were produced in full colour. 'The high quality of materials was a deliberate strategy to improve public perceptions of the party,' according to Labour's election report.[15] The trend towards increasingly glossy production values continued after the 1987 election, although this prompted growing charges of the triumph of gloss over content. Even the ordinary people whose photographs were used to illustrate publications as symbols of party support were further up the social scale.

## DIRECT MAIL

Party literature is more cost-effective when it is distributed only to selected groups and the messages it contains are tailored in content and tone to the audiences which receive them. This is the key capability of direct mail. Parties have therefore exploited it enthusiastically since computing advances made it a much more powerful medium in the 1980s. This is true at local as well as national level (local direct mail is covered in Chapter 10).

Although direct mail today seems inconceivable without computers, it was sometimes used for political purposes even at times when large mailings represented considerable feats of manual labour. Political direct mail at the national level dates back at least to the 1920s, when the Conservatives mailed target groups.[16]

In the post-war period the Tories used direct mail intermittently before the computer age. They launched an extensive direct mail programme in the months leading up to the 1950 election, sending propaganda to 94 000 individuals in selected categories who were judged likely to disseminate it further. These included barbers, newsagents, booksellers, garage owners, nurses, teachers and vets. Garages received car stickers, while barbers were sent literature in the hope they would leave it out for waiting customers to read. Party officials were aware that sending inappropriate material to particular recipients could be counterproductive. The chief organisation officer recommended that 'great discrimination be exercised in the material issued to teachers, all of whom must reach a certain mental standard'.[17]

The Conservatives ran another direct mail operation before the 1959 election. Monthly newsletters were sent to 45 000 individuals in marginal seats. This time the recipients were those thought to be opinion-formers at the hub of social networks: doctors, lawyers, clergy, teachers, barbers and publicans.[18] A similar exercise was conducted in 1963. The party compiled its own target lists – each marginal constituency was asked to supply 500 suitable names and addresses, although many failed to reach this figure. Central Office described the purpose as 'to give up-to-date material to those people who can be classed as opinion-formers and who do a good deal of talking in the course of their work'. The occupations targeted were extended to include dentists, estate agents and manicurists.[19]

In 1969 the Tories switched to computer technology in place of the mechanical envelope-addressing system they had been using. This allowed for individual letters to be fully personalised and the text to be varied according to the occupations of recipients. Prior to the 1970 election, around 10 000 opinion-formers in marginals received a series of letters from party leaders asking them to persuade others of the Conservative case.[20] A wider range of occupations was involved – people of influence were now thought also to include milkmen and postmen.[21] But constituencies still found it difficult to provide the number of names Central Office sought. The exercise was regarded as disappointing and was not repeated for the following election.

Political direct mail at the national level then lay dormant until the early 1980s, by which time commercial direct mail was booming. This was due to continuous and dramatic advances in the processing power and printing speed of computers, the better availability of lists of names and addresses, and the increasing sophistication with which these lists could be analysed, particularly with the help of census data and postcodes. These developments allowed much larger mailings which were carefully targeted and automatically personalised.

The first party to exploit this properly at a national level were the Social Democrats. From its foundation in 1981 the SDP had a national computerised membership list, in contrast to the other parties whose members were known only to their local constituencies. The SDP made some use of direct mail before the 1983 election, but the main drive occurred between then and the 1987 election. In this period it developed a continuous national programme of mailshots, based on the advice of American political consultants. Between the two elections it despatched around three million letters.[22] While the programme's goals included political persuasion, the primary purpose was fundraising and large sums were collected.

The Tories resumed national direct mail in 1982 under the influence of their director of marketing, Chris Lawson, who appreciated its potential due to his previous career in business and observation of politics in the US. In the run-up to the 1983 election, personalised letters were sent to targeted categories of individuals in marginal seats in the name of party chairman, Cecil Parkinson. The mailshots were aimed at winning political support and membership recruitment. One early recipient turned out to be Parkinson himself, which helped confirm his belief that the letters were going to the right kind of people.[23] The operation relied on what was then a powerful new mainframe computer which had just been acquired by Central Office.

But after this brief experiment prior to the 1983 election the Conservatives abandoned national direct mail entirely. The activity faced powerful internal opposition. Party treasurer Alistair McAlpine felt it cut unhelpfully across his own fundraising efforts. Many local associations thought it caused them similar problems. The Tories did not reinstitute mailshots until the summer of 1986, after Norman Tebbit took charge as party chairman. Chris Lawson was brought out of retirement to oversee a massive direct mail exercise, which started gradually and built up into a sustained barrage of around a million letters a month in the first few months of 1987. Although the Tories had failed to make the long-term investment in direct mail that the SDP did, their eventual campaign in 1986–7 was much larger than anything their political rivals had attempted. It was primarily a communications exercise aimed at building support and winning votes rather than gathering money or members.

Altogether the party sent out eight million letters before the 1987 election.[24] The largest group mailed were the 1.4 million shareholders of recently privatised British Telecom. They were warned in menacing terms of Labour's plans for 'social ownership' of privatised utilities. Mailshots were also sent to shareholders in other newly privatised industries. These represented an excellent opportunity for the Tories – large, easily available lists of people who had a financial stake in Conservatism and were likely to support one of the party's leading policies.

Other groups who were sent specially tailored literature included young householders, members of private health schemes, people with incomes over £20 000, company directors, council house buyers, farmers, headteachers, power workers, lecturers, doctors and nurses.[25] Letters about government policy on jobs, education and training were sent to 450 000 first-time voters, but much of this was done through constituencies. The mailings included policy questionnaires (typically asking for issues to be ranked in order of importance) and provided opportunities to give money. Response levels were such that the whole operation, while intended mainly to win political support, was also financially profitable.

Labour was much slower to adopt direct mail nationally, although it did produce mailshots from 1984 when a marketing manager was appointed. On arrival Steve Bilcliffe was horrified to discover that the lists of donors to the party were recycled as scrap paper for memos, but he managed to salvage L to Z.[26] The party then gradually built up its direct mail programme, which at the national level remained largely for fundraising.

The impact of direct mail was felt in the approach to the 1987 campaign rather than during it. Following legal advice, the Conservatives and SDP both abandoned plans for persuasional mailshots to large numbers of voters in the campaign proper. They were warned that this would not be considered national campaigning, and the expenditure involved would probably have to count towards the expenses of their candidates in constituencies where letters were received. The SDP and Labour persisted in sending fundraising mail to known supporters during the campaign.

As political parties' experience of direct mail grew, they exhibited greater clarity of purpose behind mailings. After the 1987 election the parties moved further towards concentrating on fundraising rather than persuasional mail at national level. Simultaneously they encouraged constituencies to develop vote-winning mail at local level. This reflected the realisation that the law on expenses meant that direct mail during elections had to be organised locally. But it also made sense because targeting was done more effectively at the grass-roots by party workers, who could link it to canvass returns and other local campaign activities. However, the parties have done large-scale mailings organised nationally and targeted locally. In the months prior to the 1992 election both the Conservatives and Labour sent a mailshot in the name of their party leader to over a million voters, the personalisation and distribution being done locally.

## AUDIO-VISUAL RECORDINGS

The use of film for electioneering in the aftermath of the second world war was a continuation of pre-war techniques. In the mid-1920s the Conservatives had established a fleet of mobile cinema vans to show political films to outdoor crowds in daylight. Each van had a hooded viewing screen at the rear and a projector which back-projected onto the screen. The party also provided portable projectors for indoor meetings. By the 1930s film was an important element in campaigning by the Tories and their coalition allies. In the months leading up to the 1935 election they showed films to an estimated 1.5 million people.[27] Labour was much slower to adopt the idea, although by 1935 it had acquired a much smaller fleet of just two cinema vans.[28]

When the 1945 election was approaching the parties agreed with each other not to deploy films in that campaign.[29] Following the election the Conservatives re-established their film service, involving both daylight cinema vans and portable indoor projector units. By 1949 they had 18 short political films available for showing to the public (average length about 7 minutes, maximum 20 minutes) plus three instructional films for activists. (The party also distributed

entertainment features such as Laurel and Hardy to provide audiences with some relief from politics.) Several Tory
productions featured a steadfast bowler-hatted character called
Joe, who dispensed homely Conservative wisdom to other
members of his family on subjects such as inflation and
nationalisation. Others included clips of speeches from party
conference and interviews with leading Tory politicians. One
film was a documentary attacking socialism as the 'doorstep
to communism'.[30]

The point of the films was not only to convey their own
political messages, but also to attract crowds who would have
to listen to political speeches as well. They were highly valued by some local Conservative associations – one described
the film service as 'the best possible way of preaching Conservatism in a rural area'.[31] But overall the response was
less eager than before the war. In the 1950 campaign 'the
Areas were not particularly enthusiastic' about the vans and
indoor units, according to a Central Office internal report.[32]
This applied particularly to the vans in towns and cities, as
new regulations forbidding traffic obstructions impeded their
use in built-up areas.[33] The vans were sold off by the mid-
1950s. For several years the party continued to distribute
films for indoor meetings, but by the early 1960s this activity had fallen through decline into desuetude because of
growing competition from television.

Labour's cinema vans do not seem to have survived the
war,[34] but the party did produce and distribute films to local
constituencies to show on their own projectors. These included *Their Great Adventure*, a 30-minute narrative made in
1949 about the record of the Labour government.[35] In 1954
the party issued one of its earliest televised party political
broadcasts in the form of a film. Entitled *Meet the Labour
Party*, it featured a range of carefully selected ordinary party
members explaining to a potential recruit why he should
join. The image-conscious plan behind it was 'not so much
to put party arguments across . . . as to give a convincing
demonstration of the friendliness, honesty and wisdom of
the Labour people'.[36]

Enthusiasm for Labour's films fluctuated. In 1958 party
headquarters reported that 'enquiries are not very numerous and only a very limited stock of films is available'.[37] Three

years later it stated: 'interest in films has been maintained and new films have been added to the catalogue'.[38] The new additions included recent party political broadcasts and a colour documentary about the Durham Miners' Gala. The party continued to convert most of its television broadcasts into films for several years.[39] Labour carried on distributing its own films into the late 1970s.

By the early 1980s, however, due to technical developments videotape was replacing film as a more convenient medium for the recording of visual images. All three main parties have now taken to making videos, from extracts of party conferences to training materials for party workers. Early Labour videos included one issued for its 1982 campaign on unemployment[40] and another for the 1984 European elections.[41] Since then, others have included the occasional party political broadcast and cinema advertisement, and videos of major election rallies. At the 1987 general election the Conservatives had the idea of producing a video to accompany their manifesto. It featured Margaret Thatcher and several other senior ministers talking about the party's policy proposals. Two hundred copies were available for the media at the manifesto launch,[42] and it was also distributed to local associations for use at meetings.

Although it is now routine for parties to produce videos, and ordinary voters may see them at public meetings, they are mainly watched by party activists or members. Despite the fact that, unlike film, videotape can be watched inside most people's own houses, the production cost is such that no party has yet attempted mass distribution of videos.

Audio recordings were also first employed in the early part of the century. The Conservatives issued gramophone records with political messages as early as 1910.[43] However, unlike film, this never became a central part of electioneering.

The Tories resumed the use of gramophone records soon after the second world war ended. At their 1947 conference they sold records of the speech by the party chairman Lord Woolton – in fact it was a recording, prepared in advance, of him rehearsing his speech.[44] (Nowadays, conference delegates can obtain more or less instant recordings on tape of the speeches made by their party leaders.)

The Conservatives used gramophone records for direct

electioneering at the 1950 election. The party prepared a
record with a 4-minute talk from the leader Winston Churchill
on one side, plus briefer statements from Woolton and the
deputy leader Anthony Eden on the other. The messages
were aimed at voters, and the record was for playing at
meetings or from loudspeaker vans touring a constituency.
Local associations were instructed by the party's chief publicity officer not to play the records too early in the campaign 'to minimise the danger of the Socialist Party copying
this idea'.[45] The Tories also issued recordings of selected
party political broadcasts (then all on radio). Sales of the
broadcast by the 'radio doctor', Charles Hill, were described
as 'phenomenal'.[46]

For the 1951 election the party produced five records.
One repeated the Churchill/Eden/Woolton formula, while
another entitled *It's Time for a Change* consisted of 22 ordinary people explaining their support for removing Labour
in favour of the Conservatives. In 1955 the Tories stuck to
the party leader record, now simply featuring messages from
Eden (since he had succeeded Churchill) and Woolton. But
interest from constituency associations in this form of communication was declining rapidly. The leader's message record
sold 260 copies in 1950, 81 in 1951 and about 20 in 1955.[47]

The Conservatives then tried a new approach, aiming at
mass distribution rather than sales to constituencies for loudspeaker vans and meetings. In its 'Roll-Call for Victory' campaign in 1958, the party issued 250 000 recordings of a brief
message from Eden's successor as leader, Harold Macmillan.[48]
After this the Tory use of gramophone recordings of political talks declined, although in 1964 the party issued probably around 250 000 copies of a record called *Songs for
Swinging Voters*. This consisted of several satirical songs about
Labour and the Liberals, with titles such as *Nationalisation
Nightmare*. It was distributed free, partly through Young
Conservative branches.[49]

Labour also used gramophone recordings in the 1950s.
For the 1951 election it produced a record with a message
from party leader Clement Attlee. Copies were sold to 150
constituencies.[50] In 1955 another Attlee message was supplemented by recordings targeted at women and voters in
rural areas.[51]

Labour then moved into audiotape. In 1957 the party produced a tape-recorded discussion on pensions, a key issue at the time. The following year it established a service for the regular production and distribution of audiotapes.[52] The tapes consisted mainly of talks by or interviews with senior party figures on topical themes. They also included conference speeches and the occasional musical compilation, such as *Songs of the American Trade Union Movement*.[53] Generally, at least six tapes were produced annually. At times Labour's party political broadcasts on radio were also issued in this format. The regular service lasted until 1984, when it was abandoned due to falling sales.[54] Since then the party has produced occasional audiotapes including 'talking manifestos' for blind and visually impaired people, the pop song it commissioned in 1989 (*Meet the Challenge, Make the Change*) to accompany a phase of its policy review, and a version of Brahms' first symphony which was Neil Kinnock's campaign theme tune in 1987.

# 10 Local Campaigning

*It had been love at first sight . . . with the irresistible canvass-cards and the marked-up registers that could not be denied.*
Roy Hattersley, describing his boyhood initiation into electioneering in 1950[1]

*I tried a new sort of bus canvassing – getting on a bus and meeting everyone on the top and bottom decks and getting off again at the next stop. . . . It has suddenly hit me like a shaft of light that there are such public meetings criss-crossing my constituency all day just waiting to be addressed.*
Tony Benn, diary entry, 1963[2]

*Shake hands with **everybody**, slap backs (where appropriate), take hold of arms (be gentle with the elderly – their joints hurt), pat shoulders, pat babies, pat dogs, stroke cats, make funny noises to budgerigars. Pressing the flesh is essential in any politician's armoury. . . . Most of all, make eye contact: look people straight in the face, between the eyebrows, and concentrate on what they are saying. Nothing's worse than a candidate who can't hold a gaze and appears shifty. And only kiss people and babies if you are **sure** (though very old ladies like it), and not if you have a cold.*
Advice for candidates on how to 'press the flesh', published by Conservative Central Office, 1991[3]

*The local campaign is becoming an arcane irrelevance, a background noise which distracts from the decisive national campaign coming over the box. When canvassers call in the day they deposit rubbish in empty houses. At night they interrupt the election by dragging people from the TV to the door.*
Labour MP Austin Mitchell, 1987[4]

Elections are fought not only by national politicians, party managers and their publicity advisers, but also by candidates and activists in constituencies across the country. This chapter examines the development of the methods of communication with the electorate employed in local electioneering.

Local campaigns have long been regarded as sideshows to the main event taking place on the national stage. During the nineteenth century general elections shifted from being a collection of disparate local battles between individual candidates into an increasingly cohesive and homogeneous countrywide contest between national political parties. This trend was reinforced by the new mass communications methods of the twentieth century – popular newspapers, radio and, above all, television. Nevertheless, local political parties have continued to devote an enormous amount of time and effort to electioneering, involving many more people than participate at national level. And there are recent signs that the local campaign is reviving.

The extent of local electioneering varies enormously from one area to another. It is much greater in marginal constituencies. Otherwise parties are usually more active in their safe seats than hopeless ones. But it is also dependent on the numbers and calibre of local party workers and their resources.

Local campaigning faces one important legal constraint which national activity does not – limits on campaign expenditure. This dates back to the Corrupt and Illegal Practices (Prevention) Act 1883, passed in the wake of the extravagant sums laid out in the 1880 general election. Ever since then legislation has imposed tight restrictions on the level of expenses which can be incurred on behalf of any candidate. But it does not affect national campaigning, which promotes the party generally rather than particular candidates. In 1883 the cost of national electioneering was negligible. Despite the fact that it is now considerably larger than the amount disbursed locally, it is still ignored by the law.

Legislation lays down ceilings for local spending in general, local and European elections. In 1948 the maximum for general elections was set at £450 plus $1\frac{1}{2}$d per elector in borough constituencies, and £450 plus 2d per elector in county constituencies (recognising the higher cost of campaigning in rural areas). From 1969 this was increased regularly, so that in 1992 it stood at £4330 plus 3.7 pence per elector in borough seats, and £4330 plus 4.9 pence per elector in county ones. These figures mean that the vast majority of candidates faced a ceiling in the £6000–8500 range. In real terms the 1992 maxima work out at roughly half those in 1948, depending on the size of the constituency. Thus since the 1940s the real limits on spending have tightened considerably, effectively because the restrictions went unchanged from 1948 to 1969.

## DOORSTEP CANVASSING

Electoral canvassing started in the eighteenth century, largely as an exercise in corruption and intimidation. Thus did personal contact win over individual voters before the days of the secret ballot and the mass electorate. Since then canvassing has remained an important, labour-intensive feature of local electioneering, although its aims and methods have changed.

The main purpose in more recent times has not been to convert opponents, whether through bribes, threats or rational argument, but instead to identify the political affiliations of individuals so that parties can mobilise their own voters. Canvassing results are noted on the 'marked register' (which today in many constituencies is held on computer), combined with whatever information has been retained from previous years. Lists of supporters can then be prepared for polling day. These are traditionally called 'Reading pads' or 'Reading sheets' by Labour (as they were first used in a by-election at Reading) and 'Shuttleworths' by the Liberal Democrats (after a firm of printers), while the Conservatives favour the more purely descriptive term 'NCR pads' (no carbon required). On the day, tellers at polling stations collect the electoral register numbers of those who have voted. This information is passed to the local party office (the 'committee room'), and party workers are then despatched to 'knock up' or 'call up' laggardly supporters who have yet to vote.

While that is the primary purpose of canvassing, other subsidiary goals include locating electors who need postal or proxy votes, want transport to the polling station, are willing to display posters in their windows or could be won round through some further contact.

However, all this is the ideal described in party manuals. There have always been many less organised constituency parties who canvass, if at all, as a matter of ritual or simply to be seen to be seeking votes and do little with the knowledge gained.

Canvassing and knocking up operations along these lines have been regarded as essential by Conservative and Labour party headquarters throughout the period since 1945. (Except in a few constituencies and in recent elections the third party has generally lacked the number of workers necessary: its canvassing has been more limited and often done as a means of publicising itself.) In the view of Lord Woolton, the Conservative chairman from 1946 to 1955 who reformed the party's electioneering capability, 'it is necessary to have a marked register; and there is nothing more laborious – or more important – in political organisation than the preparation of this register.'[5] Party manuals ever since have warned activists that all else may be wasted if they fail to identify supporters and get them to the polls. This is despite the fact that canvass returns are far from completely accurate, due to bias or incompetence of canvassers and evasiveness or deceitfulness of canvassees.

The extent of canvassing by the two main parties has declined since the 1950s. In the 1951 election, 44 per cent of the electorate reported that their homes had been canvassed by the Conservatives, 37 per cent by Labour.[6] In 1987 the figures were 25 per cent for the Conservatives and 26 per cent for Labour.[7]

This is partly due to the fall suffered by both parties in the number of active members available to do the job. In contrast, third party canvassing has increased. In 1951 the Liberal Party was extremely weak on the ground and only managed to canvass the homes of 4 per cent of voters; in 1987 the Alliance, a much stronger electoral force, hit 20 per cent. But the drop in Tory and Labour canvassing also reflects changes which have made contemporary society less conducive to canvassing. The spread of the telephone means that unexpected callers are less common and treated as more intrusive. Now that more women work, fewer contacts can be made during the day. Increased fear of crime makes some people more reluctant to open their doors at night. And, due to television, voters are more likely to be annoyed if interrupted by the doorbell. This last point was made at least as early as 1954, when a senior Labour official was quoted as saying: 'I would certainly never send canvassers to call when *What's My Line* is on.'[8]

In the 1950s and 1960s the Conservatives used to do significantly more canvassing than Labour, but this difference has since been eroded. In the six elections from 1951 to 1970, polls reported that the Tories canvassed on average 27 per cent more voters than Labour did (their margin of superiority ranged from 9 per cent in 1964 to 55 per cent in 1970).[9] In contrast, during the 1983 and 1987 elections the numbers canvassed by the two parties were consistently found to be more or less identical.[10] (Polls during the 1992 election showed Labour to be doing slightly more canvassing than the Conservatives,[11] but this situation is complicated by the increasing use of telephone canvassing by the Tories.) The elimination of the gap has more to do with a greater decline in Conservative activity rather than an increase on the part of Labour.

In recent times canvassing has been more highly concentrated into actual election campaigns than it was during the two decades or so after the war. In that period party organisations, especially the Conservatives, encouraged their workers to update the marked register continuously so that it was as comprehensive as possible even before the campaign proper started. The Tories launched such a project in 1947 under the heading 'Operation Knocker'. The more active Conservative associations maintained extensive networks of 'district wardens' and 'street captains' to fulfil this task, modelled on the wartime air raid warden service.[12] The party complemented this system with paid full-time canvassers called 'missioners' – during 1947–57 these visited nearly 8 million households.[13] Labour also employed paid canvassers in marginals in the 1950s and 1960s, mainly students on vacation, but to nothing like the same extent. The use of paid canvassers has since ceased.

Parties still exhort their supporters to canvass outside campaign periods to build up their knowledge of the electorate and create a favourable impression in advance of elections. In 1995 Labour launched an ambitious programme in which the party aims to contact 80 per cent of voters in marginal seats. It is nationally coordinated and involves telephone canvassing via regional phonebanks to bring in help from outside the key constituencies. Pre-campaign canvassing often entails seeking more than voting intention or previous voting record: canvassers may gather views, for example, on which national and local issues are considered most important. A variety of terms are used to refer to this activity: survey canvassing, issues canvassing, questionnaire canvassing, listening canvassing, soft canvassing.

Reliable data on political affiliation for use on polling day needs to be recently collected. 'Society has changed since the 1950s, when households were Tory or Labour,' says Sir John Lacy,[14] the Conservatives' general director of party campaigning from 1988 to 1992 and a party official at local, regional or national level since 1950. 'Now there is a far greater possibility of people changing their minds. There are fewer core voters, and more tactical voters and floaters.'

For most of the past 50 years the actual process of canvassing has been remarkably unchanged, but it has evolved since the mid-1980s thanks to computerisation. Computers are ideally suited to the mundane administrative tasks of basic electioneering: printing canvass cards (instead of the manual cutting-and-pasting of photocopies of the electoral register), recording canvass data, analysing it statistically, producing envelope labels for delivery of the election address and other literature, and generating lists of those to be knocked up or driven to the polls on election day. As well as this, they make it much easier to target specific messages at selected audiences (see the section on direct mail below). Computerisation also assists organisational memory. Canvass data are more likely to be preserved from one election to the next when kept on computer rather than pieces of paper.

Some early attempts to use computers to assist with canvassing and knocking up were made by individual enthusiasts in the 1983 election. This was followed by several developments which accelerated computerisation.

First, the parties started to employ computers copiously in by-elections and to experiment with increasingly sophisticated approaches. The Conservative computer journal even attributed the Liberals' narrow victory in the 1985 Brecon and Radnor by-election to the ability of their computer program to convert an electoral register partly organised alphabetically into a geographical listing much more convenient for canvassing.[15]

Second, computerisation became much more affordable through the availability of cheaper personal computers, particularly the Amstrad IBM-compatible machine launched in 1986.

Third, the Representation of the People Act 1985 required local authorities holding the electoral register on computer to make it available in computerised form, not just as hard copy. Activists could then avoid the arduous chore of typing in tens of thousands of names and addresses. Parties still had the substantial problem of converting local authority data into a format compatible with their own electoral software and the hardware used by their constituency organisations. This remains a troublesome task, which is generally performed for local parties by their national computer experts. The charges levied to constituencies for this operation throw an interesting sidelight on local party finance. In 1994 Labour normally charged £135 for an initial register conversion, the Liberal Democrats around £140, and the Conservatives the somewhat larger sum of £323.[1]

Fourth, computer enthusiasts within each party have developed electoral software dedicated to assisting electioneering. Labour's is called Elpack, sometimes nicknamed 'Hellpack' in those constituencies which find modern technology difficult to cope with. The first program used within the SDP/Liberal Alliance was called Polly, but amid some acrimony the large majority of computerised Liberal Democrat constituencies have since opted for a rival package, EARS (Election Agent's Record System). Advocates of EARS now like to describe Polly as 'a dead parrot'. Conservative associations could also choose between two competing programs, Fileplan and Consort Register, but from 1994 Central Office has recommended a new, more advanced piece of software, BlueChip, which integrates membership administration and campaigning, and is designed to work within Windows.

Over the years the packages have become much more sophisticated. Numerous revisions have added additional features and eliminated bugs. The initial version of Elpack, for example, was so basic it had no provision for noting telephone numbers or carrying over previous canvass data. One new feature of version 4, issued in 1995, is that it can hold information about addresses even if there is no occupant on the electoral register. This facilitates voter registration drives. Software development represents a more direct form of competition between the parties than any other electioneering technique.

Fifth, although much of the impetus has come from technically minded local activists, the parties centrally have also put a great deal of effort into promoting local computerisation (particularly in target seats) through advice, training and other backup. In all parties, however, plenty of constituencies have remained resolutely technophobic.

By the time of the 1987 election a significant minority of constituencies in all parties used computerised versions of the electoral register: this applied to around 90 Conservative associations, 50–60 Labour parties and 80 Alliance campaigns.[17] In 1992 the comparable figures were approaching 400 for the Conservatives, around 320 for Labour and 180 for the Liberal Democrats.[18] However, in both elections the expertise of those using them was often insufficient for anything approaching their full potential to be exploited.

As a result of computerisation the parties have started to collect more detailed canvassing information. In the past, canvass cards for all three parties often provided for just three categories of voters: 'For', 'Against' and 'Doubtful'. Now they tend to have several headings, dividing the againsts into different parties, and often noting second party preference and distinguishing according to strength of party allegiance or between classifications like 'probable' and 'undecided'. The parties have experimented with numerous variants, particularly in by-elections since the mid-1980s. In some cases canvassers are also now more likely to be encouraged to note down additional information, such as sex, housing tenure, approximate age and concerns about particular issues. The use of computers makes it easier to store this level of detail and also for well-resourced campaigns to exploit it, particularly through targeted direct mail.

## TELEPHONE CANVASSING

The use of the telephone for voter contact is not a new idea. As early as the 1920s, when the proportion of households with phones was still small, one Conservative association in south London phoned as many known supporters as possible to knock them up on polling day.[19] But despite the advantages which the telephone offers for canvassing and getting out the vote, its application remained extremely rare until the mid-1980s. This reflected deep-seated British cultural attitudes towards the phone, particularly an aversion to unsolicited calls.

Widespread telephone canvassing started during by-elections in the 1983–7 Parliament. By this time about four out of five households had phones, and cold calling by commercial companies was increasingly familiar and accepted. By-elections had also become major national political events into which the parties put all the effort they could muster.

Since then all three parties have greatly expanded their telephone work, due to its numerous advantages. Telephone canvassing is much quicker. It reaches parts of the electorate that doorstep canvassing does not, such as voters (disproportionately old and female) who are reluctant to answer the door at night, residents in blocks of flats with entryphones, and dispersed households in rural areas. It is also unaffected by the weather and utilises party workers such as the elderly or infirm who will not go out on the doorsteps. On top of this, it facilitates long-distance help: activists in safe seats can easily assist their colleagues in marginals, while phonebanks in national or regional party headquarters may also be used.

In the opinion of some, but not all, it has one additional advantage – accuracy. Opponents may be less embarrassed to confess their opposition on the telephone than during a face-to-face encounter on the doorstep. 'People are more truthful on the telephone as they are talking to a blank face,' says Sir John Lacy,[20] the former Tory director of party campaigning. A similar view is expressed in Labour guidance[21] to its activists: 'Doorstep canvassing is often intimidating to electors. They tell canvassers the information they think they want to hear, either to get rid of them or "to please". Because the telephone is more impersonal there is less of an obligation to please.'

But telephone canvassing and knocking up also have a downside. Some voters find it unpleasantly intrusive and, unlike doorstep canvassing, it cannot be combined with the distribution of posters or literature. Around 25 per cent of telephone subscribers are ex-directory, and this proportion is increasing. They may be irritated if their numbers are discovered by other means. Ten per cent of households are still not on the phone at all.

More importantly, telephone calls cost money. Telephone work done during an election should therefore feature in expenses returns, and extensive phoning could lead to breaches of the limits (individuals can spend up to £5 of their own money without it counting towards expenses, but only provided there is no collusion with others). On the other hand, the law is difficult to police when calls are made from individuals' homes rather than organised phonebanks. Campaigning guidance issued by the Association of Liberal Democrat Councillors states:[22] 'Telephone costs are difficult to quantify. Most activists waive the cost – but obviously something has to go down on election expenses.' This situation provides parties with temptation. It is noticeable that discussion of this topic often seems to make party organisers nervous.

The Conservatives have led the field in the use of the telephone to communicate with voters. The party has generally been quicker to adopt commercial marketing methods and is better able to meet the costs. Voters not on the phone are comparatively unlikely to be Tories, so missing them out is of little importance. And armchair activism suits a party whose members have an average age of 62.[23]

In 1987 Central Office advised target seats to do telephone canvassing in the last week of campaign.[24] In 1992 safe Tory seats were encouraged to assist marginals with phone work in the run-up to and during the election. Party workers in one well-organised safe seat near London made 8000 long-distance calls to voters in a northern marginal.[25] In the campaign some telephone canvassing was carried out by the Tories in around 54 per cent of seats (for Labour the figure was 38 per cent).[26] To the other parties this represented a kind of invisible campaign by the Conservatives. 'At the last election there was a feeling that the Tories weren't out and about,' says Joyce Gould,[27] then Labour's director of organisation. 'They have gradually removed themselves from the street, not putting up posters, not wearing rosettes, and so on. Instead they do a great deal of telephone work.' Since 1992 Labour has gone to great lengths to encourage its party workers to do more telephone canvassing.

The telephone has now become a recognised tool of political communication. All parties are exploiting it more and more, not only for canvassing and getting out the vote, but also for fundraising, membership recruitment and retention, survey canvassing and other activities which are performed outside election periods and thus avoid expenses problems. And the phone is used particularly heavily during by-elections, in which much greater expenditure has been allowed since 1989. But because of its drawbacks it is still only a complement to and not a replacement for doorstep work.

## LITERATURE AND DIRECT MAIL

The main element of party propaganda at local level has been the printed word. Literature in its various forms usually accounts for the majority of constituency campaign spending. Although important for all three parties, printed material has been particularly critical for the third party. Often unable to supply the number of workers required for extensive canvassing, it has made a greater priority of the quicker task of delivering literature.[28]

Traditionally, the most important leaflet has been the election address, a prominent feature of local electioneering since the nineteenth century. This has represented a kind of personal manifesto from the candidate, with greater authority than other circulars. Until recently nearly all candidates from the main parties have produced one particular item of literature as their election address. They have generally used their freepost facility to distribute it – since before the war every parliamentary candidate has had the right to use the Post Office for one free delivery to each elector. This right was also given to European election

candidates when direct elections to the European Parliament
began in 1979. (For many years much time of party workers
was devoted to the laborious procedure of addressing the
envelopes required, until the gradual spread of computerisation and also the Post Office concession from 1987 that it
would deliver one leaflet to each household – though not
each elector – even if unaddressed.) So the leaflet selected
for this often has a much wider distribution than other
materials which the local party must deliver itself.

The format of election addresses has changed surprisingly
little over the years. Their size is constrained to suit the
convenience of the Post Office, but the content has been
just as familiar from one election to the next. As well as
summaries of national policy, the most common elements
have remained a personal message from the candidate, combined with biographical details and photograph(s). The pictures often include spouse, children and pets.

The parties have tended to treat the candidate's family as
their main weapon to help create a sympathetic human image
for their standard-bearer. The SDP's advice on the production of election addresses stated:[29] 'Select the facts most likely
to appeal to electors in the constituency: whether the candidate is married or not, whether he has any children, etc.'
The use of family photographs was well established by the
1950s – in 1959 they appeared in 45 per cent of Conservative addresses and 29 per cent of Labour ones. In their study
of the 1959 election David Butler and Richard Rose also
related that Labour candidates liked to be photographed
with pipes, whereas Tories and Liberals preferred to be seen
in the company of dogs.[30]

The much ridiculed 'wife's message' is declining but has
still been remarkably persistent ('husband's messages' for
women candidates have always been rare). In 1964 one in
three addresses carried this spousal endorsement of her
partner.[31] In 1987 the proportions were down to 7 per cent
for the Tories and 6 per cent for Labour.[32]

In recent years, however, the value of the ritualised election address as a distinct form to other publicity material
has been increasingly questioned. So too has the traditional[33]
exemplary schedule for constituency leafleting – an initial
circular introducing the candidate, followed by the election

address and then a final message in the last week. With the help of computers it is now easy to use the Post Office free-post, the customary delivery mechanism for the election address, to send different individually addressed mailings to different electors in the same household. Parties are also devoting more effort to other literature, such as direct mail, newsletters, leaflets in minority languages and 'Good morning' flyers delivered early on polling day. In 1992 David Butler and Dennis Kavanagh reported that in many cases it would be arbitrary to single out a specific leaflet as the election address.[34] 'Election addresses are going out of fashion,' says Sir John Lacy.[35] 'The older candidates still feel that they must do one, but their days are numbered.'

The greater variety of printed propaganda has been fostered by technological change which made producing such material simpler and quicker. The expansion of offset litho printing around the 1970s in place of letterpress facilitated the use of straightforwardly prepared do-it-yourself artwork. Since the mid-1980s the design of publications has been assisted by desktop publishing software. This has made it much easier for more advanced constituencies to produce their own high-quality literature.

These developments have been reflected in the illustrations services provided by national parties for constituencies – diagrams, cartoons, photographs, slogans and logos, issued for incorporation into local material. The original motive was to help enliven local literature and make it more readable, although more recently the parties became equally concerned about ensuring that the visual style of local campaigning fitted with that at the national level. These illustrations were originally produced in the form of 'stereos' – blocks for letterpress printing – but then switched to 'clipsheets' for cutting-and-pasting into offset litho artwork. Now all three main parties have graphics, layouts and fonts available on computer disk or bulletin boards for desktop publishing.

Local newsletters and newspapers in particular have become increasingly popular forms of party propaganda. Parties believe them to be a good means of communication because voters are used to treating this format as authoritative and to assimilating information in this way. Regular newsletters help to build up the relationship between party and electorate in advance of elections. Although they were particularly favoured by Labour before the war and in its aftermath, their main post-war development was due to the Liberals.

In the early 1960s, Liberals in parts of Liverpool started to produce regular newsletters outside election periods. The title *Focus*, which was to become virtually standard across the country, was first used in 1962.[36] These newsletters were an integral part of 'community politics', the vigorous activism on bread-and-butter local issues pioneered in the city by Liberal campaigners Cyril Carr and Trevor Jones (later nicknamed 'Jones the Vote' for his by-election winning exploits). The theory of community politics was to identify grass-roots grievances, campaign about them aggressively and tell the voters what was happening. This implied avoiding conventional electioneering literature in favour of regular, hard-hitting, snappy newsletters with campaign reports.

This approach to communication spread across the Liberal Party in the 1970s, strongly pushed by the Association of Liberal Councillors (ALC) and its dedicated organising secretary, Tony Greaves. Newsletters entitled *Focus* became a common feature of Liberal activity, although in practice they varied enormously in the extent to which they followed the philosophy of community politics.

ALC advice emphasised keeping the articles short, including plenty of cartoons, action photos of the prospective candidate and large headlines, and minimising white space. While this prevented large, forbidding slabs of text accompanied by boring mugshots of the candidate, it also meant the newsletters were generally cluttered and untidy in appearance. But the better ones were lively, topical and punchy, clearly demonstrating how the newsletter format could be much more readable and interesting than traditional political party literature. In many areas these newsletters constituted the main form of local communication between the party and the electorate. Numerous local Liberal parties acquired cheap offset litho machines to print them themselves.

Community politics was derided by opponents as concerned only with trivial grumbles. But it proved effective in winning council seats for the Liberals, particularly in decaying

inner cities where residents had much to grumble about
and the local Labour Party was complacent or moribund.
The strategy also helped the party score some notable by-
election victories from 1969 on. But it encountered difficulties in the early 1980s following the Liberal partnership with
the newly formed SDP, whose emphasis on professionalism
and centralisation was ill-suited to this kind of guerilla politics.

The disparity of approach was evident from Alliance publicity material in by-elections. A Liberal candidate was usually promoted by cheap literature about local issues; an SDP
candidate by glossy literature about national ones. 'We had
a much tidier presentational style,' says Alec McGivan,[37] then
the SDP's national organiser. 'The Liberal view was that, as
long as you kept churning out more and more leaflets, it
didn't matter what they looked like.' In fact, the culture
clash went further than styles of literature. McGivan adds:
'The Liberals thought we were too cautious about legal
niceties.'

Since the Liberal Democrats were formed after the 1987
election the name *Focus* has lived on, featuring on the mast-
head of many local party newsletters and being particularly
conspicuous in by-election literature.

The success of the *Focus* concept was such that in the
early 1980s the idea was directly copied by the Conservatives, who urged their associations to produce regular newsletters entitled *In Touch*. These shared the emphasis on brief
news items about local issues, but tended to concentrate
more blatantly on publicising the names and activities of
MPs, councillors and prospective candidates, than did some
community action-oriented Liberal versions. The Tories even
followed the Liberal policy of giving as the name of a newsletter's 'editor' that of the local prospective candidate, to
boost his/her name recognition in advance of the election.

Labour has never borrowed the *Focus* concept wholesale
in the way the Tories did. It was led into giving its constituencies much more encouragement to publish newsletters,
but it rejected the standardised national conception employed
by the other parties on the basis that this undermined local
credentials. Nevertheless the party clearly felt it could learn
from *Focus*: the content of some lengthy Labour guidance
in the mid-1980s about producing local newsletters bore a

detailed and striking resemblance to advice previously issued by the Liberals.[38]

Since the mid-1980s there has been a move towards parties producing local four-page tabloid newspapers. The idea was pioneered by the SDP, particularly in its target seats in the run-up to the 1987 election. It has since been adopted by other parties, especially in by-elections. While newsletters usually relate to a ward, tabloid papers generally cover an entire constituency or council. This format has become more cost-effective in printing terms, encourages a chattier and more accessible tone of communication, and exploits the familiarity and credibility of an accepted medium. Such party newspapers often resemble local freesheets. Parties can even ape newspaper style by having 'editorials', 'guest columns', 'advertisements' for party meetings, and articles 'by our political correspondent'.

But the most important change in local election literature has been the rapid growth since the mid-1980s in direct mail. Computers have made it simple for parties to send a specific message to selected electors, generally in the form of a personalised letter (posted or hand-delivered as resources and expenses limits allow).

Targeted direct mail is not new, but existed even when the selection of recipients and addressing of envelopes was a cumbersome manual process. Its most common forms were probably letters to supporters and doubtfuls as indicated by the canvass, to young people attaining voting age (21 until 1970, then 18) who were easily identifiable from the electoral register after 1951,[39] and to residents in particular areas. Some local parties devoted considerable effort to such exercises.

There were also numerous instances of more specific mailings, at least in the better organised and more energetic seats. In 1955 the Tories in a Manchester constituency systematically sent relevant literature to Jews, long-term hospital patients and people recently rehoused from slums.[40] In 1964 in Barons Court, west London, Labour sent letters to 500 nurses and to 2500 tenants who would benefit from the party's plans for rent control.[41] In the same election the Liberal candidate in Finchley wrote to Labour supporters to persuade them to vote tactically for him to beat the Tory (which in this case was Margaret Thatcher).[42]

So the principle is longstanding, but what has been transformed is the ease and sophistication with which such targeting can be done. Computers were initially used for direct mail, as for canvassing, on a limited basis by a few local pioneers in the 1983 election. The next key developments happened in by-elections during the 1983–7 parliament. The trail was blazed by the Liberals, who in 1985 sent a variety of personalised mailshots to certain groups of electors, notably farmers, in the rural seat of Brecon and Radnor. The party elaborated its tactics the following year, squeezing the Labour vote in Liberal–Tory battles and creating more complex software which could for example automatically select addresses with the word 'Farm' in.

Labour and the Conservatives also adopted the technique in by-elections in 1986. Labour started with the Fulham contest, when it not only mailed the elderly about pensions and teachers about education, but sent letters to first-time voters in the name of pop stars. Targeting was extremely crude in these early stages – the party also sent a letter to all the women in the constituency. The SDP were enthusiastic direct mailers in by-elections when they supplied the Alliance candidate, being particularly keen (in line with advice from US political consultants) on writing to perceived opinion formers such as doctors, headteachers, vicars, publicans and owners of takeaway food restaurants. 'We go for people that are known to talk to people and can have an influence,' explained Alec McGivan.[43] 'If we could get a list of taxi drivers we'd undoubtedly write to them.'

Since the mid-1980s local direct mail has become increasingly widespread and sophisticated. In the 1987 election Labour direct mail often consisted of standard, pre-printed letters with merely the name and address added by computer.[44] But by 1992 all three parties ensured that the vast majority of their target seats had proper computerised direct mail capability. In addition, they provided a variety of sample letters and detailed advice based on the experience of the commercial direct mail industry, such as the importance of the 'PS' and the need to avoid cheap brown envelopes which look like they contain bills. The increased speed and reliability of computer printers has also boosted the number of letters which one constituency can manage to produce.

It is now easy for well-run local parties to target messages to different groups of voters according to any combination of data they have recorded about them. So voters may be sent mailshots particularly relevant to their age, housing tenure, sex, size of household, occupation, neighbourhood, interest in particular issues, party affiliation and its strength, or likelihood to vote tactically. Thus council tenants get mailings on the right to buy, owner-occupiers receive letters about mortgages, and so on.

Some of these attributes can be inferred from the electoral register. Electoral software can even identify characteristic ethnic minority surnames and produce letters in the appropriate language. Other information is available from public sources or commercially. But much also comes from more detailed canvassing, signatures on petitions, responses to surveys and previous contact with the MP/candidate/party.

The Conservatives have gone furthest in systematically trying to collect data on political views. Before the 1992 election over 100 Tory associations circulated questionnaires to selected voters asking them to rank in importance various national and local political issues.[45] As well as helping to target mailings, this kind of exercise informs campaigning and strengthens the local party's relationship with the electorate.

## THE MEDIA AND ADVERTISING

Influencing the local media is now treated as a much more central part of campaigning than it used to be. Many constituency organisers adopt a more proactive and sometimes imaginative approach to this task than their predecessors did twenty or more years ago. They also receive greater support from national and regional officials. Media work matters particularly outside election periods when other party communication activity is reduced. However, this does depend partly on the locality. The reach and importance of the local media vary enormously from one constituency to another.

In 1972 the material on 'press publicity' in Labour's detailed manual for local parties on electioneering merited less than a full page, a small proportion of the space given to how to organise public meetings. The section on running a 'propaganda week' with special events, meetings, leafleting, and so on, contained no suggestion of informing the local press.[46] Today advice on using the media – from developing contacts to organising an effective stunt – is one of the main elements in the guidance for constituencies issued by all three parties.[47]

There have always been some flamboyant campaigners who have favoured publicity-seeking gimmicks, such as touring the constituency by horse and cart. But for most candidates their media strategy used to consist largely of seeking to ensure – or just hoping – that their public meetings were adequately reported.

Now the more energetic local parties can manage a barrage of press releases, photocalls, press conferences and letters to the editor, even before the campaign proper starts. In the run-up to the 1992 election one Labour candidate in a marginal seat had issued 178 press releases by the time polling day was announced.[48] An analysis of media campaigning by local parties in west Yorkshire found that among Labour agents the traditionalist view that press coverage was unimportant and difficult to influence had been eliminated between 1987 and 1992.[49] Constituencies now use visiting frontbenchers not, as in the past, to address a public meeting, but instead to utter a soundbite and pose for a photo opportunity.

This reflects not only the decline in the public meeting (see below) but also a change in reporting styles. Local newspapers are now less concerned with formal events, and prefer shorter, punchy reports and pictures rather than lengthy, verbatim accounts of speeches. Furthermore, freesheets which have expanded enormously since 1970 at the expense of paid-for weeklies have fewer journalists and are more dependent on outside news sources. As a result, the extent of party coverage is more reliant on forceful and opportunistic publicity gathering by media-conscious candidates and activists.

The tremendous growth in local radio has also presented new openings (not least the airtime filling phone-in). The first BBC local radio station began broadcasting in 1967, the first commercial one in 1973. They spread rapidly across the country so that by the time of the 1992 election there were 39 BBC stations and over 100 commercial ones, nearly all broadcasting at least some local news. Together with the increase in current affairs shows on regional television, it means that candidates today are much more likely to do broadcast interviews than they were two or more decades ago. Parties now provide advice and training for this, which was previously unnecessary.

While local parties have become more zealous in seeking free publicity in the media, they have also become less prepared to pay for it. Extensive election ad campaigns have been impossible due to the limits on campaign spending, but limited advertising has been feasible. In the past, press advertisements were often a key means of publicising public meetings, and ads making political points were also not uncommon. The parties' headquarters designed and circulated standard advertisements for their constituencies to insert in the local press, both before and during the campaign. In the February 1974 election, every Scottish weekly paper carried some party political advertising, most containing 'a significant volume'. The most frequent elements were slogans, details of meetings, party symbols and photographs of candidates. Others included reporting of favourable canvass returns, reprinted extracts from speeches, celebrity endorsements, appeals for help with the campaign or attacks on rival candidates.[50] However, as national party advertising during the campaign has become accepted since 1974, local ads have been declining. In 1992 fewer than half the local papers in west Yorkshire featured party ads.[51]

Much the same applies to poster advertising. Until the mid-1970s the better resourced local parties, usually Conservative, often paid for posters on commercial hoardings. Sometimes when an election was called and national advertising was terminated, they took over sites which had been part of a national campaign – the posters frequently had space for the local candidate's name to be added. Local Conservative associations occupied 10 500 poster sites in 1950, 5800 in 1951, and 4500 in 1955.[52] But since national billboard advertising has continued during elections without counting towards candidates' expenses, constituencies have been reluctant to spend their own money on this form of activity. (Local parties have, of course, continued with displaying posters at free locations, such as window bills and poster boards on stakes in gardens and fields. But due to the Town and Country Planning Act 1947, which tightened up the law on flyposting, in most areas there is nothing like the pre-war clutter when posters were plastered on everything, including trees, fences, walls, lamp-posts and letter boxes.)

## PUBLIC MEETINGS

Public meetings have declined in importance not only at the national level (see Chapter 5) but also at the constituency level. Local meetings were still an integral feature of electioneering in the 1950s. From their adoption meeting to their eve-of-poll rally, candidates would tour schoolrooms, municipal halls and factory canteens to be heard and questioned by voters. They would also speak in the open air, standing on their soapboxes in market squares or at street corners. Today all this is a much less frequent and largely irrelevant activity.

Local parties have gradually abandoned public meetings given persistently declining audiences, even for visiting national figures. Fewer and fewer politicians have been able to draw decent crowds, while ordinary candidates have often found themselves speaking to a mere handful, and sometimes no one. The proportion of the electorate claiming to have listened to a candidate at an indoor meeting during the campaign has fallen dramatically: from 24 per cent in 1951 and 18 per cent in 1959 to 8 per cent in 1964 and 5 per cent in 1970.[53] Since then it has remained low – the 1992 figure was 4 per cent.[54]

Parties are aware that there is little point in preaching to a few committed supporters who should instead be out on the doorsteps doing something useful. According to Labour's campaign handbook,[55] 'Holding public meetings or rallies that just attract the party faithful is not a sensible use of resources. Even with a star speaker you can probably get better value by taking them out to meet people.'

In the 1950s candidates usually had extensive meeting programmes, many speaking at least once a night.[56] In 1970 Labour and Conservative local parties each held an average of eight meetings during the campaign, while for the Liberals the figure was six.[57] By 1992, Labour and the Liberal Democrats were down to two, the Tories to four.[58] Similarly, the proportion of local campaign expenditure devoted to meetings has fallen consistently since 1950, from 6 per cent then to 1 per cent in 1992.[59]

The disappearance of public meetings has been more marked in urban than rural areas, where canvassing tends to be impractical and it has been customary for candidates to address a meeting in each town or village. After the 1970 election the Conservative director of organisation reported internally that meetings 'can be cut down in urban areas, but there is a always a strong plea in country areas for villages to be visited.'[60] In some places this tradition lingers on.[61]

The continuous decline of the public meeting was interrupted by one blip – the original intense enthusiasm surrounding the SDP in 1981–2. The new party's meetings were often packed to overflowing, sometimes with four-figure audiences, notably but not only during by-election campaigns. Roy Jenkins claimed that his drawing power as SDP leader was several times what it had been as chancellor of the exchequer 12 years previously, and described the SDP as 'a party of public meetings'.[62] This revitalisation of a dwindling means of campaigning was not to last, and no party has since succeeded in reproducing the spirit that can make such large numbers of people want to listen to political speeches.

As the public meeting has waned so too has the art of heckling. In the past parties not only held their own meetings but also sought to make their presence felt at those of their opponents. The press often complained that things were going too far. In 1950 one report stated that 'Heckling is going beyond all reason in this election', and that 'continual barracking of speakers at political meetings' was being organised 'all over the country'.[63]

Acute and well-timed heckles would embarrass the speaker in front of the audience and often merit inclusion in newspaper stories. For candidates the jousting with hecklers was frequently as important as their formal speech. Parties were generally reluctant to be seen to be organising heckling, but undoubtedly did so. In the late 1940s, Tory agents were asked to supply the names of hecklers to party headquarters so that they could be briefed with the most effective points to make at Labour meetings.[64] In 1966 the Conservative chief organisation officer advised in an internal memo that 'Irresponsible heckling at our opponents' meetings can do us much more harm than good. . . . To be effective, there should be a corps of really intelligent hecklers to go with prepared questions and a prepared plan of campaign.'[65] Today, however, heckling is rare, and if it occurs would probably be treated with great hostility rather than as part of the game.

## OTHER MEANS OF VOTER CONTACT

Local parties have used a wide variety of other methods to communicate with voters.

The walkabout developed in the 1970s. Before this candidates had, of course, worked crowds in shopping centres and marketplaces, but it was only after Harold Wilson introduced the tactic as part of his national tour in the 1970 election that it became a distinct and recognised aspect of campaigning which ought to be properly planned. Wilson and his assistant, Marcia Williams, were inspired by the success of the Queen's novel walkabouts on her trip to Australia and New Zealand in 1969. They decided to copy the technique for Wilson's local visits. The resulting sympathetic television coverage of Wilson mingling easily with appreciative crowds impressed Conservative strategists, and later in the 1970 campaign the idea was also taken up by Edward Heath.

Since the 1970s local parties have organised walkabouts for their own candidates and for visiting celebrities, often accompanied by the media. In the words of Roy Jenkins, the object is 'to shake as many hands and engage in a snatch of direct conversation with as many people as possible'.[66] If it is well managed, party workers ensure the media do not get in the way and carefully marshal the public to maximise the number of voters processed. The effervescent Conservative

MP Edwina Currie states that her 'usual contact rate is about 200 people an hour'.[67]

There are also traditional forms of electioneering which have been employed throughout the post-war period. Visits to old people's homes, clubs, religious groups, community centres, workplaces and anywhere else where a number of voters may be gathered together are and have been an extensive part of any serious candidate's programme of action.

'House meetings' or 'cottage meetings' – informal gatherings of friends and neighbours in someone's house to talk to the candidate – were common in the 1950s[68] and have continued since. Such events need to be friendlier affairs than orthodox public meetings. Labour's guidance in the 1970s advised that the speaker must talk 'to the little gathering in a pleasant, homely way'.[69] Today Labour regards house meetings as a good way to meet those generally at home during the day, such as women with small children and pensioners. The Conservatives also describe these forums as 'increasingly popular'.[70]

Loudspeaker cars have been a feature of electioneering since the 1920s. Usually plastered with posters, they can tour the constituency blaring slogans, advertising meetings or events, drawing attention to a mass canvass, playing recorded messages from party leaders or allowing the candidate to address a captive if changing audience. These mobile propaganda tools were a highly conspicuous aspect of early post-war campaigns. In 1945 they were described as 'one of the great public nuisances of election time'.[71] The Nuffield study of the 1950 election claimed that 'No constituency organisation, however modest, would think nowadays of fighting an election without one.'[72]

Loudspeakering is now not as prominent as it used to be. Although an easy way to get noticed by large numbers of voters, it is unsuitable for all but the briefest messages and may be irritating and therefore counter-productive. It has also been restricted by legislation and local by-laws intended to combat noise pollution. Nevertheless, some candidates still devote much time to loudspeaker tours during the campaign. In 1992 the large majority of constituencies in all three parties used them to help get out the vote on polling day.[73]

## CONCLUSION

In the period since 1945, local electioneering has changed and developed much less than its national counterpart. While the national campaign has been completely transformed, the local electoral battle of today would not be that unfamiliar to a candidate from the 1950s. Methods of voter contact such as doorstep canvassing, the election address, leaflet delivery, mobile loudspeakering and visits to community groups still have much in common with forty or fifty years ago.

The comparative continuity in local campaigning is due to a number of factors. First, by far the most important post-war development in communications – the spread of television – has affected national rather than local activity. (However, the current growth of local cable TV should have implications for constituency campaigning in future.)

Second, the law on expenses has obstructed local developments which would cost money, for example in terms of the quantity and quality of printed literature and wider use of advertising, polling and telephone canvassing. Most active local parties in marginal seats – the ones most likely to innovate – already spend close to the maximum.

Third, despite numerous exceptions, local electioneering has generally not possessed an innovatory ethos. Party workers have tended to be creatures of habit and ritual, largely concerned about procedure and organisation. This traditionalist culture was illustrated by a survey after the 1966 election. Around 100 MPs and candidates were asked if there had been any innovations in their campaign. Almost all said none. Those novelties that were reported were hardly momentous – 'the use of hats and balloons with the candidate's name' or 'a candidate's promenade across the main shopping centres escorted by Young Conservatives with large badges'.[74]

However, although changes are small compared to the national scene, there have been some important developments at local level. Some traditional aspects have declined in importance – particularly the public meeting, but also doorstep canvassing and the formal election address. Other methods have grown – direct mail, local newsletters, telephone canvassing, walkabouts and using the media. And some longstanding activities are being modernised, such as doorstep canvassing due to computerisation.

But as well as these developments in particular methods of voter contact, the overall strategic approach of parties has altered too. The buzzword in local electioneering today is targeting. Parties have always targeted, if crudely, for example by canvassing their strong areas more thoroughly than weak areas and by producing special appeals to women. But all three parties are now generally better organised in the targeting of their campaign than they used to be, resulting in more efficient and effective use of resources. In the electoral shooting range the rifle is slowly replacing the blunderbuss. This has a lot to do with computerisation, which makes it easier to print out lists of electors in specific categories for particular communications and to store data from campaign to campaign, for example on which electors are consistent opponents or non-voters. But targeting applies to other sides of campaigning as well, such as leafleting, visits and meetings with community groups.

Targeting has two aspects. The first is concentrating the campaign on certain parts of the electorate and disregarding others. The Conservatives in particular have tried harder in the last 15 years to focus their canvassing, leaflet delivery and other efforts on their actual and potential supporters and ignore definite opponents.[75] The second is communicating different messages to different parts of the electorate. Labour, for example, in 1991 identified its primary target groups for specifically tailored messages as women, pensioners, young people, ethnic minorities and students. Secondary groups included trade unionists, parents, council tenants, private tenants, council house buyers and opinion formers.[76]

Local targeting in this way of specific electoral groups has also been accompanied by greater national targeting of resources into marginal constituencies. The parties have always paid more attention to supporting campaigning in marginals, but over the years this has become more extensive and systematic. Now it may involve regular monitoring of their strengths and weaknesses, a flow of advice and information, special training programmes for officers and candidates, extra visits from frontbench politicians, financial assistance (for example, to purchase computers) and the supply of free campaign materials. There has also been greater national coordination of the arrangements through which safe seats help out marginal ones, a process known as 'mutual aid' by the Conservatives and 'twinning' by Labour. And the assessment by party headquarters of the marginality of seats has become more sophisticated, increasingly reflecting detailed local factors and demographic changes as well as vulnerability to national swing.

Since 1950 the local campaign has generally declined. This is illustrated by the level of spending by local parties (the main component of which is for printed material). In 1950 the average expenditure for a Conservative candidate was 93 per cent of the legal maximum and for a Labour candidate 83 per cent.[77] In 1992 the figures were down to 80 per cent for the Conservatives and 71 per cent for Labour[78] – despite the fact that in real terms the 1992 maxima were about half the 1950 rate. (The averages do disguise significant variation, such as high spending in marginals.)

This drop has occurred in two stages. From 1950 to 1966 the average proportion spent out of the legal maximum possible remained roughly constant. So spending fell in real terms, because the maximum was unchanged. From 1970 to 1992 the proportion of the maximum spent has been significantly lower than in 1950–66, but spending has stayed much the same in real terms because the maximum has been regularly increased.[79] This analysis applies both to the Tories and Labour. (Third party spending cannot be assessed in this way because average spending per candidate depends on whether the party puts up a full slate of low-spending candidates in hopeless seats, which the Liberals did not always do.)

Compared to the 1950s the two main parties now have fewer members to do the work and fewer full-time agents to organise them. In 1959 the Conservatives had 506 qualified full-time agents in local constituencies, but by 1992 this had dropped to 299.[80] The number of Labour full-time agents in place fell from 296 in 1951[81] to 68 in 1987.[82]

In 1952 the Conservative Party claimed a total of 2.8 million members, falling to 2.2 million in 1958.[83] In the 1970s and 1980s most estimates suggested around 1.5 million.[84] A study in 1991 indicated a figure of around 750 000,[85] while in 1993 the party chairman Sir Norman Fowler talked of 'half a million-plus'.[86] In 1994 the level was put by one researcher at 'probably below half a million'.[87] Exact figures are not available because membership is administered locally by the party's autonomous constituency associations rather than nationally by Central Office.

Labour's (individual as distinct from union-affiliated) membership also peaked in the 1950s. In 1952 the party reported a membership of just over one million. Official figures for the 1960s and 1970s are not reliable. In 1981 the level stood at 280 000, and it then fluctuated in the 260–330 000 range. Since 1994 membership has risen remarkably rapidly, boosted by the party's popularity under Tony Blair, a more efficient national processing system and reduced rates for some trade unionists. At the end of 1995 it stood at 365 000.[88]

The long-term reduction in party membership reflects a variety of social as well as political trends. These include the growth in television viewing and other leisure activities, the spread in non-party forms of political and voluntary activity, the emphasis the parties have themselves placed on national rather than local electioneering, the decline in staunch political partisanship, and a widespread general dissatisfaction with politics and politicians. The Conservatives in particular have also been affected by the much higher proportion of middle-class women who now work and thus have less disposable time.

But despite the falls in spending, agents and members, and the decline in forms of activity like canvassing and public meetings, there have been other factors (especially in recent years) which in contrast have promoted local campaigning. Often these have not required large numbers of members to exploit them.

In the late 1960s and 1970s positive factors included the Liberal development of community politics and campaigning newsletters, the availability of cheap and quick offset litho printing, and the increases in expenses limits.

However, it was in the 1980s that more significant advances in local electioneering started to occur: computerisation, direct mail, desktop publishing, telephone canvassing, growing media awareness. By-elections played an important role in piloting and refining many techniques involved, as the parties nationally devoted much more effort to these than in the past. In fact, by-elections were events of such national political importance and contested so fiercely that gross overspending undoubtedly occurred. In 1989 the law was changed to allow by-election campaign expenses to be four times those in general election constituency campaigns.

Initially, these modern methods were used in a small minority of constituencies. The parties have since tried to ensure that they are at least employed in all marginal seats. They have spread rapidly during the 1990s, but there are still many local parties which they have yet to reach.

The most important development is computerisation. (This can assist the more technically minded local parties not only with the electioneering work already described, but with all sorts of other activities: post-election statistical analysis of voting patterns, casework management, membership administration and speedy communication via email with national headquarters, as well as word processing and accounts.) An internal report on the 1992 election by Sir John Lacy, Conservative general director of party campaigning, commented: 'The computer operation . . . is the basis upon which all future campaigns will be built.'[89]

Until the 1980s the electioneering manuals issued by party headquarters were a symptom of the unchanging nature of local campaigning. These hardly altered from one edition to the next. The new methods of the 1980s meant their content was radically revised. The overall approach changed too. Previous handbooks tended to be task-oriented, running through how best to carry out the established procedures of electioneering. This reflected the mundane and routine organisational nature of local campaigning. The newer advice is more goal-oriented, structured in terms of how to achieve the aim of winning. The extent to which this has yet influenced the culture of local parties is unclear.

The overall pattern in the development of local campaigning is similar for all three parties, but there are also important differences.

In the 1950s the Conservative Party on the ground was a formidable electoral force far superior to Labour, as illustrated by the numbers of members and agents. This point was most famously made after the 1955 election by a Labour committee of inquiry (chaired by Harold Wilson) into the party's local organisation. It stated: 'Compared with our opponents, we are still at the penny-farthing stage in a jet-propelled era, and our machine, at that, is getting rusty and deteriorating with age.'[90] Despite the call to action of the Wilson report, Tory organisational superiority persisted over the following years.

In some respects this gap remains. The Conservatives still have many more agents, and they are more thoroughly trained than their Labour counterparts. Tory local associations tend to be better off than their Labour rivals, and have been quicker to adopt some new techniques such as computerisation and telephone canvassing.

But in other ways the gap has closed. The Tories no longer beat Labour in doorstep canvassing. Their large lead in membership numbers is disappearing. Labour Party members are younger and more active than their Conservative equivalents. Labour is also much better at concentrating effort into marginal constituencies. In marginals in 1992 it greatly outscored the Tories in leaflet and poster delivery. Many of the best-resourced Conservative campaigns are in safe seats where they count for little.[91]

The traditional consensus in British political science, influentially and regularly expressed by David Butler and others in the *British General Election* series, has been that local campaigning makes very little difference to the result. Butler and his co-authors were struck by the lack of individual constituency variation in the national swing from election to election, even in seats identified in advance by party officials as having particularly improved organisation. And in 1969 one important rationale for local electioneering disappeared altogether. The law was changed to allow party affiliations on the ballot paper, so campaigners no longer had to drum home at all costs the name of the candidate in that constituency.

In recent years, however, this verdict has been increasingly questioned. Its opponents draw attention to higher turnout in marginal seats and, since 1979, the greater variation in swing and increase in tactical voting. Several recent studies have argued that there is a considerable connection between local party activity and votes won.[92] These have relied on surveys of party members, reports from party agents or the use of campaign spending as a surrogate measure for activity. All these approaches have been subject to criticism on methodological grounds. Nevertheless, taken together these studies do suggest that local campaigning can significantly affect election results.

There is also some evidence that an incumbent MP can establish a personal vote, of perhaps 750–1000 votes.[93] This may be linked to the incumbent fighting a personal 'permanent campaign' of media publicity, appearances at local meetings, direct mail to constituents, and so on, of the kind which challengers are unable to mount.

Furthermore, the position of the Liberal Democrats in a particular seat is undoubtedly often influenced by the strength of their local work over a long period. Local campaigning is also potentially more important in local than general elections. With their lower turnout and smaller voting units, their results are easier to sway. And local activity is, of course, crucial in by-elections, which frequently have political consequences of national importance.

It is at least clear that while party campaigners in safe seats (which most seats are) may be involved in a fairly pointless ritual at general election time, this is not true in marginals. Local campaigning can certainly determine the result in narrowly fought constituencies, and in a sufficiently close election can therefore affect which party forms a government. 'Butler says local campaigning makes little difference, only 1 or 2 per cent,' says Sir John Lacy, 'but that's all I'm after.'[94]

# 11 Cross-campaign Themes

*While ABC1s can conceptualise, C2s and Ds often cannot. They can relate only to things they can see and feel. They absorb their information and often views from television and tabloids. We have to talk to them in a way they understand.*
Conservative deputy chairman John Maples, 1994[1]

*'It seems to me that Neil has to be statesmanlike. Being statesmanlike doesn't go with celebrities.'*
*'Neil can be statesmanlike on Wednesday. Thursday's the day for celebrities.'*
Exchange at Labour election planning meeting, 1992[2]

*Maurice [Saatchi] is a brilliantly talented man at understanding communications strategies. . . . I would be very good at saying what the politicians thought, and how they thought it was going, and he would be very good at ignoring that, and saying, 'Fine. Well, they don't know what they're talking about – now let's work out a good communications strategy.'*
Tim Bell, 1988[3]

The preceding chapters have examined how individual aspects of party political campaigning have developed since 1945. There have also been important changes which have affected electioneering across the board. Many of these themes have been touched on in earlier chapters, but this chapter pulls together some of the strands.


INTEGRATION

The first trend has been towards greater coordination or integration of the different elements of party communications. A modern campaign is now designed as a coherent whole, in which the same tune should be played by all the various instruments in a carefully orchestrated manner. This principle applies not only to electioneering, but also to party publicity outside election time.

At its most comprehensive, the fully integrated campaign involves the gamut of publicity weapons: advertising, party political broadcasts, rallies, speeches, press conferences, media interviews, photo opportunities, printed literature and other campaign materials. Outside elections it can also bring in parliamentary debates and (for the party in power) government actions. The integrated content covers not only key messages and slogans and the arguments and facts used to bolster them, but even the exact phraseology and (where appropriate) visual symbolism and theme music.

In the past coordination was less systematic. Some electioneering initiatives would be conceived in combination, others in isolation. Leading politicians toured the country speaking where and when they wanted on the subjects of their own choosing and deploying their own favourite lines of argument, often without any link to the activities of their colleagues or party headquarters. Even those forms of communication controlled at the centre were frequently not meshed together. Until the late 1970s party political broadcasts and advertising were prepared separately and by different groups of people (this applies to both the main parties), so that often they did not reinforce each other.

The level of integration gradually increased over the years. This reflected the way in which political campaigning generally has become a much more tightly organised activity. Another factor was the growing influence of professional communicators from advertising and other sectors. For these people it is a basic tenet that an organisation maximises its persuasional impact on the public mind when it drives home the same point through every means at its disposal. This was accepted by the political parties by the mid-1980s. It was epitomised both by Labour's 'Freedom and Fairness' campaign in April 1986, which unleashed a synchronised barrage of propaganda on social issues, and also by the Conservative party conference later in the same year which, backed by other means of publicity, set out the government's 'next move forward'.

Labour took the idea a step further in the 1987 election, when it adopted a highly disciplined approach to setting and pursuing 'themes for the day'. On the day when the daily press conference dealt with health, and the party's health spokespeople did media interviews, Neil Kinnock visited a hospital and was pictured talking to nurses, and then delivered a speech on the subject in the evening. Press conference, photo opportunity, interview and speech soundbite all tied in. It helped produce excellent media coverage for Labour in that election. However, this can be a difficult and inflexible strategy to maintain in face of the need to use media opportunities to respond to unexpected campaign events. The Conservatives intended to copy it in 1992, but their plans went awry as they kept changing their daily themes at the last minute. But both parties were more successful in their use of weekly themes in the 'long campaign' over the three months before the 1992 election was finally called.

## AGENDA-SETTING

Over the years the parties moved towards planning their campaigning more consciously in terms of attempting to 'set the agenda', trying to persuade voters not so much what to think as what to think about. Elections often came to be seen as battles to control the agenda – in other words, to determine which issues the media and campaigning concentrated on. Or, as the point was put after the 1987 election by two key Labour strategists, Peter Mandelson and Patricia Hewitt:[4] 'Competition between rival agenda-setting is at the heart of election campaigning.'

This strategy is based on the following reasoning. Most voters, and especially floating voters, prefer one party's approach to some topics and another party's approach to other topics. And, in some cases, voters possess inconsistent preferences for party positions on different aspects of the same topic – for example, favouring Conservative policy on levels of taxation and Labour policy on levels of public spending. These preferences can be difficult to modify, since they are often based on deeply ingrained stereotypical views of the parties and their relationship to certain policy areas. It is a longlasting feature of British political culture that health as an issue favours Labour and defence favours the Conservatives. But what is easier to influence is the comparative importance or salience which public opinion attaches to the various issues or aspects of them. So votes can be won by ensuring that the electorate has the right subjects at the forefront of its mind on polling day. This means seeking to focus media coverage onto favourable terrain, even where necessary at the cost of failing to contest the claims which the other side is making on its best points.[5]

This argument gets stronger as the next election gets nearer, since it becomes more and more difficult to modify voters' party preferences on particular issues in the diminishing time available. By the beginning of the campaign itself it certainly will be too late.

But it cannot be a complete philosophy of electioneering. First, it is impossible to dictate the agenda entirely (and the third party cannot hope to set it at all). The political agenda is forged through competition with other parties, the media themselves who have their own priorities, and external events which are outside the control of any party and may suddenly intervene. Second, some issues are so important that, whatever their favourability, to ignore them is reckless. This applies as a rule to economic prosperity, and sometimes to other topics according to the political conditions of the moment. Third, some challenges from the enemy are so damaging that they have to be countered. Fourth, over the longer-term issues can be neutralised or even swap camps. Industrial relations/trade unions was a powerful Labour issue in the 1960s, and a powerful Conservative issue by the late 1970s.

Politicians have always faced the choice of which issues to campaign on, when to stick to exploiting perceived strengths or when also to fight back on perceived weaknesses. It is a difficult question of judgement which has to be made in the light of all the circumstances. The answers have depended on the predilections of leading politicians and the opportunities presented by the media for responding. In 1959 the novelty of broadcast news coverage of the campaign prompted an enthusiasm for 'quick retorts' between the parties.[6]

The general strategic dilemma involved became much starker thanks to the establishment of opinion polling in the 1950s and 1960s. For the first time, party managers possessed reliable evidence on the favourability and salience of issues. Thus they had to take an unfamiliarly explicit decision between counter-attacking on unfavourable but important themes or raising the profile of favourable themes.[7] By 1970 a conventional wisdom had become established: 'Each party tends to campaign on its self-chosen battleground against straw men of its own devising. There is no obligation to answer the challenges of the other side; the general view is that it is a strategic mistake ever to do so.'[8] The term 'agenda-setting' has been used in this context since the early 1970s.

The agenda-setting battle has been particularly clear in certain elections. The February 1974 campaign was largely fought as a contest over whether the key issue should be 'who governs Britain – government or unions' (as the Conservatives wanted) or inflation (as Labour wanted and gradually achieved). 1987 saw a particularly sharp contrast between the Tory agenda of overall economic performance, tax and defence, and the Labour agenda of health, education and unemployment. In 1992 the rigorously enforced Conservative strategy in the run-up to and during the campaign was based single-mindedly on increasing the prominence of tax as an issue, to the virtual exclusion of everything else.

Since 1992 the Conservatives have largely stuck to the conventional principle of trying to tilt the political agenda towards favourable items and away from the unfavourable. As the party's deputy chairman, John Maples, wrote frankly in a leaked memo in 1994:[9] 'We can never win on this issue [health]. The best result for the next twelve months would be zero media coverage of the national health service.'

Labour, however, has revised its approach. After a series of election defeats, it has turned to vigorously contesting such traditional Tory terrain as crime and tax levels, trying to shed its longstanding image as weak on crime and keen on tax. The party has also adopted a new philosophy of speedily rebutting Conservative charges. Party strategists have been deeply influenced by the experience of the Democrat candidates in the 1988 and 1992 American presidential campaigns. It is received wisdom in the US that one reason why Bill Clinton succeeded where Michael Dukakis failed was the Clinton team's policy of responding immediately and aggressively to all Republican attacks. Labour strategists now talk of 'never letting a Tory charge go unanswered'. To be effective and prevent the enemy's challenges leading to a running and damaging controversy, rebuttal must be both factual and quick. Labour has tried to ensure it can meet these criteria by establishing an extensive computer database which includes speeches, publications and statistics.

'The party made a serious error for years,' according to shadow home secretary, Jack Straw,[10] 'when we went for Tory weaknesses like health and education, and ignored their strong points such as capping local authority spending and being seen to stand up for Britain. Because we didn't tackle these, voters thought we accepted the Tory story. Military history shows you win battles by attacking the enemy at their strongest point.'

## TARGETING

Targeting has become an increasingly important element in overall campaign planning at national as well as local level. Parties target their campaigning for three reasons: first, different categories of voters are swayed by different tactics or messages; second, some voters are more easily swayed than others and are therefore more productive to concentrate on; third, influencing voters in marginal seats is more important than influencing those elsewhere.

Politicians have always devised sectional appeals aimed at portions of their electorate. But targeting became a much more important element in election strategy thanks to the development of polling, since this told party managers what mattered most to different groups of voters and which sort of voters were most volatile. The landmark report by Harold Wilson's committee on the dismal state of Labour Party organisation in 1955[11] was written as if Labour was solidly backed by 51 per cent of the electorate and merely needed to upgrade the party machine so that it could mobilise its firm supporters. By the time Wilson became party leader in 1963, the party's publicity advisers were relying on the contrasting analysis produced by pollster Mark Abrams that the electorate divided roughly into three more or less equal groupings – committed Tory, committed Labour and uncommitted. They were focusing their efforts on this latter category, whom Abrams was probably the first to call 'target voters' (see Chapter 6).

But the combination of polling and targeting has not provided parties with a short cut to electoral success. Most polling, from the time of Mark Abrams' pioneering work to the present day, has found that while floating voters are disproportionately likely (if not by much) to have certain demographic characteristics, they are nevertheless a very heterogeneous bunch found in all social groupings. Furthermore, being socially dispersed, they are difficult to reach. All that unites them is their lack of political commitment, and this does not provide a route to contact them – there are not, for example, any magazines published specifically for floating voters. A similar point applies to marginal constituencies. In social and demographic terms these have been fairly representative of constituencies as a whole.[12] All this means that, as well as their efforts at targeting, parties still have to mount national campaigns on a broad front.

While successful targeting partly depends on developing policies to suit target groups, it is also based on using the right methods and styles of communication. This involves tailoring the content of the message to its recipients (especially in local campaigning), using different channels of communication to reach different categories of voters, and giving priority to reaching those categories identified as most volatile. Parties have most often worked in terms of class, age, gender and ethnicity, although at times they have also employed other criteria such as region, housing tenure or trade union membership.

In terms of social class, parties have frequently treated skilled manual workers or C2s as the electoral battleground, targeting publicity at them. This was apparent in the Conservative advertising campaign of 1957–9, which was aimed at the more prosperous section of the working class. The same group has featured repeatedly in Conservative thinking since then, most notably in the 1970 and 1979 campaigns. The prominence both parties attached to C2s was boosted by the 1979 result, when they swung much more heavily to the Tories than did voters in other classes. But in other elections before and since they have not deviated so significantly from the overall pattern, and in general they have not been particularly volatile. Nevertheless, they are important because they constitute nearly 30 per cent of the electorate.

From time to time parties have also focused on other social class groupings. For classifying the electorate according to class, they have generally relied on the A, B, C1, C2, D, E grading of occupations employed as standard in the market research industry since the 1950s. This system may sometimes be frowned on by academics, but the parties' polling companies are really market research firms with a political specialism and are accustomed to working on this basis.

Parties have also adopted specific strategies for appealing to women, ever since they were first enfranchised in 1918. When the franchise was extended to younger women (aged 21–9) in 1928, party managers talked of how to win the 'flapper vote'. One 1920s electioneering manual[13] advised candidates: 'You may talk to women electors about "this great Empire upon which the sun never sets" till you are blue in the face, but if your rival is telling them why the purchasing power of the £ has declined, why prices are high, and why their daily task as chancellors of the domestic exchequer is so much more difficult, you may depend on it that you are wasting your breath and he is winning votes.' This emphasis on the primacy of family prosperity is similar to the kind of advice that would be given today.

Since the war all the parties have intermittently produced literature, broadcasts and advertisements aimed at women. The most comprehensive attempt to improve popularity among women has been made by Labour since the mid-1980s. The party's private research showed that, while women were often closer to Labour policies (for example, on the 'caring issues'), many nevertheless regarded the party as male-dominated. Labour has tried to counteract this not only through policy changes, but also by increasing the visibility of Labour women politicians. This includes a higher profile in campaigning, such as at press conferences, rallies and photo opportunities, and positive discrimination in shadow cabinet elections and the adoption of parliamentary candidates. Over this period, Labour has done well among young women and badly among older women. The 'gender gap' in party support is now really a 'gender and generation gap', in which Labour's majority over the Tories among young women is more than exceeded by its deficit among older women.

The parties have usually treated young voters, especially first-timers, as a prime target, because they have not had the chance to establish fixed voting habits. Parties want to attract the young for the same reason that banks do – it may be a decision for life. On the other hand, they can be also be a more difficult target because registration and turnout are lower among young people. Party publicity aimed at young voters has included special literature, cinema commercials and youth-related photo opportunities, as well as attempts to mobilise youth culture. The most notable of these was Red Wedge, an organisation of pop musicians led by Billy Bragg, which promoted Labour through pop concert tours in 1985–7.

Targeting of minority ethnic groups has increased in importance. In the past, parties did not exert themselves in this direction. In 1951 the Conservative deputy chief organisation officer noted:[14] 'With few exceptions, reports indicated that the coloured electors play little or no part in our organisation, and that no special efforts are made by the Socialists to organise them.' At that time the Conservatives estimated the 'coloured population' as 40 000–50 000. This number has grown rapidly – by 1992 there were nearly two million ethnic minority electors. As the ethnic minority proportion of the electorate grew, parties had to court their votes, through, for example, advertising in the ethnic press and producing leaflets in languages other than English. Labour has made the most effort to do this. It receives the bulk of ethnic minority support, although in recent elections the Conservatives have made inroads into the Asian vote.

## PROFESSIONALISATION

Outside experts from communications professions are now an obligatory and central feature of electioneering, not an optional extra. This applies whether they are employed in the shape of formally contracted companies (such as pollsters or advertising agencies) or an informal grouping of largely unpaid individuals.

Their role has varied according to the scope that politicians and party officials have been prepared to give them. Often they have worked in the face of hostility from politicians and officials who regarded them (sometimes correctly) as interlopers in the political process with little political nous. Their use is now widely accepted, although tensions often recur and some politicians remain resentful and contemptuous. Nigel Lawson, the former chancellor, wrote that debate about preferences for one ad agency over another left him 'inescapably reminded of Dr Johnson's remark: "Sir, there is no settling the point of precedency between a louse and a flea."'[15] By the 1980s outside professionals had acquired a more central strategic function and responsibility for the full range of party communications activities, but not the final decision-taking which has generally remained in the hands of leading politicians.

This has been accompanied by parties themselves increasingly employing more specialist staff with expertise in various fields of communication acquired outside political activity, from journalism and television production to conference presentation and direct mail.

Professional communicators have brought to party politics not only a range of marketing skills and techniques to make communication more compelling, but also professional discipline: the use of research, the defining of target audiences, the relating of content and tone of message to those audiences, and an emphasis on simplicity, consistency and repetition. Jeremy Sinclair, who worked on the Conservative campaigns from 1979 to 1992 at Saatchi and Saatchi, says:[16] 'What an ad agency brings to a political party is discipline of thought. You ask a politician "What is your proposition?", and they say they don't understand. You ask "What is the argument for voting for you?", and they list ten things. You say "You're only allowed one", and they can't cope. But this is how big brands are sold – you pick an angle and keep hammering it.'

*Table 11.1*  Overall campaign expenditure

| | Conservatives | | Labour | | Liberals/SDP/Liberal Democrats | |
| | Current prices | 1992 prices | Current prices | 1992 prices | Current prices | 1992 prices |
|---|---|---|---|---|---|---|
| 1945 | 50–100 | 1000–2100 | 51 | 1050 | ? | ? |
| 1950 | 270 | 4500 | 84 | 1400 | ? | ? |
| 1951 | 112 | 1700 | 80 | 1200 | ? | ? |
| 1955 | 142 | 1800 | 73 | 950 | ? | ? |
| 1959 | 631 | 7100 | 239 | 2700 | ? | ? |
| 1964 | 1233 | 12300 | 538 | 5400 | ? | ? |
| 1966 | 350 | 3200 | 196 | 1800 | ? | ? |
| 1970 | 630 | 4900 | 526 | 4100 | 70–100 | 550–780 |
| 1974 (Feb.) | 680 | 3700 | 440 | 2400 | | |
| 1974 (Oct.) | 950 | 4500 | 524 | 2500 | 300 | 1500 |
| 1979[a] | 2333 | 5800 | 1566 | 3900 | 213 | 530 |
| 1983 | 3908[b] | 6300 | 2300[e] | 3700 | 1934[h] | 3100 |
| 1987 | 9028[c] | 12100 | 4700[f] | 6300 | 1750[i] | 2300 |
| 1992 | 11196[d] | 11196 | 10597[g] | 10597 | 2089[j] | 2089 |

*Note*: Estimates of sums spent centrally on campaigning relating to general elections, in thousands of pounds.
*Sources*: See note 38.

## EXPENDITURE

Over the few most recent elections the cost of campaigning has been rising. However, the current level of party spending is not historically unprecedented, either in the post-war period or even beforehand (see Chapter 1). Table 11.1 shows estimates of overall central party expenditure on campaigning related to general elections from 1945 on. Comparison with Table 2.1 on advertising expenditure shows that it presents much the same pattern of a rise peaking in 1964, a fall, and another rise. This similarity reflects the fact that advertising has been the largest component of spending on electioneering (generally accounting in the Conservative case for at least half the money spent).

There is an important difference between the current spending peak and the previous high spending time of 1959 and 1964. The earlier peak was based on prolonged advertising campaigns which ran for over a year prior to the election (see Chapter 2). Current spending is now concentrated much more intensively into the campaign proper and the weeks immediately prior to it.

While the general pattern is clear, the detailed figures in Table 11.1 do have to be interpreted with some caution. They include grants to local constituencies which are then deployed on local rather than central electioneering. This constitutes a substantial proportion of third party spending (24 per cent in 1992).[17] More importantly, they are not limited to expenditure during the campaign period itself, but also include election-related spending prior to the campaign. This relies on a distinction between parties' routine and election-related spending which is important, but can be difficult to draw, is sometimes arbitrary, and may on occasions be simply a matter of accounting convention. This approach has been criticised by the Labour Party.[18] Nevertheless, these are the best set of figures available for an indication of spending trends over several elections.[19]

## PERSONALISATION

Electioneering is a conflict not simply between parties but also between politicians, most notably the party leaders. Campaigning in Britain possesses a longstanding and important 'presidential' aspect. The media foster a personality-based approach to politics, and the parties use their leaders as vehicles to project the party as a whole.

Broadcast coverage of elections is strongly focused on the activities of the leaders. Since broadcasters started to report the campaign, party leaders have usually accounted for the majority of quotes from politicians in the main news bulletins.[20] On this criterion there has been no consistent trend towards this preponderance growing or receding. However, it has become more important as the quantity of broadcast coverage has increased enormously. These figures also do not take into account non-verbal campaigning such as photo opportunities, which have seized much airtime in elections from 1979. Taking this into account increases the dominance of party leaders.[21]

As for the press, the tabloids share with television a general tendency towards personalisation, whether in politics or any other field of human activity. And there is evidence that since the 1940s broadsheets have given an increasing proportion of their political coverage to party leaders compared to their senior colleagues.[22]

The extent to which party campaigning itself has focused on the leader has fluctuated. It has partly been dependent on the leader's own desire or determination to be at the centre of things, but usually the most important factor has been the leader's own popularity. Parties have naturally tried to give a high profile to a popular leader. Given an unpopular leader, they tend to accentuate the rest of the 'team', especially when its members are more popular than their opposite numbers. The parties cannot control the distribution of exposure between the leader and other politicians, since the media have their own preferences. But parties do have considerable scope, particularly through the structuring and content of their election press conferences, broadcasts, advertisements and literature, and the ways in which politicians talk about their colleagues in interviews.

Thus in 1945 the Conservatives based their campaign on Churchill. He gave four of the party's ten radio broadcasts, and his face was plastered on hoardings all over the country accompanied by the slogan 'Help him finish the job'. Labour built up Harold Wilson's prominence in the 1964, 1966 and 1970 elections, but placed more stress on the team in the 1974 elections when he was less popular. For the same reason the Conservatives downplayed Edward Heath and highlighted his colleagues in October 1974. Margaret Thatcher played a more dominant part in the 1983 Conservative campaign in the wake of her post-Falklands popularity than she did in 1979 or 1987. In 1983 Labour attempted desperately to minimise the focus on its highly unpopular leader, Michael Foot. And Neil Kinnock fulfilled a paramount role in Labour's 1987 campaign far more than in 1992, when he was less popular and party strategists tried hard to create a high profile for the well-regarded shadow chancellor, John Smith. The Conservatives tried to capitalise on John Major's popularity in 1992, through the bio-pic party political broadcast and their advertising posters which featured him.

## NEGATIVE CAMPAIGNING

As H. L. Mencken said, 'Under democracy, one party always devotes its chief energies to trying to prove that the other party is unfit to rule,' adding, 'both commonly succeed, and are right'. Politics is an adversarial activity. A limited number of rival parties compete for the prize of power, and victory for one depends not on its absolute popularity, but on its comparative popularity relative to the alternatives. Voting is a choice between certain fixed options, and is often motivated not by liking for one party, but by dislike for the others. So it is not surprising that parties try hard to draw attention to political and personal defects of their opponents.

As well as being a natural part of democracy, negative campaigning can be particularly effective. This is despite the fact that in opinion research people say they don't like it. Indeed, it may well put them off politics in general, but the negative content can still strike home. At a time when the public is generally disillusioned with politicians, negative messages are more credible than positive ones. And psychologically, negative information has more impact on our thinking, is more easily remembered and is a more powerful motivating force than positive information.[23]

Negative campaigning has been an important component of party politics throughout the post-war period. Its content has changed according to political circumstances: in the early post-war period the Conservatives attacked Labour over nationalisation, while Labour claimed the Tories would return to the unemployment of the 1930s; in the 1992 campaign, the Conservatives attacked Labour on tax, while Labour claimed the Tories would privatise the NHS. But politicians have always devoted a good proportion of their speeches, broadcasts, literature and other propaganda to castigating the record, proposals and leaders of the other side. Many elections have been fought partly on the basis of 'time for a change' versus 'fear of change', or, to put it another way, whether the devil you know is really better than the devil you don't.

After the 1955 election, Labour's general secretary reported that 'it would seem that most Labour candidates spent most of their time at meetings and space in election addresses in attacks upon the government'.[24] During the 1970 campaign,

Harold Wilson devoted 75 per cent of the content of his
speeches to attacking the Conservatives, while Edward Heath
devoted 70 per cent of his speeches to condemning Labour.
For their senior colleagues, the figures were an average 47
per cent negative content for other leading Labour politicians, and 77 per cent for other leading Tories.[25] In 1979,
the figures were lower, but still substantial. James Callaghan
allocated 39 per cent of his speeches to attacking his opponents, Margaret Thatcher 49 per cent and David Steel 40
per cent. In this election an analysis of party political broadcasts on TV also showed that they contained a substantial
amount of negative material: for Labour the proportion was
44 per cent, the Conservatives 51 per cent, and the Liberals
59 per cent.[26]

The parties' enthusiasm for assailing their foes is reflected
in news coverage. The media generally like to report conflict, whether in politics or otherwise. In the elections of
1983, 1987 and 1992, between a third and a half of the
election lead stories in the main TV news programmes were
based on parties attacking one another.[27] During the 1992
campaign specifically, 40 per cent of lead items on the main
TV news bulletins mentioned the Conservatives attacking
other parties, which was more common than references to
them presenting their own policies or defending themselves
against attacks from others. The position for the other two
parties was similar, although the Liberal Democrats had an
even higher negative/positive ratio and Labour a slightly
lower one.[28]

The partisan tabloids tend to be even more devoted to
negative messages than the parties themselves. The Conservative papers generally devote more space to items about
Labour than their own party, while similarly the *Daily Mirror*
gives more space to the Tories than Labour. This space is
filled up with derogatory knocking copy.[29]

Nevertheless, at times parties have made attempts to make
certain aspects of their electioneering more positive. Early
newspaper advertising was predominantly positive until the
late 1960s, since when advertising has been one of the most
negative facets of campaigning (see Chapter 2). In the 1974
elections both main parties were worried by the Liberal revival
and attributed it partly to public distaste for the ritual

exchange of denunciations between Wilson and Heath. The Liberals seemed above the fray, if only because their own denunciations of Wilson and Heath – as often as not for too much mud-slinging – failed to get reported. Both parties decided to cut back on the personal wrangling between the two leaders.

While negative campaigning is a longstanding democratic tradition, there has been one recent development which encourages it further. Parties have improved their negative capability by collecting much more material about their opponents – broken promises, misdeeds, failures of policy, gaffes, inconsistencies, hostages to fortune, extremist or eccentric statements, and so on. This has been facilitated by computer databases which can easily store, sort and retrieve large quantities of information. The parties have always been at war with each. Now they have a faster supply of more deadly ammunition.

In 1946 Conservative Central Office had only one file on the Labour Party, which covered everything from the time of Keir Hardie. This appalled the new head of publicity, Toby O'Brien. When he asked what happened to press cuttings, he was told that 'when everyone has seen them, we throw them away'.[30] The party soon embarked on a more assiduous collection of intelligence about its enemies. In the 1951 campaign the party's research department met 120 requests for dossiers on Labour candidates.[31] In more recent years Central Office has amassed files on MPs and candidates of other parties, containing material from press reports, speeches, *Hansard*, press releases, interviews, articles and books. This is used to inform party publications and broadcasts, to assist local campaigning and to provide background briefing for the media. The files are often detailed and thorough. In 1992 Central Office provided the BBC's *Panorama* programme with a 52-page dossier on Paddy Ashdown. It consisted mainly of information about his past and present political views on topics ranging from Europe to Salman Rushdie, but also contained material about his family life, career before politics, and smoking and drinking habits (all taken from public sources).[32]

In 1992 Labour was far behind the Conservatives in the extent and quality of its opposition research. It operated with a quotes database of 1500 quotes from opposing politicians[33] (the Tories had hundreds from Ashdown alone). Even this was a significant step forward on its previous system – a smaller, unmethodical manual card index of quotes. However, the new computer database which Labour has established since the 1992 election for its rapid rebuttal strategy contains and makes easily accessible far more information about its political opponents than the party has ever been able to deploy in the past.

## CELEBRITIES

The cast list of a modern election campaign is not limited to politicians. It also includes soap opera stars, stand-up comics, Shakespearean actors, pop musicians, DJs, bestselling authors, playwrights, TV presenters, leading scientists, high-profile businesspeople, footballers, swimmers, athletes and snooker players – or anyone else who is sufficiently famous and might be worth a few votes.

The parties use these celebrities in a variety of ways: to appear at rallies; to deliver endorsements in broadcasts, ads, leaflets or press conferences; to pose for photo opportunities with politicians; and to engage the attention of the public on walkabouts. Celebrities add glamour to an event. They are often an easy way to get favourable publicity or attract interest. And the parties hope to borrow for themselves some of the celebrity's popularity or credibility, and to associate their cause with the values which the celebrity represents.

The role of non-political celebrities in electioneering is much greater now than in the past, but the idea itself is not a recent development. During the large Tory advertising campaign of 1957–9, the party ran a series of ads entitled 'You're looking at a Conservative'. Those featured included not only ordinary people, but also sporting stars such as the cricketer Colin Cowdrey and the show jumper Pat Smythe.[34] Labour's party political broadcasts on television in 1959 contained endorsements from several well-known non-politicians (see Chapter 3). Harold Wilson was always an enthusiast for exploiting popular culture, and in the 1960s Labour gave entertainment celebrities a leading role at some election rallies. In the 1970 campaign, famous names who appeared in Labour literature to explain their backing for the party included Sybil Thorndike, Warren Mitchell, Pat Phoenix and Jackie Charlton.

Celebrity electioneering became more prominent in the 1980s, especially at major election rallies which were full of showbiz razzmatazz (see Chapter 5). The Conservatives led the way, but in due course Labour went further. It wanted to show it had support from a wide range of successful people. In 1992 Labour even organised an event specifically for celebrities on the last Sunday of the campaign. Described by the party as a collection of 'Britain's best and brightest', it was derided by others as 'Luvvies for Labour'.

Since 1992, Labour has been rethinking its approach to celebrities. Its internal election postmortem report argued: 'Undoubtedly, the most successful use of celebrities is in local events, attracting otherwise unlikely publicity to events at regional and key seat level. Future activity should be primarily directed at this, although use in rallies and other events is effective. The use of stars on PEBs [party election broadcasts] and press conferences should be treated with some circumspection.'[35]

The pattern of celebrity support throws an interesting sidelight on the politics of different branches of British culture. Labour has performed better in the fields of drama and music (from Sir Ian McKellen to Nigel Kennedy), while the Conservatives have scored well in sport (from Freddie Trueman to Sharron Davies). Comedy has been divided by a generational split: the Conservatives have had the old ones (Jimmy Tarbuck, Bob Monkhouse); Labour the young ones (Ben Elton, Stephen Fry). The third party has tended to favour a more intellectual brand of fame (Bamber Gascoigne, Magnus Magnusson). Sometimes celebrities swap sides. In 1983, Sir Richard Attenborough announced that Gandhi (the subject of his Oscar-winning film biography) would have backed the Alliance if given the chance.[36] Who Gandhi would have voted for in 1992 is not known, although by then Attenborough himself had switched to supporting Labour. But the prize for political volatility must go to Jimmy Savile, who in February 1974 appeared in a Liberal television and Conservative radio broadcast on the same day.[37]

# 12 Conclusion

*When I was in my early teens, I used to occasionally erect a soapbox. I had two soapboxes, one that I used to erect in Brixton market and the other in Brixton Road, and I used to talk about political matters of the day, and everyone was very tolerant. Some people used to listen, some used to engage in badinage.*

John Major, 1992[1]

In a television interview during the 1992 general election, Sir Robin Day quizzed John Major about his apparently faltering campaign and asked: 'What has happened to the soapbox you used to speak from in your younger days in Brixton? Couldn't you bring that into play somehow?'[2]

It must have struck Major as a good question, because two days later he stood on a packing crate in Luton and shouted at a surprised crowd of Saturday shoppers through a loudhailer. In the campaign until then the prime minister had spoken in the contrasting environment of carefully planned, high-tech settings to ticket-only gatherings of the party faithful. But from that time the 'soapbox' became his electioneering trademark.

It was presented by Conservative officials as a return to an older, less artificial form of campaigning, when political leaders stumped the country and addressed rowdy outdoor gatherings of allcomers. This line was also taken up in some news coverage. One ITN report described Major's new approach as 'old-fashioned soapbox electioneering that has not been seen from a prime minister for some 30 years'.[3]

In fact, Major's soapbox oratory exemplified many of the changes that have taken place over the past few decades. It was a form of contemporary soundbite politics, not traditional soapbox politics. The whole exercise was laid on for the benefit of the media. Major wasn't allowed to arrive at a location and mount his crate until the television cameras and press were ready and waiting. His staff recognised that the main impact depended on the brief clips on that night's TV news bulletins. The images of Major on the soapbox

272

may have evoked an impression of authentic and direct contact between a politician on the hustings and real people, but this was an authenticity staged for television.

The political points that Major repeatedly proclaimed through his loudhailer – that 'the average taxpayer would pay £1250 extra tax a year under Labour', and so on – were derived from the tightly integrated Conservative strategy. They were exactly the same as those retailed in the party's ads, broadcasts, literature and press conferences, and had been worked out partly on the basis of extensive opinion research. And Major was accompanied by a huge entourage of assistants and advisers, who travelled on an immensely expensive 'battlebus' full of the latest communications technology which kept them instantly in touch with campaign developments.

It was all a far cry from the modest prime ministerial election tour in 1950 by Clement Attlee. Attlee travelled in the family car, accompanied from place to place only by his wife (who was the driver), one sympathetic journalist and one detective.[4] He addressed several open-air meetings a day, speaking off the cuff, without a TV camera in sight, relying on newspaper reports and the party's radio broadcasts to take his message beyond his immediate audience.

The modern election campaign was born between the mid-1950s and the mid-1960s. The parties then embraced the three key defining features of the contemporary era of party political communication: the all-encompassing drive to maximise the value of television coverage, the use of mass advertising and the influence of polling. Other innovations during this period included daily election press conferences, more adventurous party political broadcasts and the celebrity-based rally. And by 1965 party strategists talked of targeting the uncommitted voter, took care over their leader's personal image on television, and regarded the party conflict as partly a quasi-presidential contest between Wilson and Heath.

The two elections of 1959 and 1964 thus constitute the most rapid phase of change in party campaigning since the war. The next most innovatory election was 1979, when the Conservatives were responsible for several developments: the systematic use of the photo opportunity, the creation of party political broadcasts and advertising by the same ad agency, the first cinema commercial, the rebirth of the showbiz-type rally, and the extensive employment of focus groups. Elections at other times have also produced important innovations, but change has been more gradual and evolutionary.

There are two particularly influential factors behind the rate of development of electioneering techniques since 1945. First, the media context – the growth or decline of different forms of media, and changes in the way they cover politics and relate to political parties (as described in Chapter 4). Second, technological change, from printing methods and film-making techniques to the increasing power of computers and the introduction of the personal computer. New technologies enable better communication with voters, and also faster internal communication (for example, via email and mobile phones) which promotes consistency of message and coordination of activity.

Second-order factors include the level of resources possessed by parties and electoral law. Shortage of cash has prevented parties from launching desirable but costly innovations; it has also meant having to choose between different forms of activity. Limited finance has always been a significant difficulty for Labour, and a major handicap for the third party. It has been less restricting for the Conservatives, at least at times. Michael Dobbs, Conservative chief of staff in 1987, says:[5] 'I can't recall a good campaigning idea turned down in 1987 for lack of money. One always knew one had enough money in the kitty.' However, the Tories have been forced into cutbacks following periods of particularly great expenditure, such as the high-spending times of 1963–4 and 1989–92.

The law has mainly acted as a constraint, for example on constituency expenses and paid TV advertising, but the occasional legal development such as the Tronoh Mines case relating to advertising during the campaign period (see Chapter 2) has given parties greater flexibility.

And beyond all these factors there is the attitude of politicians and party officials themselves, ranging from those who will jump at any new-fangled gimmick they think will boost their popularity to those who disdain all modern methods of presentation.

Resistance to change has been common. This has partly stemmed from inertia and complacency among tradition-ally-minded individuals, who felt attached to their time-honoured methods of electioneering. In many cases it also reflected a belief that the new methods were in some way unethical and unsuited to politics, whether because they were undignified, superficial, associated with commercialism or a challenge to the paramountcy of policy over presentation. As the young Tony Benn said derisively of Aneurin Bevan, 'He has the absurd idea that all publicity is unimportant and that all you need is the right policy.'[6]

These attitudes are much rarer today. The opposite com-plaint has become more common – that too many of those involved in electioneering believe that all policy is unim-portant and all you need is the right publicity. The contem-porary ethos of party political campaigning propels parties in the direction of enthusiastic espousal of modern tech-niques. The parties now constantly seek to update their approach. They learn promptly from their opponents. They frequently pick up quickly on developments in commercial marketing, whether directly or through professional advis-ers. And they import from overseas, especially but not only from the US. Political parties used to be persistent laggards in the use of new communication techniques. Now they are often early adopters.

# Appendix:
# General Election Results

| Election | Conservative | Labour | Liberals/ Alliance/ Liberal Democrats | Others |
|---|---|---|---|---|
| **5 July, 1945** | | | | |
| % of votes cast | 39.8 | 48.3 | 9.1 | 2.7 |
| Seats won | 213 | 393 | 12 | 22 |
| **23 February, 1950** | | | | |
| % of votes cast | 43.5 | 46.1 | 9.1 | 1.3 |
| Seats won | 299 | 315 | 9 | 2 |
| **25 October, 1951** | | | | |
| % of votes cast | 48.0 | 48.8 | 2.5 | 0.7 |
| Seats won | 321 | 295 | 6 | 3 |
| **26 May, 1955** | | | | |
| % of votes cast | 49.7 | 46.4 | 2.7 | 1.1 |
| Seats won | 345 | 277 | 6 | 2 |
| **8 October, 1959** | | | | |
| % of votes cast | 49.4 | 43.8 | 5.9 | 1.0 |
| Seats won | 365 | 258 | 6 | 1 |
| **15 October, 1964** | | | | |
| % of votes cast | 43.4 | 44.1 | 11.2 | 1.3 |
| Seats won | 304 | 317 | 9 | 0 |
| **31 March, 1966** | | | | |
| % of votes cast | 41.9 | 47.9 | 8.5 | 1.6 |
| Seats won | 253 | 363 | 12 | 2 |
| **18 June, 1970** | | | | |
| % of votes cast | 46.4 | 43.0 | 7.5 | 3.1 |
| Seats won | 330 | 288 | 6 | 6 |
| **28 February, 1974** | | | | |
| % of votes cast | 37.8 | 37.1 | 19.3 | 5.8 |
| Seats won | 297 | 301 | 14 | 23 |
| **10 October, 1974** | | | | |
| % of votes cast | 35.8 | 39.2 | 18.3 | 6.7 |
| Seats won | 277 | 319 | 13 | 26 |

| | | | | |
|---|---|---|---|---|
| **3 May, 1979** | | | | |
| % of votes cast | 43.9 | 37.0 | 13.8 | 5.3 |
| Seats won | 339 | 269 | 11 | 16 |
| **9 June, 1983** | | | | |
| % of votes cast | 42.4 | 27.6 | 25.4 | 4.6 |
| Seats won | 397 | 209 | 23 | 21 |
| **11 June, 1987** | | | | |
| % of votes cast | 42.3 | 30.8 | 22.6 | 4.3 |
| Seats won | 376 | 229 | 22 | 23 |
| **9 April, 1992** | | | | |
| % of votes cast | 41.9 | 34.4 | 17.8 | 5.8 |
| Seats won | 336 | 271 | 20 | 24 |

*Source:* Adapted from Butler and Kavanagh, 1992, pp. 284–5.

# Notes

## 1 INTRODUCTION

1. Houston and Valdar, 1922, p. 14.
2. *Campaign*, 30 June 1978.
3. See Pinto-Duschinsky, M., 1981, pp. 98–101.

## 2 ADVERTISING

1. *Hansard*, House of Commons debates, 21 July 1960, vol. 627, col. 788.
2. Rutherford, 1992.
3. Issued by the Committee of Advertising Practice, February 1995 edition (similar provisions existed in earlier editions).
4. *Hansard*, 7 June 1815, col. 663.
5. Pinto-Duschinsky, M., 1992.
6. Labour Party annual accounts, 1992.
7. Nicholas, 1951, facing p. 241.
8. CCO 500/24/19, Conservative Party Archive (CPA), Bodleian Library, Oxford.
9. Quoted in Cockett, 1994, p. 567.
10. Windlesham, 1966, pp. 259–60.
11. Ibid., p. 54.
12. Butler and Rose, 1960, p. 27.
13. Abrams, 1963a, p. 18.
14. Rose, 1967, pp. 49–50.
15. Ibid., pp. 55, 81–2; Abrams, 1963b, p. 7.
16. Rose, 1967, p. 81.
17. Abrams, 1964, p. 16.
18. Rose, 1965, pp. 370, 372.
19. Butler and Pinto-Duschinsky, 1971, p. 289.
20. Ibid., p. 312.
21. Ibid., p. 133.
22. Interview, 7 April 1994.
23. The advertisement's place in political folklore was enhanced after the 1970 election when the BBC used 'Yesterday's Men' as the title of a famous programme about Wilson and his colleagues. This show led to an extremely bitter and well-publicised dispute between the BBC and Wilson, who was outraged when asked about the money he had made from his memoirs.
24. Butler and Pinto-Duschinsky, 1971, p. 313.
25. Ironically, a Saatchis subsidiary was in a sense the Labour agency at the previous election. At that time Labour had not used an agency

278

for creative work, but usually employed one to buy advertising space. For October 1974, it had contracted Notley Advertising to purchase space. Two weeks before polling day, Notley was taken over by Saatchi and Saatchi.

26. Bell, 1982, p. 12.
27. Ibid., p. 16.
28. Interview, 29 April 1994.
29. Bell, 1982, p. 16.
30. Harrop, 1984, p. 209.
31. Parkinson, 1992, p. 229.
32. Saatchis also sometimes kept in reserve anti-Labour ads to be used if things got tight. In 1987 this included a picture of a Soviet bomber with its bomb doors open, captioned 'If Labour dropped our bomb, would the Russians drop theirs?' (interview with Norman Tebbit, 10 May 1994). Tebbit, the Tory party chairman in 1987, says: 'It would have been hairy and controversial, with risks attached of opening up big debates on, for example, how willing are you to drop yours? But if the election had been close, we would have got this out of the locker.'
33. Tebbit, 1989a, p. 47.
34. Interview, 10 May 1994.
35. Butler and Kavanagh, 1988, p. 40.
36. Thatcher, 1993, p. 580.
37. Principally Tyler, 1987, and Young of Graffham, 1991.
38. Thatcher, 1993, p. 585.
39. For a Saatchi account, see Sharkey, 1989; for the Young and Rubicam view, see Stothard, 1987.
40. 'Tebbit leads the charge on the expensive ad-machine', *Guardian*, 20 June 1989.
41. Interview, 28 April 1994.
42. Hogg and Hill, 1995, p. 238.
43. Interview, 29 April 1994.
44. Saatchi, 1994.
45. Butler and Kavanagh, 1980, p. 134.
46. 'Labour's publicity men vow death to all dragons', *Guardian*, 1 March 1979.
47. Interview, 20 April 1994.
48. Wright, 1986, p. 80.
49. Labour national executive committee (NEC) annual report 1992, p. 16.
50. Wilson, 1987, p. 294.
51. CCO 500/24/19–20, CPA.
52. Rose, 1967, p. 42.
53. Interview, 22 February 1995.
54. 'How the money has been spent', *Marketing Week*, 19 June 1987.
55. Fallon, 1988, p. 181.
56. Thatcher, 1993, p. 302.
57. Baker, 1993, p. 292.
58. Labour Party annual accounts, 1984.

59. *Register-MEAL Quarterly Digest,* April–June 1994.
60. Linton, 1994, p. 23.
61. Cambray, 1932, p. 157.
62. CCO 500/24/20, CPA.
63. Rose, 1967, p. 169.
64. Bell, 1982, p. 14.
65. FitzGerald, 1986, p. 219.
66. Pinto-Duschinsky, M., 1981, p. 145.
67. Bell, 1982, p. 14.
68. Pinto-Duschinsky, M., 1989, p. 201.
69. Pinto-Duschinsky, M., 1992.
70. Linton, 1994, p. 23.
71. Information supplied by staff at Poster Publicity, Labour's poster-buying agency.
72. Interview, 29 April 1994.
73. Interview, 20 April 1994.
74 a. Estimated from papers in CCO 500/24/19–20, CPA.
   b. Butler and Rose, 1960, p. 21.
   c. Rose, 1967, p. 58.
   d. *Statistical Review of Press and Television Advertising 1965, 1966* (this figure only reflects press advertising and not posters).
   e. Estimated from Pinto-Duschinsky, M., 1981, pp. 143–4, and Butler and Pinto-Duschinsky, 1971, p. 290.
   f. *MEAL Monthly Digests* 1973, 1974 (this figure only reflects press advertising and not posters).
   g. Estimated from Butler and Kavanagh, 1975, p. 242.
   h. Pinto-Duschinsky, M., 1981, p. 145.
   i. Pinto-Duschinsky, M., 1985a, p. 63.
   j. Pinto-Duschinsky, M., 1989, p. 198.
   k. Pinto-Duschinsky, M., 1992.
   l. Butler and Rose, 1960, p. 28.
   m. Rose, 1967, p. 79.
   n. *MEAL Monthly Digests* 1969, 1970 (this figure only reflects press advertising and not posters).
   o. Estimated from *MEAL Monthly Digests* 1973, 1974, and *Adweek,* 11 January 1974.
   p. Kleinman, 1974.
   q. Labour Party annual accounts, 1979.
   r. Labour Party annual accounts, 1983.
   s. Pinto-Duschinsky, M., 1989, p. 201.
   t. Labour Party annual accounts, 1992.
   u. *MEAL Monthly Digests* 1969, 1970 (this figure only reflects press advertising and not posters).
   v. Butler and Kavanagh, 1974, p. 240.
   w. Butler and Kavanagh, 1975, p. 242.
   x. Pinto-Duschinsky, M., 1981, p. 202.
   y. Estimated from Pinto-Duschinsky, M., 1986, pp. 285–6, and Pinto-Duschinsky, M., 1985b, p. 338.
   z. Estimated from data supplied by Register-MEAL.
  aa. Linton, 1994, p. 23.

3   PARTY POLITICAL BROADCASTS

1. Quoted in White, 1992.
2. Rees, 1992, p. 43.
3. Menneer and Bunker, 1992.
4. Reith, 1949, p. 96.
5. McCallum and Readman, 1947, p. 154.
6. CCO 500/24/1, CPA.
7. Briggs, 1979, p. 673.
8. Butler, 1955, p. 57.
9. Rhodes James, 1986, p. 305.
10. Adams, 1992, pp. 141–2.
11. Butler and Rose, 1960, p. 90.
12. Harrison, 1966, p. 141.
13. Wyndham Goldie, 1977, p. 61.
14. Ibid., pp. 97–8.
15. Cockerell, 1988, pp. 11–13.
16. Wyndham Goldie, 1977, p. 136.
17. Cockerell, 1988, p. 17.
18. Benn, 1994, p. 172.
19. Cockerell, 1988, p. 34.
20. Ibid., pp. 29–30.
21. Ibid., p. 36.
22. Labour NEC minutes, June 1955.
23. Butler, 1955, p. 52.
24. Ibid., p. 110.
25. 'The new hustings', *The Times*, 23 May 1955.
26. Butler and Rose, 1960, p. 93.
27. Benn, 1994, p. 304.
28. Harrison, 1965, p. 178.
29. Home of the Hirsel, 1978, p. 214.
30. Cockerell, 1988, p. 110.
31. Some politicians had used comparable but simpler devices in the past for cinema newsreels. In the 1930s Baldwin read newsreel talks off a roller mechanism located just to one side of the camera. See Ramsden, 1982, pp. 130–1.
32. Cockerell, 1988, p. 36.
33. Clark, 1986, p. 183.
34. Macmillan, 1971, p. 196.
35. Benn, 1987, p. 8.
36. Howard and West, 1965, p. 212.
37. Evans, 1981, p. 178; Cockerell, 1988, p. 81.
38. Harrison, 1966, p. 140.
39. Windlesham, 1966, pp. 261–4; Howard and West, 1965, p. 136.
40. Windlesham, 1966, p. 75.
41. Interview, 2 June 1994.
42. Day, 1982, p. 7.
43. Interview, 12 April 1994.
44. Harrison, 1974, p. 160.
45. Harrison, 1975, p. 159.

46. *There Now Follows* . . ., BBC2, 8 October 1993.
47. 9 June 1978.
48. Delaney, 1982, p. 27.
49. Pinto-Duschinsky, M., 1981, p. 145.
50. Parkinson, 1992, p. 216.
51. Bell, 1982, p. 21.
52. Interview, 22 April 1994.
53. Interview, 22 April 1994.
54. BBC, 1984, p. 165.
55. Interview, 22 April 1994.
56. Interview, 20 April 1994.
57. 'TV gimmicks storm', *Daily Express*, 18 April 1979.
58. Butler and Jowett, 1985, p. 64.
59. MORI, 1987.
60. Harrison, 1988, p. 157.
61. 'Adman comes to the aid of the party', *Independent*, 15 November 1989.
62. Pinto-Duschinsky, M., 1993, p. 32.
63. Bruce, 1992b.
64. Scammell, 1995, p. 252.
65. For the best evidence of this, see Clifford and Heath, 1994.
66. Whitty, 1992.
67. Pardoe, 1989, p. 57.
68. Crewe and King, 1995, p. 330.
69. Interview with Peter Luff, former SDP official, 14 September 1995.
70. Interview, 12 April 1994.
71. Cockerell, 1988, p. 220.
72. Scammell, 1995, p. 111.
73. *The Times*, 25 March 1995.
74. Interview, 22 April 1994.
75. Young of Graffham, 1991, p. 241.
76. Hughes and Wintour, 1990, p. 27.
77. MORI, 1987.
78. Hogg and Hill, 1995, p. 222.
79. Ibid., pp. 221–2.
80. Information derived from annual BBC *Handbooks*.
81. Information derived from annual BBC *Handbooks* and Labour NEC annual reports.
82. Interview, 12 April 1994.

## 4  USING THE MEDIA

1. Diary entry quoted in Benn, 1994, p. 263.
2. *Panorama*, BBC1, 8 June 1987.
3. *Dispatches*, Channel 4, 18 March 1992.
4. Hurd, 1994.
5. Blair, 1987.
6. Butler and Rose, 1960, p. 93.

7. Ibid., 1960, pp. 78, 80.
8. Butler and Stokes, 1969, pp. 219–20; see also Blumler and McQuail, 1968, p. 43.
9. See, for example, Blumler and McQuail, 1968, p. 43, for an early instance, and Kellner, 1992, for a poll conducted in the run-up to the 1992 election.
10. Interview, 22 April 1994.
11. Hurd, 1979, p. 15.
12. Interview with Peter Mandelson, 21 April 1994.
13. *Dispatches*, Channel 4, 18 March 1992.
14. See, for example, Dunleavy and Husbands, 1985, p. 111.
15. Henderson, 1945, p. 4.
16. Nicholas, 1951, p. 149.
17. See, for example, Harrop, 1986, pp. 140–3; Seymour-Ure, 1991, pp. 198–202.
18. Quoted in Horne, 1989, p. 264.
19. Thatcher, 1995, p. 294.
20. Just in case: 'You cannot hope to bribe or twist, / thank God!, the British journalist / But, seeing what the man will do / unbribed, there's no occasion to'.
21. Unattributable interview.
22. For example: Margach, 1978; Cockerell et al., 1984; Harris, 1990; Ingham, 1991.
23. Pearson and Turner, 1966, p. 179.
24. *Independent*, 1 July 1989.
25. Linton, 1995.
26. Millar, 1993, p. 287.
27. Ramsden, 1982, p. 129.
28. Butler and Rose, 1960, p. 78.
29. Evans, 1981, p. 266.
30. Day, 1982, p. 8.
31. Harrison, 1965, p. 171.
32. Harrison, 1982, p. 77.
33. Cockerell, 1988, p. 56.
34. Cook, 1992.
35. See, for example, International Press Institute, 1992, p. 4.
36. McCallum and Readman, 1947, p. 191.
37. *At the Hustings*, BBC Television, 14 November 1983.
38. Castle, 1993, p. 313.
39. Young, 1990, p. 128.
40. Quoted in Fallon and Grice, 1992.
41. Quoted in 'Communicating Labour values', *Tribune*, 27 January 1989.
42. For some other examples from the 1992 election, see Billig et al., 1993, p. 119.
43. Internal memo quoted in Butler and Kavanagh, 1988, pp. 61–2.
44. Cockerell, 1988, p. 81.
45. Woolton, 1959, p. 361.
46. CCO 4/2/152, CPA.
47. Woolton, 1959, p. 361.

48. Vicker, 1962, pp. 93–4.
49. Macmillan, 1972, p. 40.
50. Internal memo quoted in Cockett, 1994, p. 566.
51. Labour NEC annual report 1958, p. 42.
52. Labour NEC annual report 1964, p. 43.
53. Cockerell, 1988, p. 137.
54. Magee, 1966, p. 57.
55. Interview, 2 June 1994.
56. Cockerell, 1988, p. 150.
57. Pease, 1969.
58. Quoted in King and Sloman, 1973, p. 90.
59. Barry Day, interview, 12 April 1994.
60. Cockerell, 1988, p. 230.
61. Young of Graffham, 1991, p. 87.
62. Bull and Mayer, 1991; 1993.
63. Quoted in BBC, 1992, p. 4.
64. Day, 1989, p. 245.
65. Interview, 27 April 1994.
66. Cockerell, 1988, p. 104.
67. Interview, 21 December 1994.
68. Quoted in Kavanagh, 1995, p. 202.
69. This requirement is now laid down in paragraph 5.1(c) of the BBC's Agreement, and sections 6 (regarding independent television) and 90 (independent radio) of the 1990 Broadcasting Act.
70. Cockett, 1994, p. 558.
71. Moran, 1966, p. 390.
72. Briggs, 1979, p. 645.
73. Cockerell, 1988, p. 7.
74. Ibid., p. 25.
75. Phillips, 1959, p. 11.
76. Williams, 1964, p. 13.
77. CCO 20/17/8, CPA.
78. Williams, 1975, pp. 189–90.
79. Blumler, 1969, p. 228.
80. Quoted in Cockerell, 1988, p. 310.
81. Tebbit, 1989b, p. 324.
82. Owen, 1992, p. 624; see also Crewe and King, 1995, p. 270, for details of content analysis of TV coverage of the 1983 and 1987 elections which confirms Owen's statement.
83. Tebbit, 1989b, p. 325.
84. Scammell, 1995, p. 136; see also Blumler et al., 1989, pp. 166–7.
85. *Dispatches*, Channel 4, 18 March 1992.
86. Leapman, 1992; Phillips, 1992.
87. Campbell, 1995.
88. Butler and Rose, 1960, p. 53.
89. Butler and Pinto-Duschinsky, 1971, p. 243.
90. Woodward, 1995, p. 33.
91. Cockerell, 1988, p. 281; Kellner, 1985, p. 74.
92. 'Labour changes colour to suit TV', *Guardian*, 26 January 1996.

93. Jones, 1992, p. 23.
94. Interview, 9 November 1994.
95. Thatcher, 1993, p. 577.
96. See, for example, Thatcher, 1995, p. 445; Linton, 1986, pp. 151–2, 159.
97. Kavanagh and Gosschalk, 1995; Linton, 1986, p. 153.
98. Information supplied by David Deacon, Loughborough University.
99. Labour NEC annual report 1992, p. 15.
100. Boorstin, 1962.
101. BBC, 1992, p. 21.
102. Tyler, 1987, p. 196; cf. Thatcher, 1993, pp. 582–3.

## 5   RALLIES AND CONFERENCES

1. *Panorama*, BBC1, 15 June 1987.
2. Quoted in Hill, 1992, p. 239.
3. *Dispatches*, Channel 4, 25 September 1992.
4. Atkinson, 1988, pp. 57–82; see also Heritage and Greatbatch, 1986, for quantitative evidence confirming Atkinson's microanalysis.
5. Speech to Labour Party conference, 2 October 1995.
6. Interview, 9 November 1994.
7. Thatcher, 1993, p. 258.
8. Interview, 6 April 1994.
9. Interview, 9 June 1994.
10. Hogg and Hill, 1995, p. 132.
11. Harris, 1982, p. 443.
12. Nicholas, 1951, p. 94.
13. Howard and West, 1965, p. 142.
14. Home of the Hirsel, 1978, p. 213.
15. Falkender, 1983, p. 50.
16. Campbell, 1993, p. 275.
17. Falkender, 1983, pp. 51, 53.
18. Ibid., pp. 56, 53.
19. Ibid., pp. 56–7; Cockerell, 1988, pp. 197–8, 210.
20. Millar, 1993, p. 261.
21. Interview, 17 May 1994.
22. Kellner, 1985, pp. 75–6
23. *Dispatches*, Channel 4, 18 March 1992.
24. Interview, 6 April 1994.
25. The broadcasters deny that they use film of party events supplied by the parties themselves (see for example Tait, 1995, pp. 61–2). However, Jim Parish (interview, 12 February 1996) maintains that in 1992 the broadcasters did use film of Labour events provided by the party.
26. Gould, 1995, p. 250.
27. Labour NEC annual report 1992, p. 14.
28. Jones, 1992, p. 31.
29. Labour had already allowed cinema newsreel filming, but this had led to claims from some in the party that the resulting films were

biased and showed its conference from unfavourable angles.
30. Crossman, 1981, p. 257.
31. Cockerell, 1988, p. 22.
32. Pickles, 1959, p. 56.
33. Cosgrave, 1989, p. 329.
34. Minkin, 1978, pp. 214–16, 232.
35. For example, 'Parties on the screen', *Economist*, 3 October 1953.
36. Interview, 17 May 1994.
37. Interview, 17 May 1994
38. Quoted in Wintour, 1990.
39. Interview, 6 April 1994
40. Interview with Jim Parish, 6 April 1994.


6   OPINION RESEARCH

1. Butler and King, 1965, p. 49.
2. Memo dated 8 July 1983, in MORI, 1983.
3. See Gallup, 1976, p. 14.
4. CRD 2/21/1, CPA.
5. Quoted in Abrams, 1963a, p. 11.
6. Davies, 1995, p. 267.
7. Nicholas, 1951, p. 283.
8. Butler and Rose, 1960, p. 23.
9. Abrams, 1963a, p. 12.
10. Worcester, 1991, p. 20.
11. Later republished in book form as Abrams et al., 1960.
12. Butler and King, 1965, pp. 68–70.
13. Interview, 7 April 1994.
14. Rose, 1967, p. 81.
15. Rose, 1965, p. 370.
16. Teer and Spence, 1973, pp. 159–60.
17. Windlesham, 1966, p. 78.
18. Butler and King, 1966, p. 33.
19. Ibid., p. 68.
20. Taylor, 1977, p. 78.
21. Teer and Spence, 1973, pp. 173–5.
22. Butler and Kavanagh, 1980, pp. 275–6.
23. Interview, 19 October 1994.
24. Cockerell, 1988, p. 234.
25. Interview, 29 April 1994.
26. Sharkey, 1989, p. 63.
27. Cockerell, 1988, p. 309.
28. Jones, 1992, pp. 44–5.
29. MORI, 1974.
30. Interview, 21 April 1994.
31. Butler and Kavanagh, 1980, p. 272.
32. Benn, 1990, p. 260.
33. MORI, 1979.

34. Delaney, 1982, p. 28.
35. Butler and Jowett, 1985, pp. 65–6.
36. Shaw, 1994, p. 68.
37. Mandelson, 1988, p. 12.
38. Hewitt and Mandelson, 1989, p. 51.
39. Butler and Kavanagh, 1988, p. 133.
40. Gould et al., 1989, p. 72.
41. Hughes and Wintour, p. 170.
42. Kavanagh, 1992, p. 520.
43. Liberal Democrats, 1992, p. 69.
44. Butler and King, 1965, p. 70.
45. Butler and Pinto-Duschinsky, 1971, p. 154.
46. MORI, 1974.
47. Worcester, 1991, pp. 51–3.
48. Interview, 19 October 1994.
49. Butler and Kavanagh, 1980, p. 276.
50. MORI, 1987.
51. Butler and Kavanagh, 1992, pp. 149–51.
52. Butler and Kavanagh, 1984, p. 144.
53. Interview, 14 March 1995.
54. Stothard, 1987.
55. Interview, 2 June 1994.
56. For two conflicting accounts see Stothard, 1987; and Tyler, 1987; pp. 225–7.
57. 'Saatchi issues writ for libel against BBC', *Daily Telegraph*, 17 June 1987.
58. Interview with John Banks, 14 March 1995.
59. Butler and Kavanagh, 1992, pp. 36–7.
60. Baker, 1993, p. 328.
61. *The Vote Race*, BBC Television, 15 March 1992.
62. Conservative Party annual accounts 1990–1 (it is described as 'special political research').
63. Butler and Kavanagh, 1988, p. 132.
64. Bruce, 1992a, p. 86.
65. Rentoul et al., 1995, p. 112.
66. Butler and Rose, 1960, p. 3.

7 PERSONAL IMAGE

1. 'The new hustings', *The Times*, 23 May 1955.
2. Television interview, quoted in 'Healey claims Kinnock TV looks helped lose election', *Guardian*, 7 December 1992.
3. *Thatcher: The Path to Power and Beyond*, BBC1, 10 June 1995.
4. Falkender, 1983, p. 209.
5. Letter from Tucker (Conservative director of publicity) to Heath, 22 May 1969.
6. Thatcher, 1993, p. 586.
7. Quoted in Cockerell, 1988, p. 71.

8. Many media trainers and image consultants now like to quote the following 'fact': that your impact on others is based 55 per cent on how you look, 38 per cent on how you sound, and only 7 per cent on what you actually say. Given the wide currency of this assertion, it is worth noting that it represents a gross over-generalisation of the academic research from which it stems. These studies reported a much narrower finding: that in judging whether someone making a statement was expressing a positive or a negative attitude, respondents relied 55 per cent on that person's facial expression, 38 per cent on tone of voice, and 7 per cent on the meaning of the words uttered. This result derives from two small experiments involving Californian students in the 1960s (Mehrabian and Ferris, 1967; Mehrabian and Wiener, 1967; see also Mehrabian, 1971, pp. 42–5). It illustrates how an isolated academic finding, decontextualised and distorted, can become recycled as common wisdom. And thus, to adapt Keynes, do those in authority distil their beliefs from some academic scribbler of a few years back.
9. Ballantyne, 1993, p. 18.
10. Moran, 1966, p. 756.
11. Cockerell, 1988, p. 45.
12. Horne, 1989, pp. 144–5.
13. Evans, 1981, p. 180.
14. Benn, 1994, p. 291.
15. Cockerell, 1988, p. 105.
16. Butler and King, 1965, p. 147.
17. Cockerell, 1988, p. 87.
18. Wilson of Rievaulx, 1986, p. 172.
19. Williams, 1975, p. 100.
20. 'Mr Wilson's "family doctor" image on TV', *Guardian*, 30 April 1966.
21. Horne, 1989, p. 145; Cockerell, 1988, p. 210; 'Nothing but the whole tooth', *Daily Mail*, 11 March 1994.
22. Thatcher, 1993, p. 576.
23. Millar, 1993, p. 338.
24. Wapshott and Brock, 1983, p. 81.
25. Cockerell, 1988, p. 234.
26. Thatcher, 1995, p. 255.
27. Ibid., pp. 294–5.
28. *Angela Rippon Meets the Image Makers*, BBC1, 15 September 1981.
29. Baker, 1993, pp. 270–1.
30. 4 May 1982.
31. Thomson, 1989, pp. 81–2; Webster, 1990, p. 94.
32. Thatcher, 1993, p. 576.
33. Millar, 1993, pp. 313–14; Tyler, 1987, pp. 187–8.
34. Lawson, 1993, p. 127.
35. Ibid., p. 249.
36. Television interview quoted in 'Lawson's economic miracle came into view after dinner', *Guardian*, 30 October 1992.
37. Young of Graffham, 1991, p. 225; see also the varying accounts of Tyler, 1987, pp. 187–8; Millar, 1993, pp. 313–14; Lawson, 1991,

p. 702. Millar claims in his memoirs that he overheard Thatcher's side of a telephone conversation with Lawson during the 1987 campaign in which she asked him to have a haircut. Lawson states (letter to author, 6 December 1995) that he has 'no recollection of any such conversation'. Millar insists (letter to author, January 1996) that he did hear such a conversation, but that 'it's just possible that the exchange was with an aide at Number 11 rather than the chancellor himself'.

38. Foot, 1984, p. 27.
39. Heffernan and Marqusee, 1992, p. 108.
40. Jones, 1995, p. 71.
41. Unattributable interview.
42. Jones, 1995, p. 71.
43. Interview with Mary Spillane, 24 November 1995.
44. Interview, 22 April 1994.
45. Thatcher, 1995, p. 295.
46. Atkinson, 1986, p. 47.
47. '10 years at Number 10', *Observer*, 30 April 1989.
48. Woolton, 1959, p. 418.
49. Interview, 2 June 1994.
50. Campbell, 1993, p. 256.
51. Butler and King, 1966, p. 70.
52. Alexander and Watkins, 1970, pp. 172–3.
53. Cockerell, 1988, p. 212.
54. Crossman, 1975, p. 481.
55. Williams, 1975, pp. 183–4.
56. Cockerell, 1988, pp. 145–6, 154, 88, 151.
57. Butler and Kavanagh, 1992, p. 191.
58. Hogg and Hill, 1995, p. 174.
59. Bruce, 1992a, p. 70.
60. Howard and West, 1965, p. 41.
61. Interviews quoted in Webster, 1990, pp. 9–10.
62. Bruce, 1992a, pp. 78–9.
63. Interview, 28 September 1995.
64. Cockerell, 1988, p. 204.
65. Letter to Heath from Tucker, 8 April 1971.
66. Interview, 2 June 1994.
67. Thatcher, 1995, p. 294.
68. Interview, 12 April 1994.
69. *The Wilderness Years*, BBC2, 18 December 1995.

## 8   PARTY IDENTITY

1. Benn, 1992, p. 474.
2. *The Wilderness Years*, BBC2, 17 December 1995.
3. Nicholas, 1951, p. 242; CCO 4/3/211, CPA.
4. Owen, 1988, p. 206.
5. Quoted in Stephen, 1981.

6. Quoted in Riddell, 1987.
7. Bennett, 1992.
8. Interview, 6 April 1994.
9. Bruce, 1992a, pp. 120–1.
10. Interview, 12 February 1996.
11. Wring, 1996.
12. Interview, 21 April 1994.
13. Labour NEC annual report 1987, p. 35.
14. Mandelson, 1988, p. 13.
15. Woolton, 1959, p. 334.
16. Benn, 1994, p. 317.
17. Crewe and King, 1995, p. 100.
18. Interview, 19 February 1996.

## 9 CAMPAIGN MATERIALS AND DIRECT MAIL

1. Naughtie, 1986.
2. Approximate calculations based on Craig, 1975; Craig, 1990; and Topf, 1994, p. 153.
3. Manifesto wordage figures taken from Topf, 1994.
4. Labour NEC minutes, 22 March 1950.
5. Labour NEC minutes, 7 November 1951.
6. Labour NEC annual report 1964, p. 9.
7. Labour NEC annual report 1960, p. 8.
8. Labour NEC annual report 1987, p. 5.
9. Information from Labour Party.
10. Butler and Pinto-Duschinsky, 1971, p. 312.
11. Information from Conservative Central Office.
12. Innes, 1983.
13. Aldhouse, 1950, pp. 143–4.
14. CCO 500/24/1, CPA.
15. Labour NEC annual report 1987, p. 5.
16. Pinto-Duschinsky, M., 1981, p. 98.
17. CCO 500/24/26, CPA.
18. Butler and Rose, 1960, p. 24.
19. CCO 500/44/1, CPA.
20. CCO 500/44/2, CPA.
21. Butler and Pinto-Duschinsky, 1971, p. 290.
22. Trenear-Harvey, 1987, p. 22.
23. Interview with Cecil Parkinson, 9 June 1994.
24. Scammell, 1995, p. 128.
25. Ibid.
26. Douglas, 1987.
27. Hollins, 1981, p. 366.
28. Swaddle, 1990, p. 186.
29. Labour NEC minutes, 28 March 1945.
30. CRD 2/21/2 and CCO 4/2/153, CPA.

31. Cockett, 1994, p. 560.
32. CCO 500/24/1, CPA.
33. Hollins, 1981, p. 366.
34. Swaddle, 1990, p. 186.
35. Labour NEC annual report 1949, p. 28.
36. Labour NEC annual report 1954, p. 6; Cockerell, 1988, p. 32.
37. Labour NEC annual report 1958, p. 42.
38. Labour NEC annual report 1961, p. 35.
39. See for example *Labour Organiser*, February 1970, p. 22.
40. Labour NEC annual report 1982, p. 36.
41. Butler and Jowett, 1985, p. 67.
42. Tyler, 1987, pp. 132–3, 162.
43. Cockett, 1994, p. 547.
44. Pearson and Turner, 1966, p. 180.
45. CCO 4/3/235, CPA.
46. CCO 500/24/78, CPA.
47. CCO 500/24/78 and CCO 600/3/4/1, CPA.
48. Butler and Rose, 1960, p. 24.
49. CCO 600/3/5/1, CPA.
50. Labour NEC minutes, 7 November 1951.
51. Labour NEC minutes, June 1955.
52. Labour NEC annual reports 1957, p. 36; 1958, p. 42.
53. Labour NEC annual report 1963, p. 37.
54. Labour NEC annual report 1984, p. 53.

10  LOCAL CAMPAIGNING

1. Hattersley, 1990, p. 180.
2. Benn, 1987, p. 50.
3. Steen, 1991, p. 30.
4. Mitchell, 1987.
5. Woolton, 1959, p. 341.
6. Butler, 1952, p. 143.
7. British Election Study 1987 (Economic and Social Research Council Data Archive, Essex University).
8. Goodhart, 1954.
9. Calculated from polls summarised in the Nuffield general election series: Butler, 1952, p. 143; Butler, 1955, p. 112; Butler and Rose, 1960, p. 140; Butler and King, 1965, p. 220; Butler and King, 1966, p. 197; Butler and Pinto-Duschinsky, 1971, pp. 317–18.
10. *Gallup Political Index*, June 1983 and June 1987; Butler and Kavanagh, 1988, p. 215; British Election Studies 1983 and 1987 (Economic and Social Research Council Data Archive, Essex University).
11. See *Gallup Political and Economic Index*, April 1992; Butler and Kavanagh, 1992, p. 242. Similarly, Whiteley et al. (1994, p. 74) suggest that in the 1992 election there were more Labour than Conservative canvassers.
12. McKenzie, 1955, pp. 255–6; Labour Party, 1955, p. 4.

13. CCO 4/7/280, CPA.
14. Interview, 19 April 1994.
15. Swaddle, 1989, p. 32.
16. Computing for Labour, 1994; *EARS – The Party's Favourite Software* (leaflet); Conservative Central Office, 1994a.
17. Swaddle, 1989, p. 33.
18. Calculated from data supplied by Gordon Hands, Lancaster University.
19. *Conservative Agents' Journal*, August 1927, quoted in Swaddle, 1990, p. 210.
20. Interview, 19 April 1994.
21. Labour Party, 1995, p. 1(ii).
22. Association of Liberal Democrat Councillors, 1993, p. 52.
23. Whiteley et al., 1994, p. 42.
24. Scammell, 1995, p. 133.
25. Butler and Kavanagh, 1992, p. 239.
26. Calculated from data supplied by Gordon Hands, Lancaster University.
27. Interview, 28 April 1994.
28. Rennard, 1988, p. 92; Denver and Hands, 1992, p. 538.
29. Social Democratic Party, 1986, p. 47.
30. Butler and Rose, 1960, p. 133.
31. Butler and King, 1965, p. 223.
32. Butler and Kavanagh, 1988, p. 223.
33. See for example Butler, 1952, p. 141; Butler and Pinto-Duschinsky, 1971, p. 311.
34. Butler and Kavanagh, 1992, p. 234.
35. Interview, 19 April 1994.
36. Interview with Chris Rennard, 9 November 1994.
37. Interview, 28 September 1995.
38. See Labour Party, circa 1984; Greaves, 1981.
39. Butler, 1952, p. 31.
40. CCO 600/14/4, CPA.
41. Holt and Turner, 1968, p. 158.
42. Butler and King, 1965, p. 249.
43. Douglas, 1987.
44. Swaddle, 1989, p. 37.
45. Rosenbaum, 1992.
46. Labour Party, 1972, pp. 41, 47–8.
47. Although much of this guidance is similar, there are occasional differences in approach: the SDP (see Social Democratic Party, 1986, p. 96) told its workers to 'avoid saying "No comment"' as 'this is at best wet'; while in the opinion of the Conservatives (see Conservative Central Office, 1995, p. 13), '"No comment" is the most useful phrase for a political press officer.'
48. Gapes, 1992.
49. Franklin, 1994, p. 165.
50. Bochel and Denver, 1977, pp. 21–4.
51. Franklin, 1994, p. 167.

52. CCO 500/24/75 and CCO 600/14/6, CPA.
53. Butler, 1952, p. 141; Gallup, 1976, pp. 542, 763, 1099.
54. *Gallup Political and Economic Index*, May 1992.
55. Labour Party, 1991b, p. 94.
56. Nicholas, 1951, p. 235.
57. Butler and Pinto-Duschinsky, 1971, p. 224.
58. Data supplied by Gordon Hands, Lancaster University.
59. Calculated from Craig, 1989, p. 61, and Home Office, 1993, p. 5.
60. CCO 500/24/278, CPA.
61. Butler and Kavanagh, 1992, p. 241.
62. Jenkins, 1992, p. 537.
63. *News Chronicle*, 18 February 1950.
64. Scammell, 1995, p. 41.
65. CCO 500/24/214, CPA.
66. Jenkins, 1992, p. 366.
67. 'Tornado Currie is keeping her fingers crossed', *Independent*, 25 May 1994.
68. See, for example, Nicholas, 1951, p. 235.
69. Labour Party, 1972, p. 40.
70. Conservative Central Office, 1991, p. 25.
71. McCallum and Readman, 1947, p. 133.
72. Nicholas, 1951, p. 240.
73. Denver and Hands, 1992, p. 537.
74. Butler and King, 1966, p. 192.
75. Ball, 1994, p. 302; see also, for example, Conservative Central Office, 1994b.
76. Labour Party, 1991a, p. 2.
77. Nicholas, 1951, p. 17.
78. Butler and Kavanagh, 1992, p. 245.
79. This analysis is based on the figures given for average candidate expenditure by party in each volume of the *British General Election* series.
80. Ball, 1994, pp. 284–5.
81. Butler, 1952, p. 22.
82. See Butler and Kavanagh, 1988, p. 228. In 1992 Labour had 100 professional organisers 'in the field' (Butler and Kavanagh, 1992, p. 232), but as well as the full-time constituency agents this figure includes regional staff appointed to assist lay agents.
83. Ball, 1994, p. 291.
84. Whiteley et al., 1994, p. 22.
85. Ibid., p. 25.
86. Riddell, 1993.
87. Pinto-Duschinsky, 1994.
88. *Labour Party News*, January/February 1996.
89. Lacy, 1992.
90. Labour Party, 1955, p. 3.
91. Denver and Hands, 1992, pp. 534, 536; Denver and Hands, 1993, pp. 235–7.
92. See, for example, Johnston, 1987; Johnston and Pattie, 1993; Pattie

et al., 1995; Seyd and Whiteley, 1992; Whiteley and Seyd, 1992; Whiteley et al., 1994; Denver and Hands, 1993.

93. See, for example, Curtice and Steed, 1992, p. 340; Norris et al., 1992.

94. Interview, 19 April 1994.

## 11　CROSS-CAMPAIGN THEMES

1. Internal memo leaked to the press, quoted in Peston, 1994.

2. Quoted in Hare, 1993, p. 165.

3. Quoted in Fallon, 1988, p. 160.

4. Hewitt and Mandelson, 1989, p. 53.

5. This is analogous to the argument that, in terms of personal image-making for politicians, it is easier and more productive to give prominence to a politician's strong points than to try to neutralise widely perceived character weaknesses.

6. Butler and Rose, 1960, pp. 79, 80.

7. See, for example, Butler and Rose, 1960, pp. 69–70; and Lawson, 1965.

8. Butler and Pinto-Duschinsky, 1971, p. 137.

9. Peston, 1994.

10. Speech at fringe meeting at Labour Party conference, 3 October 1994.

11. Labour Party, 1955.

12. See, for example, Harrop, 1990, pp. 283–4.

13. Houston and Valdar, 1922, p. 13.

14. CCO 4/4/224, CPA.

15. Lawson, 1993, p. 699.

16. Interview, 29 April 1994.

17. Linton, 1994, p. 23.

18. See, for example, Home Affairs Select Committee, 1993, p. 126.

19. For comparison, the Conservatives put their spending during the campaign itself in 1992 at £10.1 million and Labour put its at £7.1 million (Butler and Kavanagh, 1992, p. 260).

20. Statistics taken from the Nuffield election studies for 1964 to 1987 are summarised in Holme, 1988, p. 24; for 1992, see Harrison, 1992, p. 169. For similar results about the broadcast prominence of party leaders based on different measures, see, for example, Axford and Madgwick, 1989, p. 152; Golding, 1992 (this reveals slightly less leader prominence but includes the low-rating, more analytical *Newsnight* as well as the high-rating main news bulletins); and Nossiter et al., 1995, p. 91.

21. Foley, 1993, pp. 247–8.

22. Ibid., pp. 123–5.

23. See Jamieson, 1992, p. 41.

24. Phillips, 1955, p. 6.

25. Robertson, 1971, pp. 442–5 (this analysis is based on speech texts issued by party headquarters).

26. Pinto-Duschinsky, S., 1981, pp. 309–11.

27. Kavanagh, 1995, p. 198.
28. Golding, 1992.
29. Seymour-Ure, 1992, pp. 56–9; Harrop and Scammell, 1992, p. 188.
30. Pearson and Turner, 1966, p. 179.
31. CRD 2/48/54, CPA.
32. This is based on personal sight of the 'Ashdown dossier'.
33. Labour NEC annual report 1992, p. 49.
34. Kavanagh, 1995, p. 49.
35. Whitty, 1992, p. 58.
36. Butler and Kavanagh, 1984, p. 101.
37. Harrison, 1974, pp. 163, 166.
38a. Figures for elections up to and including 1979 are taken from Pinto-Duschinsky, M., 1981, pp. 143, 167, 191, 202. The one exception is Conservative spending for the 1950 election – this is based on the sum given by Pinto-Duschinsky (p. 143) for campaign spending during the 1950 calendar year, coupled with data on advertising expenditure in 1949 obtained from files CCO 500/24/19–20 in the Conservative Party Archive.
   b. Pinto-Duschinsky, M., 1985a, p. 63.
   c. Pinto-Duschinsky, M., 1989, p. 198.
   d. Pinto-Duschinsky, M., 1992.
   e. Pinto-Duschinsky, M., 1985b, p. 335.
   f. Pinto-Duschinsky, M., 1989, p. 201.
   g. Pinto-Duschinsky, M., 1992.
   h. Pinto-Duschinsky, M., 1985b, p. 338.
   i. Pinto-Duschinsky, M., 1989, p. 204.
   j. Linton, 1994, p. 23.

## 12 CONCLUSION

1. Conservative party political broadcast, 18 March 1992.
2. *This Week*, ITV, 26 March 1992.
3. Quoted in Foley, 1993, p. 244.
4. Attlee, 1954, p. 195.
5. Interview, 25 April 1994.
6. Benn, 1994, p. 190.

# Bibliography

Abrams, M. et al., 1960, *Must Labour Lose?* (Penguin).

Abrams, M., 1963a, 'Public opinion polls and political parties', *Public Opinion Quarterly*, vol. 27, pp. 9–18.

Abrams, M., 1963b, 'Why the parties advertise', *New Society*, 6 June.

Abrams, M., 1964, 'Opinion polls and party propaganda', *Public Opinion Quarterly*, vol. 28, pp. 13–19.

Adams, J., 1992, *Tony Benn* (Pan).

Aldhouse, E., 1950, 'Posters and propaganda', in S. Chrimes (ed.), *The General Election in Glasgow, February 1950* (Jackson, Son & Co.).

Alexander, A. and Watkins, A., 1970, *The Making of the Prime Minister 1970* (Macdonald).

Association of Liberal Democrat Councillors, 1993, *Activists' Handbook No. 2: Organising to Win*.

Atkinson, M., 1986, 'The 1983 election and the demise of live oratory', in Crewe and Harrop, 1986.

Atkinson, M., 1988, *Our Masters' Voices* (Routledge).

Attlee, C., 1954, *As It Happened* (Heinemann).

Axford, B. and Madgwick, P., 1989, 'Indecent exposure? Three-party politics in television news during the 1987 general election', in Crewe and Harrop, 1989.

Baker, K., 1993, *The Turbulent Years* (Faber).

Ball, S., 1994, 'Local Conservatism and the evolution of the party organization', in A. Seldon and S. Ball (eds.), *Conservative Century* (Oxford University Press).

Ballantyne, J., 1993, *Researcher's Guide to British Newsreels*, Volume 3 (British Universities Film and Video Council).

BBC, 1984, *Annual Report and Handbook 1985*.

BBC, 1992, *Election 92*.

Bell, T., 1982, 'The Conservatives' advertising campaign', in Worcester and Harrop, 1982.

Benn, T., 1987, *Out of the Wilderness: Diaries 1963–67* (Hutchinson).

Benn, T., 1990, *Conflicts of Interest: Diaries 1977–80* (Hutchinson).

Benn, T., 1992, *The End of an Era: Diaries 1980–90* (Hutchinson).

Benn, T., 1994, *Years of Hope: Diaries, Papers and Letters 1940–1962* (Hutchinson).

Bennett, O., 1992, 'Brand leaders', *Creative Review*, April.

Billig, M. et al., 1993, 'In the hands of the spin-doctors', in N. Miller and R. Allen (eds.), *It's Live – But is it Real?* (John Libbey).

Blair, T., 1987, 'A breakdown in communication', *The Times*, 24 November.

Blumler, J., 1969, 'Producers' attitudes towards television coverage of an election campaign', in R. Rose (ed.), *Studies in British Politics* (Macmillan).

Blumler, J. and McQuail, D., 1968, *Television in Politics* (Faber and Faber).

Blumler, J. et al., 1989, 'The earnest vs. the determined: election newsmaking at the BBC, 1987', in Crewe and Harrop, 1989.

Bochel, J. and Denver, D., 1977, 'Political communication: Scottish local newspapers and the general election of February 1974', *Scottish Journal of Sociology*, vol. 2, pp. 11–30.

Boorstin, D., 1962, *The Image* (Atheneum, New York).

Briggs, A., 1979, *Sound and Vision* (Oxford University Press).

Bruce, B., 1992a, *Images of Power* (Kogan Page).

Bruce, B., 1992b, 'My biggest mistake', *Independent on Sunday*, 15 March.

Bull, P. and Mayer, K., 1991, *Is John Major as Unremarkable as He Seems?* (paper presented to British Psychological Society conference).

Bull, P. and Mayer, K., 1993, 'How not to answer questions in political interviews', *Political Psychology*, vol. 14, no. 4, pp. 651–66.

Butler, D., 1952, *The British General Election of 1951* (Macmillan).

Butler, D., 1955, *The British General Election of 1955* (Macmillan).

Butler, D. and Jowett, P., 1985, *Party Strategies in Britain* (Macmillan).

Butler, D. and Kavanagh, D., 1974, *The British General Election of February 1974* (Macmillan).

Butler, D. and Kavanagh, D., 1975, *The British General Election of October 1974* (Macmillan).

Butler, D. and Kavanagh, D., 1980, *The British General Election of 1979* (Macmillan).

Butler, D. and Kavanagh, D., 1984, *The British General Election of 1983* (Macmillan).

Butler, D. and Kavanagh, D., 1988, *The British General Election of 1987* (Macmillan).

Butler, D. and Kavanagh, D., 1992, *The British General Election of 1992* (Macmillan).

Butler, D. and King, A., 1965, *The British General Election of 1964* (Macmillan).

Butler, D. and King, A., 1966, *The British General Election of 1966* (Macmillan).

Butler, D. and Pinto-Duschinsky, M., 1971, *The British General Election of 1970* (Macmillan).

Butler, D. and Rose, R., 1960, *The British General Election of 1959* (Macmillan).

Butler, D. and Stokes, D., 1969, *Political Change in Britain* (Macmillan).

Cambray, P., 1932, *The Game of Politics* (John Murray).

Campbell, A., 1995, 'When Ally met Auntie', *Tribune*, 13 October.

Campbell, J., 1993, *Edward Heath* (Jonathan Cape).

Castle, B., 1993, *Fighting All the Way* (Macmillan).

Clark, W., 1986, *From Three Worlds* (Sidgwick and Jackson).

Clifford, P., and Heath, A., 1994, 'The election campaign', in A. Heath et al. (eds.), *Labour's Last Chance?* (Dartmouth).

Cockerell, M., 1988, *Live from Number 10* (Faber and Faber).

Cockerell, M. et al., 1984, *Sources Close to the Prime Minister* (Macmillan).

Cockett, R., 1994, 'The party, publicity and the media', in A. Seldon and S. Ball (eds.), *Conservative Century* (Oxford University Press).

Computing for Labour, 1994, *Factsheet 17: The Transfer of Electoral Register Data*.

Conservative Central Office, 1991, *Election Organisation and Law.*

Conservative Central Office, 1994a, *Constituency Computer Services.*

Conservative Central Office, 1994b, *Election Pack 1994: Targeting.*

Conservative Central Office, 1995, *Local Government Manual '95.*

Cook, S., 1992, 'Tabloids' Tory bias grows more blatant', *Guardian*, 30 March.

Cosgrave, P., 1989, *The Lives of Enoch Powell* (Bodley Head).

Craig, F., 1975, *British General Election Manifestos 1900–1974* (Macmillan).

Craig, F., 1989, *British Electoral Facts 1832–1987* (Dartmouth).

Craig, F., 1990, *British General Election Manifestos 1959–1987* (Dartmouth).

Crewe, I. and Gosschalk, B. (eds.), 1995, *Political Communications: The General Election Campaign of 1992* (Cambridge University Press).

Crewe, I. and Harrop, M. (eds.), 1986, *Political Communications: The General Election Campaign of 1983* (Cambridge University Press).

Crewe, I. and Harrop, M. (eds.), 1989, *Political Communications: The General Election Campaign of 1987* (Cambridge University Press).

Crewe, I. and King, A., 1995, *SDP* (Oxford University Press).

Crossman, R. 1975, *The Diaries of a Cabinet Minister*, Volume One (Hamish Hamilton and Jonathan Cape).

Crossman, R., 1981, *The Backbench Diaries of Richard Crossman* (Hamish Hamilton and Jonathan Cape).

Curtice, J. and Steed, M., 1992, 'The results analysed', in Butler and Kavanagh, 1992.

Davies, A., 1995, *We, the Nation* (Little, Brown).

Day, B., 1982, 'The politics of communication, or the communication of politics', in Worcester and Harrop, 1982.

Day, R., 1989, *Grand Inquisitor* (Weidenfeld and Nicolson).

Delaney, T., 1982, 'Labour's advertising campaign', in Worcester and Harrop, 1982.

Denver, D. and Hands, G., 1992, 'Constituency campaigning', *Parliamentary Affairs*, vol. 45, pp. 528–44.

Denver, D., and Hands, G., 1993, 'Measuring the intensity and effectiveness of constituency campaigning in the 1992 general election', in D. Denver et al., (eds.), *British Elections and Parties Yearbook 1993* (Harvester Wheatsheaf).

Douglas, T., 1987, 'Letter from Kinnock Steel Thatcher Owen', *Observer*, 17 May.

Dunleavy, P. and Husbands, C., 1985, *British Democracy at the Crossroads* (Allen and Unwin).

Evans, H., 1981, *Downing Street Diary* (Hodder and Stoughton).

Falkender, Baroness, 1983, *Downing Street in Perspective* (Weidenfeld and Nicolson).

Fallon, I., 1988, *The Brothers* (Hutchinson).

Fallon, I. and Grice, A., 1992, 'Fixers chase winning image', *Sunday Times*, 15 March.

FitzGerald, M., 1986, 'The parties and the "black vote"', in Crewe and Harrop, 1986.

Foley, M., 1993, *The Rise of the British Presidency* (Manchester University Press).

Foot, M., 1984, *Another Heart and Other Pulses* (Collins).

Franklin, B., 1994, *Packaging Politics* (Edward Arnold).

Gallup, G., 1976, *Gallup International Public Opinion Polls: Great Britain 1937–1975* (Random House, New York).

Gapes, M., 1992, 'Essex Man wins for Labour', *Fabian Review*, May/June.

Golding, P., 1992, 'Economy and polls hogged coverage', *Guardian*, 11 April.

Goodhart, P., 1954, 'Fireside politics', *Daily Telegraph*, 13 February.

Gould, B., 1995, *Goodbye to All That* (Macmillan).

Gould, P. et al., 1989, 'The Labour party's campaign communications', in Crewe and Harrop, 1989.

Greaves, T., 1981, *How to Produce Focus – and Live!* (Association of Liberal Councillors).

Hare, D., 1993, *Asking Around* (Faber and Faber).

Harris, K., 1982, *Attlee* (Weidenfeld and Nicolson).

Harris, R., 1990, *Good and Faithful Servant* (Faber and Faber).

Harrison, M., 1965, 'Television and radio', in Butler and King, 1965.

Harrison, M., 1966, 'Television and radio', in Butler and King, 1966.

Harrison, M., 1974, 'Television and radio', in Butler and Kavanagh, 1974.

Harrison, M., 1975, 'On the air', in Butler and Kavanagh, 1975.

Harrison, M., 1982, 'Television news coverage of the 1979 general election', in Worcester and Harrop, 1982.

Harrison, M., 1988, 'Broadcasting', in Butler and Kavanagh, 1988.

Harrison, M., 1992, 'Politics on the air', in Butler and Kavanagh, 1992.

Harrop, M., 1984, 'Press', in Butler and Kavanagh, 1984.

Harrop, M., 1986, 'The press and post-war elections', in Crewe and Harrop, 1986.

Harrop, M., 1990, 'Political marketing', *Parliamentary Affairs*, vol. 43, pp. 277–91.

Harrop, M., and Scammell, M., 1992, 'A tabloid war', in Butler and Kavanagh, 1992.

Hattersley, R., 1990, *A Yorkshire Boyhood* (Pan).

Heffernan, R. and Marqusee, M., 1992, *Defeat from the Jaws of Victory* (Verso).

Henderson, W., 1945, *Report on Campaign Publicity Services* (internal Labour Party document).

Heritage, J. and Greatbatch, D., 1986, 'Generating applause', *American Journal of Sociology*, vol. 92, pp. 110–57.

Hewitt, P. and Mandelson, P., 1989, 'The Labour campaign', in Crewe and Harrop, 1989.

Hill, D., 1992, *Out for the Count* (Macmillan).

Hogg, S. and Hill, J., 1995, *Too Close to Call* (Little, Brown).

Hollins, T., 1981, 'The Conservative Party and film propaganda between the wars', *English Historical Review*, vol. 96, pp. 359–69.

Holme, R., 1988, 'Selling the PM', *Contemporary Record*, vol. 2, pp. 23–5.

Holt, R. and Turner, J., 1968, *Political Parties in Action: The Battle of Barons Court* (Free Press, New York).

Home Office, 1993, *Election Expenses* (HMSO).

Home of the Hirsel, Lord, 1978, *The Way the Wind Blows* (Fontana).

Horne, A., 1989, *Macmillan: 1957–86* (Macmillan).

House of Commons Home Affairs Committee, 1993, *Funding of Political Parties: Minutes of Evidence and Memoranda of Evidence* (HMSO).

Houston, H. and Valdar, L., 1922, *Modern Electioneering Practice* (Charles Knight).

Howard, A. and West, R., 1965, *The Making of the Prime Minister* (Jonathan Cape).

Hughes, C. and Wintour, P., 1990, *Labour Rebuilt* (Fourth Estate).

Hurd, D., 1979, *An End to Promises* (Collins).

Hurd, D., 1994, 'What became of all the passion?', *Independent on Sunday*, 22 May.

Ingham, B., 1991, *Kill the Messenger* (HarperCollins).

Innes, J., 1983, 'The inside story of Labour's press machine', *Journalist*, July.

International Press Institute, 1992, *The Potholes on the Campaign Trail.*

Jamieson, K., 1992, *Dirty Politics* (Oxford University Press).

Jenkins, R., 1992, *A Life at the Centre* (Pan).

Johnston, R., 1987, *Money and Votes* (Croom Helm).

Johnston, R. and Pattie, C., 1993, 'The effectiveness of constituency campaign spending at recent general elections', in House of Commons Home Affairs Committee, 1993.

Jones, N., 1992, *Election 92* (BBC Books).

Jones, N., 1995, *Soundbites and Spin Doctors* (Cassell).

Kavanagh, D., 1992, 'Private opinion polls and campaign strategy', *Parliamentary Affairs*, vol. 45, pp. 518–27.

Kavanagh, D., 1995, *Election Campaigning* (Blackwell).

Kavanagh, D. and Gosschalk, B., 1995, 'Failing to set the agenda: the role of election press conferences in 1992', in Crewe and Gosschalk, 1995.

Kellner, P., 1985, 'The Labour campaign', in A. Ranney (ed.), *Britain at the Polls 1983* (American Enterprise Institute, Washington, DC).

Kellner, P., 1992, 'Tabloid newspapers earn distrust of voters', *Independent*, 27 February.

King, A. and Sloman, A., 1973, *Westminster and Beyond* (Macmillan).

Kleinman, P., 1974, 'Selling the parties', *Spectator*, 31 August.

Labour Party, 1955, *Interim Report of the Sub-Committee on Party Organisation.*

Labour Party, 1972, *Party Organisation.*

Labour Party, circa 1984, *Community Newsletters.*

Labour Party, 1991a, *Targeting to Win.*

Labour Party, 1991b, *The Way to Win.*

Labour Party, 1995, *This is Labour calling...*

Lacy, J., 1992, *General Election Report* (internal Conservative Central Office document).

Lawson, N., 1965, 'What did happen in October?', *Financial Times*, 28 April.

Lawson, N., 1993, *The View from No. 11* (Corgi).

Leapman, M., 1992, 'The heavy breathers', *Independent on Sunday*, 1 March.

Liberal Democrats, 1992, *General Election Campaign – The Final Plan* (internal party document).

Linton, M., 1986, 'Political parties and the press in the 1983 campaign', in Crewe and Harrop, 1986.

Linton, M., 1994, *Money and Votes* (Institute for Public Policy Research).

Linton, M., 1995, *Was It the* Sun *Wot Won It?* (Nuffield College, Oxford).

Macmillan, H., 1971, *Riding the Storm* (Macmillan).

Macmillan, H., 1972, *Pointing the Way* (Macmillan).

Magee, B., 1966, *The Television Interviewer* (Macdonald).

Mandelson, P., 1988, 'Marketing Labour', *Contemporary Record*, vol. 1, pp. 11–13.

Margach, J., 1978, *The Abuse of Power* (W. H. Allen).

McCallum, R. and Readman, A., 1947, *The British General Election of 1945* (Oxford University Press).

McKenzie, R., 1955, *British Political Parties* (Heinemann).

Mehrabian, A., 1971, *Silent Messages* (Wadsworth Publishing, Belmont, California).

Mehrabian, A. and Ferris, S., 1967, 'Inference of attitudes from non-verbal communication in two channels', *Journal of Consulting Psychology*, vol. 31, pp. 248–52.

Mehrabian, A. and Wiener, M., 1967, 'Decoding of inconsistent communications', *Journal of Personality and Social Psychology*, vol. 6, pp. 109–14.

Menneer, P. and Bunker, D., 1992, *1992 General Election: Audiences and Audience Reaction to Broadcast Coverage* (paper presented to conference of the Elections, Public Opinion and Parties subgroup of the Political Studies Association).

Millar, R., 1993, *A View from the Wings* (Weidenfeld and Nicolson).

Minkin, L., 1978, *The Labour Party Conference* (Allen Lane).

Mitchell, A., 1987, 'Taking it personally', *New Society*, 5 June.

Moran, Lord, 1966, *Winston Churchill* (Constable).

MORI, 1974, *Campaign Polling Presentations: Confidential Research Studies Conducted for the Labour Party, September–October 1974.*

MORI, 1979, *Campaign Polling Presentations: Confidential Research Studies Conducted for the Labour Party, April–May 1979.*

MORI, 1983, *Campaign Polling Presentations: Confidential Research Studies Conducted for the Labour Party, May–June 1983.*

MORI, 1987, *Campaign Polling Presentations: Confidential Research Studies Conducted for the Labour Party, May–June 1987.*

Naughtie, J., 1986, 'Why Kinnock is happy to invest in a glossy image', *Guardian*, 14 October.

Nicholas, H., 1951, *The British General Election of 1950* (Macmillan).

Norris, P. et al., 1992, 'Do candidates make a difference?', *Parliamentary Affairs*, vol. 45, pp. 496–517.

Nossiter, T. et al., 1995, 'Old values versus news values', in Crewe and Gosschalk, 1995.

Owen, D., 1988, *Personally Speaking* (Pan).

Owen, D., 1992, *Time to Declare* (Penguin).

Pardoe, J., 1989, 'The Alliance campaign', in Crewe and Harrop.

Parkinson, C., 1992, *Right at the Centre* (Weidenfeld and Nicolson).

Pattie, C. et al., 1995, 'Winning the local vote', *American Political Science Review*, vol. 89, no. 4, pp. 1–15.

Pearson, J. and Turner, G., 1966, *The Persuasion Industry* (Eyre and Spottiswoode).

Pease, K., 1969, 'The great evaders', *New Society*, 2 October.

Peston, R., 1994, 'Tory chief sets out wish-list to boost party image', *Financial Times*, 21 November.

Phillips, M., 1955, *The General Election 1955* (internal Labour Party document).

Phillips, M., 1959, *General Election 1959: Report by the Secretary* (internal Labour Party document).

Phillips, M., 1992, 'The siege of our screens', *Guardian*, 17 February.

Pickles, W., 1959, 'Political attitudes in the television age', *Political Quarterly*, vol. 30, pp. 54–66.

Pinto-Duschinsky, M., 1981, *British Political Finance 1830–1980* (American Enterprise Institute, Washington, DC).

Pinto-Duschinsky, M., 1985a, 'The Conservative campaign', in A. Ranney (ed.), *Britain at the Polls 1983* (American Enterprise Institute, Washington, DC).

Pinto-Duschinsky, M., 1985b, 'Trends in British political funding 1979–83', *Parliamentary Affairs*, vol. 38, pp. 328–47.

Pinto-Duschinsky, M., 1986, 'Financing the general election of 1983', in Crewe and Harrop, 1986.

Pinto-Duschinsky, M., 1989, 'Trends in British party funding 1983–87', *Parliamentary Affairs*, vol. 42, pp. 197–212.

Pinto-Duschinsky, M., 1992, 'Labour's £10m campaign spending closes the gap with Tories', *The Times*, 30 November.

Pinto-Duschinsky, M., 1993, memorandum of evidence, in House of Commons Home Affairs Committee.

Pinto-Duschinsky, M., 1994, 'Tory chiefs in danger of losing their troops', *The Times*, 10 October.

Pinto-Duschinsky, S., 1981, 'Manifestoes, speeches and the doctrine of the mandate', in H. Penniman (ed.), *Britain at the Polls 1979* (American Enterprise Institute, Washington, DC).

Ramsden, J., 1982, 'Baldwin and film', in N. Pronay and D. Spring (eds.), *Propaganda, Politics and Film, 1918–45* (Macmillan).

Rees, L., 1992, *Selling Politics* (BBC Books).

Reith, J., 1949, *Into the Wind* (Hodder and Stoughton).

Rennard, C., 1988, *Winning Local Elections* (Association of Liberal Councillors).

Rentoul, J. et al., 1995, 'People metering: scientific research or clapometer?', in Crewe and Gosschalk, 1995.

Rhodes James, R., 1986, *Anthony Eden* (Weidenfeld and Nicolson).

Riddell, P., 1987, 'Two Davids trumpet key themes with aid of Purcell', *Financial Times*, 27 January.

Riddell, P., 1993, 'Shrinking membership raises spectre of begging letters to businessmen', *The Times*, 6 February.

Robertson, D., 1971, 'The content of election addresses and leaders' speeches', in Butler and Pinto-Duschinsky, 1971.

Rose, R., 1965, 'Pre-election public relations and advertising', in Butler and King, 1965.

Rose, R., 1967, *Influencing Voters* (Faber and Faber).

Rosenbaum, M., 1992, 'Painting a wider canvass', *The Times*, 28 April.

Rutherford, A., 1992, 'Private view', *Campaign*, 10 April.

Saatchi, M., 1994, 'Can adverts win elections?', London *Evening Standard*, 12 October.

Scammell, M., 1995, *Designer Politics* (Macmillan).

Seyd, P. and Whiteley, P., 1992, *Labour's Grass Roots* (Oxford University Press).

Seymour-Ure, C., 1991, *The British Press and Broadcasting since 1945* (Blackwell).

Seymour-Ure, C., 1992, 'Press partisanship: Into the 1990s', in D. Kavanagh (ed.), *Electoral Politics* (Oxford University Press).

Sharkey, J., 1989, 'Saatchi's and the 1987 election', in Crewe and Harrop, 1989.

Shaw, E., 1994, *The Labour Party Since 1979* (Routledge).

Social Democratic Party, 1986, *Winning in the 80's*.

Steen, A. (ed.), 1991, *Tested Ideas for Political Success* (Conservative Central Office).

Stephen, A., 1981, 'Admen give the Gang a PR gloss', *Sunday Times*, 29 March.

Stothard, P., 1987, 'How "Project Blue" turned Tory débâcle into election triumph', *The Times*, 13 June.

Swaddle, K., 1989, 'Ancient and modern: innovations in electioneering at the constituency level', in Crewe and Harrop, 1989.

Swaddle, K., 1990, *Coping with a Mass Electorate – A Study in the Evolution of Constituency Electioneering in Britain* (DPhil thesis, Oxford University).

Tait, R., 1995, 'The parties and television', in Crewe and Gosschalk, 1995.

Taylor, H., 1977, 'The use of survey research in Britain by political parties and the government', *Policy Analysis*, vol. 3, no. 1, pp. 75–84.

Tebbit, N., 1989a, 'The Conservative campaign', in Crewe and Harrop, 1989.

Tebbit, N., 1989b, *Upwardly Mobile* (Futura).

Teer, F. and Spence, J., 1973, *Political Opinion Polls* (Hutchinson).

Thatcher, Baroness, 1993, *The Downing Street Years* (HarperCollins).

Thatcher, Baroness, 1995, *The Path to Power* (HarperCollins).

Thomson, A., 1989, *Margaret Thatcher – The Woman Within* (W. H. Allen).

Topf, R., 1994, 'Party manifestos', in A. Heath et al. (eds.), *Labour's Last Chance?* (Dartmouth).

Trenear-Harvey, G., 1987, 'The SDP, Liberals and direct marketing', *Direct Response*, April.

Tyler, R., 1987, *Campaign!* (Grafton).

Vicker, R., 1962, *How an Election Was Won* (Henry Regnery, Chicago).

Wapshott, N. and Brock, G., 1983, *Thatcher* (Macdonald).

Webster, W., 1990, *Not a Man to Match Her* (Women's Press).

White, M., 1992, 'Instant tea, enduring influence', *Guardian*, 11 July.

Whiteley, P. and Seyd, P., 1992, 'The Labour vote and local activism', *Parliamentary Affairs*, vol. 45, pp. 582–95.

Whiteley, P. et al., 1994, *True Blues: The Politics of Conservative Party Membership* (Clarendon Press).

Whitty, L., 1992, *The General Election 1992: The General Secretary's Report to the National Executive Committee* (internal Labour Party document).

Williams, L., 1964, *General Election 1964: Preliminary Report by the General Secretary* (internal Labour Party document).

Williams, M., 1975, *Inside Number 10* (New English Library).

Wilson, D., 1987, *Battle for Power* (Sphere).

Wilson of Rievaulx, Lord, 1986, *Memoirs: The Making of a Prime Minister 1916–64* (Weidenfeld and Nicolson).

Windlesham, Lord, 1966, *Communication and Political Power* (Jonathan Cape).

Wintour, P., 1990, 'The rise of the red rinse conference', 6 October, *Guardian*.

Woodward, S., 1995, 'The Conservative Party's strategy', in Crewe and Gosschalk, 1995.

Woolton, Lord, 1959, *Memoirs* (Cassell).

Worcester, R., 1991, *British Public Opinion* (Basil Blackwell).

Worcester, R. and Harrop, M. (eds.), 1982, *Political Communications: The General Election Campaign of 1979* (George Allen and Unwin).

Wright, J., 1986, 'Advertising the Labour Party in 1983', in Crewe and Harrop, 1986.

Wring, D., 1996, 'From mass propaganda to political marketing', in C. Rallings et al. (eds.), *British Elections and Parties Yearbook 1995* (Frank Cass).

Wyndham Goldie, G., 1977, *Facing the Nation* (Bodley Head).

Young, H., 1990, *One of Us* (Pan).

Young of Graffham, Lord, 1991, *The Enterprise Years* (Headline).

# Index

Notes:
(a) Mentions of the Conservative and Labour Parties are too numerous to be useful to index here.
(b) The notes have been indexed where they contain substantive material other than details of references.